THE LIFE CYCLE OF
THE UNION BANK OF SCOTLAND
1830–1954

THE LIFE CYCLE OF
THE UNION BANK OF SCOTLAND
1830–1954

Norio Tamaki

Foreword by
S G Checkland

ABERDEEN UNIVERSITY PRESS

First published 1983
Aberdeen University Press
A member of the Pergamon Group

© Norio Tamaki 1983

British Library Cataloguing in Publication Data

Tamaki, Norio
    The life cycle of the Union Bank of Scotland
    1. Union Bank of Scotland—History
    I. Title
    332.1′2′0941   HG2998.U/
    ISBN 0 08 030359 5

PRINTED IN GREAT BRITAIN
THE UNIVERSITY PRESS
ABERDEEN

For
Setsuko

Foreword

There are few studies of individual banks which seek to penetrate their real workings, both in banking and in human terms. Norio Tamaki, a young Japanese scholar interested in western institutions especially of a banking kind, chose the Union Bank of Scotland as the basis for his study of British nineteenth-century banking.

He did so partly because the Union Bank was an important element in the story of Scottish achievement in a field in which Scotsmen gained world eminence. It represented the attempt, in the 1830s, of the 'new men' of Scotland's industrial west centred on Glasgow to seize the banking initiative from the east, with its powerful chartered banks in Edinburgh. This rivalry was extended to the Scottish scene generally as all the banks, including the Union, strove for national coverage in terms of their competing branch systems. This struggle was closely associated with the amalgamation movement. The Union Bank, as its name implies, had its origins in that phase of banking which saw the acceleration of the trend to larger size through mergers. The leading banks in this activity were faced with complex and intriguing tactical questions involving two great matters, namely what to take over and at what valuation. The Union Bank was to become itself a counter in this game being assimilated by the Bank of Scotland in 1954.

Behind this struggle for business, for power, for deposits and for good managerial ability lay two other sets of considerations. The one had to do with the rules by which the Bank should govern its portfolio. Professor Tamaki throws much light on asset management, lending control and the geographical flow of funds. The other was concerned with the evolving anatomy of the Scottish economy from which deposits were to be attracted and to which loans, in their many directions were to be made. Here we learn of the principal lending outlets and how they changed over time, using the Union Bank as a window on the Scottish economy, especially its industrial west. Both asset management and lending were judgemental questions, the responsibility for which lay with the senior management, especially the Superintendent of Branches and the General Manager.

There was yet a further facet, namely the relationships between the Scottish banks. Here matters were regulated on what was, in effect, a cartel basis. All the way from 1865 to 1914 the Committee of General Managers met regularly to set the rates to be paid both on deposits and on lending. Within this framework, however, there was vigorous competition.

The pattern of bank control reflected Scottish society: it was a mixture of the democratic and the hierarchic. Democracy obtained in the mode of recruitment of young men as they were fed into the lowest echelon of the banks as junior clerks: it continued as the promotion of 'lads o' pairts', based upon success in the examinations of the Institute of Bankers in Scotland together with managers' reports. Thus a lad of quite modest, but good, home background could make his way up from one stool to the next highest, right to the mandarin status that attached to the General Manager of a Scottish bank. All this, however, took place in a context in which hierarchy was present, operating through the directorship. A bank like the Union needed as wide a network of information and business power as possible. This meant that the boardroom could be dominated by men who were second generation or earlier, though in the west of Scotland there were arrivists also. This aspect came to a head in the Chairman of such a bank.

The Union Bank, like so many business enterprises, went through an arc of early struggles, rapid (not to say hectic) growth reaching a peak in the 1860s, followed by a period of consolidation leading to stagnation by 1885. The latter part of the story centres in large measure around a striking example of General Managership, namely Charles Gairdner. Though a man of note, who made his contribution to monetary and banking debate, he was not able to maintain the momentum of his bank in the Scottish league standing. Thus is posed in the book the general question: what are the factors that govern the life of a banking enterprise; in particular what is needful in managerial terms when such an institution is 'mature', and so requires a renewal of dynamic? Moreover, there is the question, how should a General Manager respond to external shocks: in Gairdner's case the failure of the City of Glasgow Bank in 1878 seems to have traumatised him into conservatism.

In a Postscript the author discusses the story of the Bank from 1885 to 1954. In this phase there is a shortage of available archival material, limiting the depth of scrutiny. It is possible, however, to make a number of observations of considerable interest. The minute books have by this time become conventionalised (the business historian's great source of chagrin) and there are no policy papers. The most interesting of the post-1885 managers (apart from Charles Gairdner) was Norman Hird (in office 1920–46). Though he doubled the Bank's business, the Union nevertheless fell behind its rivals. A further monograph on this innovative but frustrated and sometimes difficult man, an implacable enemy of trade unions in banking, would be of considerable interest. Within six years of his death in office the Union Bank, in a sense and for a time the flagship of Glasgow-based banking, was assimilated to the Edinburgh dominance.

The present book by Norio Tamaki, a Japanese scholar researching and writing in English, is an impressive achievement. It gives a depth to an aspect of Scottish banking not previously available. It should attract favourable attention from all those with a real interest in the formation and functioning of British banking.

S G Checkland
Department of Land Economy
The University of Cambridge

Contents

Three   The Union Bank of Scotland at its Zenith, 1858–65

Four   Years of Difficulty, 1865–79

Maps

Diagrams

Tables

Conclusion

Postscript

Abbreviations

BEM *Blackwood's Edinburgh Magazine*
BH *Business History*
BLC British Linen Co
BS Bank of Scotland
CBS Commercial Bank of Scotland
CIB Clydesdale Bank
CWM Charles W Munn
EcHR *Economic History Review*
GH *Glasgow Herald*
GL Charles Gairdner's Incoming Letters
GUA Glasgow University Archives Collection
JEH *Journal of Economic History*
JSS *Journal of the Statistical Society*
NBS National Bank of Scotland
RBS Royal Bank of Scotland
SBM *Scottish Bankers Magazine*
SGC S G Checkland
SIH *Scottish Industrial History*
SJPE *Scottish Journal of Political Economy*
TBR Three Banks Review
TP J & G Thomson MSS Papers
UB Union Bank of Scotland
UBAAB UB (Glasgow) Abstract Annual Balance
UBAQB UB (Glasgow) Abstract Quarterly Balance
UBC UB Contract of Copartnership
UBGC UB (Glasgow) General Circular
UBGL UB (Glasgow) General Ledger
UBHC UB (Glasgow) Head Office Circular
UBM UB Minute Book of the Glasgow Committee of Directors
UBMA UB Minute Book of the Sub-Committee 'A' of the Glasgow
  Committee of Directors
UBMB UB Minute Book of the Sub-Committee 'B' of the Glasgow
  Committee of Directors
UBME UB Minute Book of the Edinburgh Committee of Directors
UBMGB UB Minute Book of the General Board of Directors
UBPJ UB (Glasgow) Private Journal
UBPL UB (Glasgow) Private Ledger
UBSB UB (Glasgow) Secretary's Private Letter Book

Preface

This book is based on material prepared for my thesis which was accepted by the University of Glasgow in 1981. The principal consideration of the work covers the period 1830–85. A concluding chapter brings the account down to the amalgamation with the Bank of Scotland in 1952/54.

The emphasis on the years before 1885 arises from the fact that this was the period of the Union Bank of Scotland's greatest activity and share in the leadership of Scottish banking. Indeed, in these years, the Union Bank showed remarkable performance which once dominated the Scottish banking scene and which may well attract interest of banking and business historians. The Glasgow Union Banking Company was created in 1830, the first joint-stock bank based in Glasgow and the West of Scotland. The Bank soon embarked upon the amalgamation movement, the first successful and substantial activity of its kind. The amalgamations greatly enhanced the resources and fame of the Bank which in 1844 dropped the local name and adopted the national title, the Union Bank of Scotland. The powerful and remarkable growth of the Union Bank continued until 1865 when the Bank ranked only second to the Royal Bank of Scotland. The British economy entering upon the so-called 'Great Depression', the Union Bank ceased to show initiative and was entirely overtaken by the Edinburgh based banks. In 1885, the Union Bank sank into sixth place from which it could not really advance during the rest of its existence down to 1954 when the final fusion between the Union Bank and the Bank of Scotland was completed. This book is an attempt to trace the life cycle of the most senior Glasgow-based Union Bank of Scotland and to investigate it in the light of a certain set of banking themes.

Scottish banking has become an important research subject in recent years. Following the commissioning by the Institute of Bankers in Scotland of a history of Scottish banking, which became Professor S G Checkland's *Scottish Banking A History* published in 1975, there have been widespread interest and considerable research. The preparation for this book encouraged the banks in Scotland to list all archive materials in their possession. This has resulted in an astonishing amount of material becoming available and I am grateful to Mr W T Liddle and Mr A J Thomson of the Bank of Scotland for permission to use the archive material of the Union Bank of Scotland held at their Glasgow Chief Office—formerly the Head Office of the Union Bank—and at their Edinburgh Head Office. This present study of the Union Bank of Scotland would not have been possible without access to a wide variety of original and hitherto unused materials. Mr A B M Scott has been especially kind in helping me to progress in every aspect of my research. A debt of gratitude is also due to Mr D Burns of the Glasgow Chief Office and Mr R Perkins of the Edinburgh Head Office, who have been of considerable assistance, giving me generous facilities in their archives.

From the outset of my research in the Department of Economic History at the University of Glasgow in 1979, I have owed a great deal to many people. I am most grateful to Professor Checkland and Dr C W Munn whose unfailing supervision, guidance and encouragement have enabled me to accomplish this work. Their writings on Scottish banking have been of invaluable assistance to me in solving questions which arose at every stage of my studies. A special vote of thanks is due to Mrs E O A Checkland who has read my drafts at all stages, giving me numerous comments and suggestions. Without her guidance, this book would not have come into existence. I am grateful to her for the generosity shown throughout my research in Glasgow and during the preparation for this book. My thanks are also due to Professor Maxwell Gaskin, University of Aberdeen, who kindly commented upon my final draft.

I am indebted to the staff of the Department of Economic History whose readiness to respond to my demands was indispensable for the progress of my work. I am especially grateful to Professor A Slaven for his helpfulness at the earlier stage of my research. The staff of the Glasgow University libraries, of the Mitchell Library and of Baillie's Library were excellent in their professional services. My thanks are particularly due to one whose knowledge of Glasgow literature is especially profound, namely Mrs M Manchester of Baillie's Library, and to Mr M S Moss, Dr D A Dow and Mr J Emery of the University Archives.

At all stages in my writing this book, Professor Checkland, Dr Munn and Mrs Checkland have corrected my faulty English. I am grateful to them all. In this respect, a special vote of thanks is due to Miss J W Taylor, who has been far more than my English teacher. I am also indebted to Mrs I Burnside for her excellent typing of my final draft. Responsibility for errors remains mine alone. The index has been prepared by Mrs A F Ballantyne.

Keio University, Tokyo, in which I have a lectureship, supported my research in Glasgow for two years. I thank Keio University and my colleagues at the Faculty of Commerce for such generosity. My thanks are also due to Professor T Kotake and Professor S Watanabe, who were responsible for kindling my interest in British banking history, to Professor C Sugiyama whose advice was essential for my preparation for the research in Glasgow and to Manuel Fernandez and Takao Matsumura who have shown very friendly interest throughout my research. Keio University has also given me generous help in publishing this book, and I am particularly grateful to Professor S Tamura. Then last, but not least, a tremendous debt of gratitude is due to my wife, Setsuko, who has assisted me in typing drafts and preparing tables and maps. Without her assistance and patience, my work could not have been done so efficiently and pleasantly.

Norio Tamaki
Faculty of Commerce
Keio University, Tokyo

Introduction

1 Scottish Banking and the West of Scotland, 1800–1829

The Scottish banks in 1800 were grouped into three categories; the public banks composed of the Bank of Scotland (est. 1695), Royal Bank of Scotland (est. 1727) and British Linen Co (est. 1746), all of which were set up on the joint-stock principle with limited liability as a product of public authority; fifteen private banks, which were small partnerships based mostly on Edinburgh, primarily non-note-issuers acting as intermediaries between the public banks and customers; and sixteen provincial banks, which were note-issuers located in towns other than Edinburgh and ranging from firms of partnerships to those formed as co-partneries.[1] At the turn of the century, Scottish banking was a three-tier structure.

Between 1800 and 1829, the Scottish system began to change. As Table 1 suggests, one constituent, that is, the private banks, lost ground. More than one third of the private banks disappeared from the Scottish scene. Only relatively large scale firms like Sir William Forbes, James Hunter & Co, could survive. Up to 1829 only three firms set up as private banks, and nine firms

TABLE 1

Scottish Banks, 1800 and 1829

		1800	*1829*
1	Public Banks	3	3
2	Private Banks		
	(a) Edinburgh	13	8
	(b) Glasgow	2	1
3	Provincial Banks		
	(a) Glasgow	3	3
	(b) West	4	5
	(c) Rest	9	13
4	Joint-Stock Banks		
	(a) Edinburgh	0	2
	(b) Glasgow	0	0
	(c) Aberdeen	0	1
		34	36

Sources: SGC, 1975, Tables 3 and 9; CWM, 1981, Tables 5, 9 and 11

[1] Notes begin on p. 195

1

TABLE 2

Liabilities/Assets of Scottish Banks, 1802 and 1825: £1,000

		1802	%	1825	%
1	Public Banks	6,645	54	11,263	46
2	Private Banks	1,100	9	1,009	4
3	Provincial Banks	4,527	37	5,735	24
	(Glasgow based)	(931)	(8)	(1,104)	(5)
4	Joint-Stock Banks	0	0	6,412	26
		12,272	100	24,419	100

Source: SGC, 1975, Tables 8 and 14

failed or retired. The provincial banks were also heading for the same fate. From 1801 to 1829, nineteen made a beginning, but fourteen failed or retired or made their business over to others.[2] Their shares in the Scottish total liabilities/assets fell, remarkably, to less than one third in 1825 as Table 2 sets out. The eclipse of private and provincial banks was due to the fact that their capabilities were overtaken by the growth of the Scottish economy.

In place of the declining private and provincial banks, there emerged a new constituent in Scottish banking, that is, the joint-stock bank, which was created on the principle of co-partnership, as indeed were the provincials, but on an unprecedentedly large scale. First, in 1810, came the Commercial Bank of Scotland, based in Edinburgh, with a capital of £3m, 673 shareholders and 14 branches by 1815, and whose success encouraged another two to enter the system in the boom of 1825; the National Bank of Scotland in Edinburgh and the Aberdeen Town & County Bank. The emergence of large scale joint-stock banking was due entirely to the expanding economy during the first quarter of the nineteenth century, during which the three public banks were not sufficiently active in supplying adequate funds.[3] The addition of three joint-stock banks to the public banks resulted in a tremendous proportion of large scale joint-stock banking, which amounted to nearly three quarters of the total Scottish liabilities in 1825. The age of large scale joint-stock banking had arrived in Scotland.

Successful joint-stock and provincial banking in Scotland, where no legal restriction was laid against it, led Thomas Joplin, 'a Newcastle timber merchant with local experience of banking disasters'[4], to argue for the adoption of the same system in England and Wales, and the monopoly of the Bank of England, was, indeed, mitigated by the Act of 1826, the process of which legislation, however, once caused a fear that the Scottish banks would be deprived of the right of small note-issues. In his argument Joplin did not forget to add that,

> In addition, however, to their success, some of the Scotch Banks have very considerable capital, particularly the Edinburgh Banks, which have from five to fifteen hundred thousand pounds each.[5]

and that,

> The Edinburgh Banks have agencies, and do business to a great amount, in all the
> principal towns of Scotland, which no doubt is on the aggregate found to pay them.[6]

Indeed, the superiority of Scottish banking over its English and Welsh
counterpart was mainly the feature of Edinburgh banking. There was no joint-
stock bank outside Edinburgh, except in Aberdeen. There was not yet a joint-
stock bank in the industrial West, where the cotton industry equipped with
power looms was rapidly growing, taking the place of the traditional linen
industry, and Neilson's hot blast was about to be adopted by the iron industry
during the late 1820s.[7] Even in Glasgow which had become the largest town in
Scotland,[8] there were only four small scale banks, whose proportion in the
total Scottish liabilities was as little as 5% in 1825 (Table 2). Consequently,
banking facilities in Glasgow and the West had to be provided by banks based
in other towns, particularly Edinburgh.[9]

Why could not Glasgow and the West take the initiative in creating their
own joint-stock bank? Were merchants and land-owners in the West reluctant
to establish their own banks? In retrospect the reverse is true, at least in the
eighteenth century. In the first place, the Glasgow merchants set up three
banking houses based on their wealth created in the tobacco trade in the
middle of the eighteenth century; the Ship Bank of Dunlop, Houston & Co in
1749, the Arms Bank of Cochrane, Murdoch & Co in 1750 and the Thistle
Bank of Maxwell, Ritchie & Co in 1761.[10] Originally the Ship and Arms
Banks started their banking business as agencies of the Bank of Scotland and
the Royal Bank and then became independent after a successful confrontation
with the parent concerns. This was the very first rivalry between the two
banking centres. Unfortunately for the Glasgow merchants, the American
war, which had broken out in 1776, damaged the basis of their banking
business. Thus, the Arms Bank dropped out in the 1793 crisis along with a
scheme for a joint-stock bank, which will be discussed later, and the younger
Merchants Bank (est. 1769), and the surviving two lost ground.[11]

The second initiative came from further west than Glasgow, from the Bank
in Ayr of Douglas, Heron & Co, established in 1769. The short life of the Ayr
Bank brought drama to banking. The Ayr Bank was the first substantial
banking concern outside Edinburgh, being led by many lowland lairds of the
first rank. It soon established seven branches, invading Edinburgh and taking
over two provincial banks. In spite of its aggressiveness, the Ayr Bank was not
openly opposed by the public banks, perhaps because 'they knew that it was
hopeless to oppose so powerful a company, with the backing of vast acres and
prestigious titles'.[12]

The initial success of the Ayr Bank seems to have been promising and its
Bank notes spread over the country through its agents. Liberal cash credits
and discounts, which the public banks tended to avoid, were given to the
proprietors as well as to the public. From this over-enthusiasm came disaster.
In 1772, when the Scottish economy witnessed overtrading which the Ayr
Bank had itself accelerated, the Bank encountered difficulties and collapsed in

the wake of the rejection of its appeal for assistance to the Bank of England and the public banks.[13] The Ayr Bank, through its wide note circulation and liberal lending policy, contributed to the setting up of note exchange and the expansion of the Scottish economy in the late eighteenth century, and left a substantial effect on the later development of banking in the West. Its performance made the West and Glasgow increasingly notorious with regard to speculation. Indeed, in 1803, thirty years afterwards, when Robert Scott Moncrieff, joint-agent of the Royal Bank in Glasgow, asked the government to help Glasgow which was at that time in great financial difficulties, the prime minister refused any assistance because Glasgow was a speculative place.[14]

The third initiative, led by Sir John Sinclair, a talented Scotsman,[15] made its appearance in 1793 as a scheme for setting up 'a major chartered bank based upon Glasgow',[16] to be 'the Royal Bank of Glasgow'. According to the prospectus, 'the Royal Bank of Glasgow' was to have a subscribed capital of £0.3m with limited liability. The project was welcomed in Glasgow, 175 subscribers signed and the public banks also seemed to accept this newly projected bank in the Scottish banking family. At this very moment, the war crisis arose and engulfed the only scheme for establishing a public bank based upon Glasgow.

The collapse of the tobacco trade, of the Ayr Bank and of the abortive scheme of a Glasgow public bank left a great gap in the growing economy in the West which the small scale Glasgow banks were unable to fill. This was filled by the Edinburgh banks. The Royal Bank took the opportunity to expand its business, especially in Glasgow. Indeed, the deposits of its Glasgow agent more than doubled between 1794 and 1807 and the advances on discounts increased from £400,000 to £636,000 in the same period. The proportion of discounts by the Royal Bank agent exceeded 40% of the total discounts in Glasgow.[17] The growth of the Royal Bank business encouraged the British Linen Co and the Bank of Scotland, which opened their Glasgow agencies by 1797 and 1802 respectively. Glasgow business was obviously profitable, and was able to be conducted best by large scale joint-stock banking, such as that of the public banks.

Profitable banking business in Glasgow inevitably attracted the attention of entrepreneurs, perhaps ironically, from another town. The partners of the Dundee New Bank (provincial bank), who were encouraged by their successful reconstruction of the Dundee Commercial Bank (provincial bank, est. 1792) in 1802, invaded Glasgow and created the Glasgow Bank (provincial bank) in 1809. The Glasgow Bank showed aggressiveness and successfully established itself in Glasgow. It is noticeable that, though the Glasgow Bank was a creation of Dundee entrepreneurs, and small compared to the Edinburgh banks, a Glasgow man, James Dennistoun of Golfhill, Glasgow, 'perhaps the most prominent citizen of Glasgow in the first quarter of the nineteenth century',[18] took office as managing director. The success of the Glasgow Bank under the management of a notable Glasgow merchant, though small scale with fourteen partners and £0.1m paid-up capital, showed what could be done in Glasgow.

The success of the relatively small scale Glasgow Bank, naturally, did little to change the Glasgow scene which was increasingly dominated by the Edinburgh banks. In 1809, there were twenty banking offices in Glasgow as Table 3 sets out. During the twenty years up to 1829, the economy in the West was making great progress but the number of banking offices became reduced to thirteen. The reduction of banking offices in Glasgow, the centre of the rising industrial West, suggests that banking business was increasingly conducted by large scale joint-stock banks, that is, the Edinburgh banks, and also that the capability of the provincial banks, including those Glasgow-based, was completely overtaken by the growth of the economy.

TABLE 3

Banking Offices in Glasgow, 1809 and 1829

	1809	*1829*
Glasgow based	1 Ship Bank*	1 Ship Bank*
	2 Thistle Bank*	2 Thistle Bank*
	3 Glasgow Bank*	3 Glasgow Bank*
	4 Watson & Co†	4 Watson & Co†
Edinburgh based	5 Bank of Scotland	5 Bank of Scotland
	6 Royal Bank	6 Royal Bank
	7 British Linen	7 British Linen
		8 Commercial Bank‡
Provincials	8 Hunters & Co (Ayr)	9 Greenock Bkg Co
	9 Greenock Bkg Co	10 Paisley Bkg Co
	10 Paisley Bkg Co	11 Paisley Union Bank
	11 Paisley Union Bank	12 Renfrewshire Bkg Co
	12 Renfrewshire Bkg Co (Greenock)	13 Leith Bkg Co
	13 Kilmarnock Bkg Co	
	14 Stirling Bkg Co	
	15 Dundee New Bank	
	16 Falkirk Bkg Co	
	17 Falkirk Union Bank	
	18 Fife Bkg Co (Cupar)	
	19 Leith Bkg Co	
	20 Perth Bkg Co	

*Provincial Bank
†Private Bank
‡Joint-stock Bank

Sources: C W Boase, 1867, p.262. J K McDowall, 1899, pp.66–9. SGC, 1975, Tables 3 and 9

2   The Union Bank of Scotland

By 1830, Glasgow and the West of Scotland were entering upon a period of great expansion and prosperity. Despite the fluctuations of the trade cycle, the general picture was of successful achievement. In 1829, in Glasgow, as already mentioned, there were thirteen bank offices, two-thirds of which were those of banks based on other towns. Above all, the Edinburgh banks were the most powerful. It was therefore perhaps inevitable that Glasgow merchants, proud of their energy and initiative, should attempt to inaugurate a new era of Glasgow-based joint-stock banking. Indeed, during the 1830s, Glasgow men founded four important banks, that is, the Glasgow Union Banking Company in 1830, the Western Bank of Scotland in 1832, the Clydesdale Bank in 1838 and the City of Glasgow Bank in 1839.

This book is an attempt to examine the history of the Glasgow Union Banking Company, later the Union Bank of Scotland, the first founded by Glasgow initiative, which led other Glasgow banks during the crucial years of Glasgow challenge by the third quarter of the nineteenth century. After 1885, following the spectacular collapse of the Western Bank of Scotland in 1857 and the City of Glasgow Bank in 1878, and despite the continuance of the Union Bank of Scotland and the Clydesdale Bank, the Edinburgh banks and the men who controlled them knew they had nothing to fear from any further Glasgow banking challenge. The influential period in the history of the Union Bank of Scotland was, thus, from 1830 to 1885, though it remained in existence until 1955 when it was taken over by the Bank of Scotland. This book considers the rise of the Union Bank of Scotland and its subsequent stagnation. The years after 1885 are of less consequence.

Scottish banking in 1830 was operated by four very different institutions—the public bank, the private bank, the provincial banking company and the joint-stock bank, the product of the nineteenth century. At the end of our period, i.e. 1885, the number of the components was reduced to two—the public bank and the joint-stock bank. By this time, the categorical difference between the two became insignificant, and only regional pattern was noticeable. Five Edinburgh-based and two Glasgow-based banks were the nationwide and three North-based were the local. Between banking based on Edinburgh and Glasgow, the former boosted its supremacy over the latter. Fifty-five years from 1830 brought drama to the Scottish banking history.

This was well exemplified by the history of the Union Bank of Scotland. Indeed, during the period of 1830/1885, the Union Bank of Scotland exhibited very strongly different types of performance. From these, seven themes emerge. These are the rise and fall of the Glasgow challenge to the Edinburgh banks, the amalgamation movement of which the Union Bank was a 'classic example',[19] the competitiveness of the Union Bank compared with the other Scottish banks, the remarkable change in the assets management, the relationship of the Bank with particular industries, the substantial money flow inside the Bank's own structure, and the conditioning character of the general manager who headed the Union Bank for thirty-three years. These themes have not been deliberately discussed. Though R S Rait's book on the Union Bank of Scotland between 1830 and 1930 remains a useful official history of the Bank, it scarcely enters into these topics. They are essential components of banking history, and it is hoped that the study of them in terms of a single bank will carry connotations for the system as a whole.

Before beginning our examination in detail, a definition of 'joint-stock bank' must be re-affirmed. 'Joint-stock' is a very ambiguous concept, because any concern composed of more than a single proprietor is 'joint-stock'. Even 'joint-stock of a large number of shareholders' might be an insufficient basis, because a legal limitation of 'six partners', stipulated in the Act of 1708 regarding England and Wales, did not apply to Scotland; as a result, some of the Scottish provincial banking companies had dozens of partners.[20] A possible and safer definition of joint-stock bank on the Scottish context, into which category the Union Bank of Scotland falls, is, therefore, that the joint-stock bank, as it emerged in Scotland during the first half of the nineteenth century, was in all terms of amount of capital and number of shareholders and branches larger by an order of magnitude than the provincial banking company. It aimed at national coverage, and was able to respond to the growing economy, ranking in scales with the public banks. The difference between the joint-stock bank, both chartered and unchartered, and the public bank was simply that the former was not by the early 1880s based on the principle of limited liability.

Chapter One

Formative Years, 1830–1844

The Union Bank of Scotland, which was the first joint-stock bank in Glasgow as well as in the industrial West of Scotland, made remarkable progress in the first fourteen years, and this was primarily due to successful amalgamations between 1836 and 1844. The successful business of the Union Bank of Scotland initiated the Glasgow challenge to the Edinburgh banks and pioneered the age of amalgamation.

1   The Establishment of the Glasgow Union Banking Company, 1830[1]

(a) THE BIRTH OF THE FIRST JOINT-STOCK BANK IN GLASGOW

In the autumn of 1829, Robert Stewart (wine and spirit merchant at Old Post Office Court, Glasgow) proposed the idea of 'setting on foot a local public bank in Glasgow'[2] to Roderick MacKenzie (WS, Edinburgh) and William Mitchell (teller of the Commercial Bank of Scotland). Ironically, one of the original promoters was an Edinburgh lawyer. Stewart made two points. In the first place, he insisted that the further deterioration of the City of Glasgow, especially around the Market Cross and the Exchange, could be prevented by the establishment of 'a bank on popular principles'.[3] His opinion must have been shared by many Glasgow businessmen. Indeed, from the summer to the autumn of 1829 when the Royal Bank was deserting the old city centre, one of the promoters, who afterwards joined Stewart, was repeatedly petitioning the City authority to take some steps 'with a view to the maintenance of the property of the centre district of the city'[4] and no bank office was situated there as Map 1 shows.

In the second place, it was believed that a joint-stock bank based in Glasgow was 'very much wanted upon a general view of the state of other banks in Glasgow'[5] and should be successful as well as profitable. Stewart, MacKenzie and Mitchell soon consulted businessmen in Glasgow and some other principal towns in the West, Central and East, and formed an interim committee, which was composed of thirty persons and appointed Mitchell and MacKenzie as interim manager and secretary respectively. A prospectus of the first Glasgow joint-stock bank, termed 'Glasgow Union Banking Company', appeared in newspapers in December 1829.[6]

Nine resolutions were attached to the prospectus. According the the first resolution, the capital stock was to be £2m which was divided into 8,000 shares of £250 each, and the partners were 'to be allowed to operate upon their shares

MAP 1

Bank Offices in Glasgow, 1830

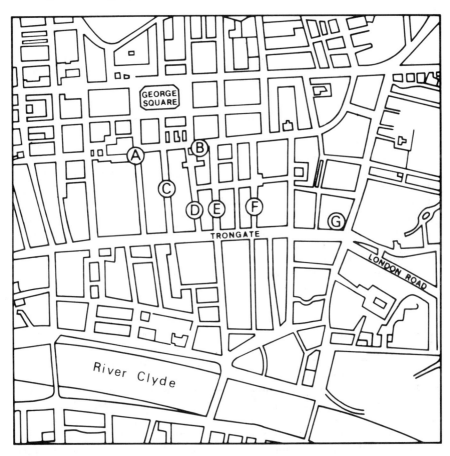

A	Queen Street	6	British Linen	E	Glassford Street
	1 Royal Bank	7	Renfrewshire		12 Ship Bank
	2 Greenock Bkg Co		Bkg Co	F	Brunswick Street
B	Ingram Street	D	Virginia Street		13 Leith Bank
	3 Glasgow Bank	8	Commercial Bank	G	Market Cross
	4 Paisley Union	9	Thistle Bank		14 Union Bank
	Bank	10	Watson & Co		
C	Miller Street	11	Paisley Bkg Co		
	5 Bank of Scotland				

Sources: Post Office Glasgow Directory, 1830/31. J K McDowall, 1899, pp. 66–7. R Renwick, 1916, vol. XI, appendix

to the extent of one half of their advanced stock upon the principle of a cash credit account'.[7] The subscription of Bank stock started immediately under the supervision of Stewart and the interim secretary. In two weeks, 3,350 shares were subscribed and a meeting of the interim committee was called in the middle of January 1830.

The meeting of 15 January carried the motion made by Stewart that 1,000 shares should be made available for eligible persons in Edinburgh. This was a wise decision because a new joint-stock bank based in Glasgow might have been unsuccessful without firm support in Edinburgh which was the financial centre of Scotland. The committee released MacKenzie from his duty of interim secretary and he thereafter devoted himself to promoting the establishment in Edinburgh. In addition, the committee set up a sub-committee including Stewart and Robert MacHaffie for the purpose of drawing up a report made before a future general meeting, and for a plan with regard to the design of notes and other indispensable matters. Upon closing discussions, the meeting gave special thanks to Robert Stewart for 'his invaluable and indefatigable exertions'.[8]

By 21 January, 4,221 shares were subscribed, including those allotted to Edinburgh, and, as a result, the committee declared in terms of the sixth resolution of the prospectus that the Glasgow Union Banking Co was constituted.[9] Although the necessary number of shares was subscribed, applications were still pouring into the office of interim secretary, which had been opened by David Wilkie (WS, Glasgow). The interim committee was delighted by the response and began to discriminate between useful applic-ants, who would give good business and deposits, and others. A new sub-committee was appointed to sort out desirable shareholders. In the meantime, MacKenzie, who had finished his task in Edinburgh, was preparing a draft of the contract of co-partnery and the first general meeting of shareholders was planned for 2 February.

Thus far there were no problems. As early as 20 January, R MacHaffie raised 'some very important matters'[10] to the interim committee, which delayed consideration of them on account of the absence of Stewart. The matters were related to the mode of election of the directorate and the authority of the chairman and deputy chairman. According to the draft of the contract, 'neither the chairman, deputy chairman, nor extraordinary direc-tors, shall be members of the committee of management, or ordinary direction'.[11] Nevertheless, it was fully expected by R MacHaffie and his party that the two senior persons of their group, that is, David MacHaffie and Joseph Bain, would be elected to the offices of chairman and deputy chairman. The result of the ballot came out as they expected.

No compromise was reached between the group led by MacHaffie and that led by Stewart and John Leadbetter (jute merchant and manufacturer, Glasgow). The general meeting was postponed for a fortnight. Meanwhile, the conflict between the parties was leaked by the Glasgow Chronicle. These disagreements might have had political undertones. Certainly the party led by MacHaffie included James Lumsden, a well-known supporter of the Liberals, and one of the leaders of the other party, Leadbetter, was a Conservative.[12]

Too much should not be made of the political interpretation, for Robert Dalglish, the Lord Provost and a Liberal, who was a partner of Dalglish, Falconer & Co (calico printers, near the Market Cross, Glasgow) and was 'far from being a reformer',[13] later became a shareholder.

Eventually, the MacHaffies and their party dropped out at the general meeting of 16 February, which had been earlier postponed, when the first ten directors including Stewart and Leadbetter were elected and the contract underwent only slight amendment. The number of the dissentients finally amounted to 46 and the withdrawal of their 416 shares was effected later in June 1830. From the dissentients, there emerged at least two joint-stock banks in Glasgow. The one was the Clydesdale Bank which was promoted by Lumsden in 1838. The other was the Glasgow Joint Stock Bank, set up in 1843, one of the creators of which was R MacHaffie. It could be argued that the struggle in the course of the birth of the first joint-stock bank was one of the important elements in the formation of Glasgow joint-stock banking.

The Union Bank started with 407 shareholders who attended, or sent letters

TABLE 4

Regional Distribution of Shareholders, 1830

Glasgow	267	66%
Rest of West	66	16
Edinburgh	55	14
Rest of East	4	—
Central	4	—
North	1	—
Western Isles	3	—
Unknown	7	—
	407	

Source: UB *List of Shareholders 1830*

TABLE 5

Occupational Distribution of Shareholders, 1830

Merchant	71	38%
Manufacturer	24	13
Retailer	48	25
Professions	35	19
Farmer	4	2
Builder	3	1
Service	4	2
	189	100%

Source: UB *List of Shareholders 1830*

of attorney to, the first general meeting held on 2 February 1830. The regional and occupational distributions of the shareholders are set out in Tables 4 and 5 respectively. Table 4 shows that the Union Bank depended overwhelmingly upon the wealth of Glasgow and the West of Scotland. No English capital was involved. It should also be noted that there was a substantial proportion of Edinburgh shareholders. Table 5 tells us only less than half of the occupations of shareholders. However, it might not be unreasonable to say that the Union Bank was based primarily on wholesale and retail trade. Consequently, the first Glasgow joint-stock bank was created from the wealth of the Glasgow merchants whose initiative pioneered a new age of Scottish banking.

(b) THE OPENING OF BUSINESS

At the first board of directors held on 17 February 1830, the directors divided themselves into four sub-committees; on bank notes, establishment, premises and London correspondents. Some preparations for opening business had already made progress before the election of directors. Designs of bank notes were produced by W H Lizars (an Edinburgh shareholder), which were formally adopted on 19 February. Plans with regard to book-keeping and regulations for agencies were prepared by Mitchell, interim manager, probably on the model of the Commercial Bank of Scotland, in which he once served.

   One of the most important tasks was recruitment of Bank staff. Although the interim manager, Mitchell, was considered competent for the pre-opening preparations, he had never been promised the post of manager and seems to have been regarded as inadequate for conducting the whole business of the Bank. Indeed, as early as under the management of the interim committee, J A Anderson (manufacturer and merchant, Brunswick, Glasgow, aged forty-five)[14] was nominated as a manager and appointed on 20 February. Objection was raised by two directors who seemed to think that no manager was necessary.[15] They must have thought that the Union Bank could manage to conduct its business without a manager. This idea was obviously wrong, and the selection and appointment of Anderson as manager proved to be successful. Anderson was bound to devote his whole time to the business of the Bank, unlike some cashiers and managers of provincial banks,[16] at the salary of £700, which was the same as that of the managers of the Commercial Bank and the National Bank and which was to be increased by £100 per year for three successive years. Mitchell was appointed cashier, with which position he was dissatisfied for he afterwards deserted the Bank to be a manager of the Western Bank of Scotland in 1832.[17]

   By the end of March, staff recruitment was completed. John Sharpe, from the staff of the Commercial Bank, was appointed principal accountant. The Commercial Bank of Scotland was seemingly a primary source of the Union Bank staff as the cases of Mitchell and Sharpe exemplified. The accountant's department employed five clerks at salaries from £50 to £130. A teller and two apprentices were also employed at salaries of £180 and £10 respectively. The staff of eleven was twice as much as that of the average provincial bank.[18] In the meantime, the Bank office was settled on the first and second floors of the building situated at Old Post Office Court, Trongate, near the old city centre, and its rental was £250 for the first year. The total amount of salaries and rental was at least £2,000 which must have been the minimum expense for setting up a joint-stock bank in the early 1830s.

The next important step for opening the Bank was the establishment of agencies in London and Edinburgh. As early as in January, Barclay, Tritton, Bevan & Co (London) offered their services, but the interim committee did not feel the need for a London agent. By the end of March, the sub-committee on agencies recommended Jones, Loyd & Co as London correspondents, and this was agreed to by the directors.[19] Robert Allan & Son had agreed to act as Edinburgh correspondents at the charge of 1%. The Edinburgh shareholders objected to this decision and insisted that an Edinburgh agency should be opened, as the contract stipulated, arguing that this could be successfully supported by them. The directors countered by stating that,

> the matter must rest on the ground of expediency and advantage to the Bank, on which subject their views were considerably changed from finding that Edinburgh business could be conducted on much lower terms than was formerly anticipated.[20]

The directors held to this opinion and, as a result, the subject of opening an Edinburgh branch was re-considered in the autumn of 1830.

Otherwise, all preparations were completed by the beginning of April when a circular was issued encouraging the shareholders that,

> each individual in his own sphere, will use every exertion to promote and advance the general interests, and I would suggest that this may be done by opening cash, current and deposit accounts, negotiation of bills and by the circulation of the notes of the Bank.[21]

The directors organised a daily committee, which was to sit in the Bank and to superintend the general business.[22] At 10 a.m. on 13 May 1830 the first Glasgow joint-stock Bank opened its doors. The first three applicants for credits were John Miller, director (for £900), J Leadbetter, director (for £375) and J A Anderson, manager (for £700).

(c) THE FIRST BUSINESS YEAR OF THE BANK, MAY 1830–MAY 1831

The directors of the first Glasgow joint-stock Bank were very conscious that,

> It must be obvious that a newly established bank is peculiarly liable to loss as well from inexperience, and natural over anxiety to extend the business and employ the capital as from the attempts that never fail to be made upon it by persons of unworthy credit.[23]

The policy of carefulness and shrewdness, i.e., 'canniness', was followed in all their business.

The directors used a seven-point scale for investigating their customers' creditworthiness; very bad (symbolised as 16), bad (16c17), fair (17), very fair (17c18), good (18), very good (18c19), and undoubted (19).[24] According to this scale, the directors considered carefully and granted credits. They generally rejected applications for credits of more than £1,000 but were very keen to distribute advances of less than £1,000 among their customers.[25]

The fifth clause of the contract of the Union Bank allowed the directors to invest surplus funds in British government securities and in the stock of chartered companies and that of the Union Bank. It took more than three months for the directors to make up their minds to commence the business of investments. At the end of August 1830, the Union Bank for the first time resolved to invest in British government securities to the extent of £25,000 through Loyd & Co and Sanderson, Sandeman & Co, though this decision was not made unanimously. This sum was not increased during the first business year which was not unreasonable. The first unhappy experience of the directors had been when the Bank suffered a loss of £2,500 by the depreciation of the market value of funds.

During the first business year, the directors considered the establishment of ten branches, among which only three were created at Greenock, Bathgate and Port Glasgow by the end of August 1830. Greenock was in the forefront of the foreign trade of the West of Scotland,[26] and the directors natually gave priority to the establishment of a Greenock branch over others, which, fortunately, proved to be very successful at the end of the first business year.[27] An Edinburgh branch, which had been a serious topic of discussion inside the boardroom, was eventually instituted in September 1830, and this took the place of the service of Allan & Son. None the less, the directors were very careful in commencing business there. It took more than three months for the Edinburgh office to open its doors. Firstly, a managership was instituted and Robert Burns was appointed in October. Detailed instructions were drawn up and sent to the manager, tellers and accountants at the Edinburgh Office in December. Furthermore, a local committee, composed of seven Edinburgh shareholders, was set up and strictly instructed by the directors to superintend closely the daily business of the branch. Finally, the Edinburgh branch opened at the end of December 1830.[28] The behaviour of the directors exhibits their carefulness, but even this policy was enterprising compared to that of the English counterparts some of whom regarded it as foolhardy to erect a branch more than around twenty-five miles away from its head office.[29] Edinburgh was forty-five miles' distance from Glasgow. This difference between two styles of banking was obviously due to the development of branch banking in which Scottish banking had considerable superiority over the English.

Plans for other branches were either delayed or abandoned. Branches at Stirling, Alloa and Kincardine were postponed because the National Bank of Scotland was offering its stock below the market price of shares and enthusiastically establishing branches in these places.[30] An Ayr branch, which had been resolved on, was also delayed, probably because the Ayrshire Banking Co (joint-stock) came into being immediately after the opening of the Union Bank. Plans for branches at Wick and Lochgilphead were abandoned.

Following the policy of canniness, the Bank made sound progress in the first business year. The first inter-bank relationship was formed in March 1830 when the Provincial Bank of Ireland offered to do business in Ireland on behalf of the Union Bank. This relationship probably resulted from the Irish connection of John Leadbetter, director, who was engaged in the linen trade. The note exchange at Glasgow was also arranged with the Royal Bank of Scotland in January 1831. The notes of the Union Bank began to cross the border, making their appearance in Carlisle in June 1830,[31] in common with the issues of several other Scottish banks.

The first balance sheet, issued in May 1831, showed the total liabilities/assets of £748,804.[32] Balance in the profit and loss account amounted to £8,779 from which the directors could have paid up to a 5% dividend if it had not been prohibited from doing so by the contract. The number of shareholders had increased to 608 by May 1831. The emergence and successful inception of the Union Bank must have had not a little effect on the banks already operating in Glasgow. Indeed, the Royal Bank, which had the biggest interest in the Glasgow business, now had a decrease in deposits.[33] Consequently, the Union Bank was firmly established in Glasgow and embarked upon the Glasgow challenge to the Edinburgh banks, though it was still a fledgling.

2 Years of Steady Growth, 1831–1836

(a) THE BEGINNINGS OF TRIAL

Financing the growing economy, especially speculative in the West of Scotland, the Union Bank, in common with other banks, inevitably began to sustain losses. In the spring of 1832, the Union Bank suffered owing to the failure of a large number of the Glasgow grain merchants and it took two years to make good the losses, but the dividend remained $2\frac{1}{2}\%$ in the three successive years. Again in the summer of 1835, one of the hectic years for the British economy in the 1830s, the Bank sustained losses in common with other banks. However, the directors managed to ride out the minor crisis and raised the 4% dividend in 1835 to 5% in 1836, leaving a surplus of more than £1,000 on their profit and loss account.

More importantly, the Union Bank entered a stage of increasing competition which was accelerated by the opening of the second joint-stock bank in Glasgow, the Western Bank of Scotland in 1832. The directors of the Union Bank, having learned of the preparation for the establishment of the Western Bank, encouraged their shareholders to exert themselves to promote its circulation.[34] It was also revealed that W Mitchell, cashier of the Union Bank, and a teller had committed themselves to set up the Western Bank, and they were immediately dismissed in the spring of 1832. Against the loss of the staff, the Union Bank took over the Paisley agent of the Western Bank, who, seemingly dissatisfied with the rather foolhardy management of his parent concern, had proceeded to make over his agency together with his associated shareholders of the Western Bank. The Paisley branch, under the charge of the late agent of the Western Bank, was thus created in October 1833. The directors of the Union Bank were very proud of this take-over and declared in their annual report that the establishment of a Paisley branch was the 'most important occurrence'[35] of the year. Entering an arena of real trial, the Union Bank grew steadily from 1831 to 1836.

(b) THE ASSETS MANAGEMENT OF THE BANK

During the first business year, the Union Bank allowed customers to borrow almost entirely on cash credits and discounts. It was from the second business year that the directors began to diversify their methods of advances according to the twenty-fifth clause of the contract. In February 1834 the directors gave a credit of £700 on the personal security of five customers.[36] Sanctions of credits on heritable securities emerged earlier in December 1831.[37]

However, the most remarkable method of advances was discounting of bills as Table 6 sets out. Surprisingly, the amount of discounts for the first year was thirteen times larger than advances on cash, or credit, accounts, though the gap between the two was reducing as the business of the Bank progressed as likewise at the Glasgow branch of the Royal Bank of Scotland.[38] Consequently, one concludes that the Glasgow-based Union Bank supplied funds primarily by discounting, as did other Scottish banks, public and provincial.[39] This runs contrary to the claim of Professor R Cameron that,

> Bills of exchange, the staple assets of many contemporary banks in other countries were the least important earning assets of the Scottish banks. . . . The largest volume of lending, however, took place by means of loans on cash accounts.[40]

Remarkable progress was also made in the management of surplus funds which was due to the general situation of the money market as well as the cautious policy of the Bank. The directors made use of two outlets for the surplus funds. Firstly, the Bank gradually increased investments in public funds such as Consols, East India bonds, Bank of England stock and Exchequer bills which were effected mainly through the London correspondents, Loyd & Co and Sandeman & Co. But, unlike during the first business year, the directors, who had increasing confidence in themselves, did not leave the management of investments totally to the discretion of the correspondents and gave detailed instructions for the first time in September 1831 to them when and how they should purchase and dispose of the public funds.[41] The Bank increased investments in government securities particularly in the autumn of 1831 and the summers of 1832 and 1833 when Consols were yielding 3.8, 3.6 and 3.4% respectively. When the market prices of securities were supposed to have reached their highest points and other profitable outlets such as inter-bank loans were found, the directors did not hesitate to dispose of them.[42]

The second outlet was, as already mentioned, inter-bank loans, chiefly to

TABLE 6

Methods of Advances, 1831 and 1836

	Credit Accounts†		Discounts†	
1831*	£27,348	(7%)	£364,316	(93%)
1836*	74,984	(16%)	405,828	(84%)

*date as in April each year
†%; proportion between two methods

Source: UBAAB

the English banks, which were probably doing business with the customers of the Union Bank. Therefore, the development of inter-bank loans was said to be a result of surplus funds as well as 'follow the customer' policy. The first inter-bank loan in this period was arranged with the National Provincial Bank of England in June 1831 which was followed by the Bank of Manchester, Bank of Liverpool and Manchester & Liverpool District Bank, the last of which took £20,000.[43] These loans were made from the excessive balance in the hands of Loyd & Co and proceeds of the sale of public funds.[44] In the course of the development of English inter-bank loans, there occurred the necessity of having correspondents in Cumbria where the Bank notes had earlier appeared. The directors soon arranged with Carrick, Sons & Starbuck (Carlisle) and Atkinson, Craig & Co (Penrith) who opened circulation accounts for the Union Bank.[45] Meanwhile, Overend, Gurney & Co (bill dealers, London) proposed to borrow money.[46] Consequently, the Union Bank developed its inter-bank relationship along the west coast of the British Isles into industrial Lancashire and London. Beyond the Irish sea, the Provincial Bank of Ireland was operating as a correspondent. This was the basic pattern of the English and Irish inter-bank relationships of the Bank.[47] Against this, the development of Scottish relationships was only seen in arrangements made with the National Bank of Scotland in 1833, the Central Bank of Scotland (joint-stock, est. 1834) and the Dundee Commercial Bank (provincial, est. 1802 and later in 1838, altered to the joint-stock Eastern Bank of Scotland) in 1834. The English and Irish relationships might have been a first priority for the Union Bank because its surplus funds would be profitably placed and quickly transferred in cities such as London and Liverpool where its customers were trading.

(c) THE ORGANISATION OF THE BANK

The election of chairman, deputy chairman and extraordinary directors, which was delayed on account of the conflict at the inception of the Bank, was eventually effected in October 1831. In the course of a steady growth of business, the directors reorganised their sub-committees into four of more permanent character; establishment, accounts, branches and loans and securities. In 1835, another sub-committee on investments was added to their system, which was considered to be essential in conducting their surplus funds in an efficient way.[48] The system of the board was strengthened.

The office of manager became increasingly important, and already in the first business year the manager had been given his own department and a secretary had been appointed. In 1834, the manager was authorised to discount bills on his own responsibility 'except in particular cases where his own information is deficient'.[49] When the sub-committee on investments was instituted, the manager was instructed to attend all five sub-committees. J A Anderson satisfied the directors who appreciated his management as 'the mainspring of the whole.'[50]

Eleven new branches were established between 1831 and 1836; Ayr, Moffat, Strathaven, Alloa and Kincardine in the year of 1831/32, Stranraer and Auchtermuchty in 1832/33, Paisley in 1833/34 and Neilston, Beith and Stewarton in 1835/36. The business at Greenock and Paisley was regarded as most important as well as successful. On the other hand, the directors were not quite satisfied with the management of the Edinburgh branch. In August 1832, the Edinburgh manager was strictly instructed to investigate the business.[51] Furthermore, there was a certain misunderstanding between the directors and the Edinburgh manager regarding the branch instructions.[52] This circumstance might be one of the reasons which led the directors to amalgamating with Sir William Forbes & Co.[53]

In establishing branches, the directors of the Union Bank were careful and not really enterprising, say, compared to the National Bank, which set up thirteen at the outset of the establishment, and the Western Bank, which created forty-nine in eight years. After 1834 when five branches were established, the directors of the Union Bank changed their minds and the two branches established in the year of 1832/33 were only for the purpose of circulating the Bank notes, one of which was soon withdrawn. In the annual report of 1834, the directors stressed that,

> The present excessive extension of banking operations throughout the country will call for increased cautions in the extension of new branches as well as increased vigilance in regard to those already established.[54]

Also in the annual report of 1835, the same opinion was expressed that,

> the directors are disposed to proceed with extreme caution in regard to any proposal for increasing their number.[55]

This opinion can be construed to be the policy of the Bank, at least, during the 1830s and was sharply contrary to the later expansionist policy of the 1850s.[56] Consequently, the North and almost the whole of the East were left vacant by the Union Bank, whose business there was, therefore, conducted by three Scottish Banks; the National Bank branch in Aberdeen, the Dundee Commercial Bank and the Central Bank in Perth.

The growing business of the Union Bank, and probably an anticipation of the opening of the Western Bank in the summer of 1832, caused the first removal with regard to the Bank premises as early as in January 1832.[57] It must have been thought that the senior Bank in Glasgow, which occupied the first and second floors of the building in Trongate, should be accommodated in more convenient and comfortable premises and also that the further western part of the city, where all the offices of other banks were situated, would be more suitable for the Bank which would increasingly commit itself to inter-bank connections. The decision on new premises was carried into effect despite the objection of two directors, R Stewart and J Drysdale, who held to the idea expressed in the prospectus that,

> The waste of time thus occasioned to Merchants in the Middle and Eastern Districts, by being compelled to proceed to Virginia Street, Queen Street, or the New Exchange, to transact their Bank business, is a very serious evil, and one universally felt.[58]

The decision against one of the main motives of, and only two years since, its own establishment, suggests that the head or chief offices of the banks tended to be located nearer to each other in the better part of the city for convenience as well as safety. Thus, curiously, at the suggestion of the Bank of Scotland, it was decided that the new premises of the Union Bank were to be in the building at the foot of Virginia Street, formerly occupied by J & R Watson & Co, the oldest private bankers, who were sequestrated in 1832. The Union Bank moved into these new premises in the summer of 1833.[59]

First of all, in May 1834, the Union Bank considered an application for a charter. The directors were probably wishing to raise the prestige of the Bank in competition with the aggressive Western Bank and, thus, specially emphasised that the Union Bank was 'the first Bank established in the West of Scotland on the joint-stock principles',[60] in the petition of a charter made in December 1835 on the model of that of the National Bank, which obtained it in 1831 along with the Commercial Bank. The petition was unsuccessful probably because of objections by the public banks and the government which intended to introduce new legislation to control joint-stock banks, and was not repeated until Sir William Forbes & Co could join forces in the application.

3   The Age of Amalgamation, 1836–1844

(a) AMALGAMATION AND COMPETITION

The business of the Union Bank grew by leaps and bounds from 1836 to 1844 primarily due to five amalgamations; these were with the Thistle Bank, Sir William Forbes & Co, the Paisley Union Bank, Hunters & Co and the Glasgow & Ship Bank. Five successful amalgamations in seven years could well have been a world record in banking history. The dimension of total liabilities/assets of the Bank increased from £1.2m in 1836 to over £6m in 1844.

As the substantial growth of the Bank implies, the business made good progress without interruption from 1836 to 1841. The directors paid a 6%

dividend both in 1837 and 1838 which was raised to 7% in 1839 and 1840, and further to 8% in 1841. When the 7% dividend was reported in 1839, the directors were proud that this was 'above the rate generally paid by the Scotch banks'.[61] Even the financial difficulties of 1837/38 did not cause any problem with regard to the growth of the Bank and in the period of cheap money from the spring of 1838 to the summer of 1839 when the Bank of England rate stood at 4%, the Union Bank experienced a great increase in transactions in which the total liabilities grew by 25% to over £2m in 1839,[62] though the difficulties of the Eastern Bank of Scotland (a re-organised version of the Dundee Commercial in 1838) caused a certain anxiety. The profits of the Union Bank amounted to nearly £40,000 in 1841, which was the largest sum between 1836 and 1844. The reserve also increased from £20,000 in 1837 to £111,974 in 1841. Meanwhile, the nominal amount of capital stock was raised to £2.5m in 1839 by the creation of 2,000 shares of £250 each. Thus far the Union Bank was tremendously successful in all respects.

In 1842 when a severe financial crisis occurred in Paisley in which at least twenty firms collapsed,[63] the Union Bank encountered real danger for the first time in its history. Three provincial banks failed in the crisis, in two of which the Royal Bank was involved. The losses of the Union Bank amounted to £34,292, nearly half of which was incurred at the Paisley branch. The reserve decreased by 25% to £83,897 in 1842. In 1843, the Paisley branch suffered from losses amounting to £2,900.

Paisley was the centre of the cotton industry which was becoming increasingly equipped with power looms and one of the places where serious competition between the banks was going on. In addition to two provincials, the Paisley Bank (est. 1783) and the Paisley Union Bank (est. 1788), the Commercial Bank first invaded Paisley earlier in 1825. Next in 1833, the Western Bank established a branch which was soon taken over by the Union Bank. The Bank of Scotland and the Royal Bank created branches in 1836. The British Linen Co took over the Paisley Bank in 1837 establishing itself there. When the Union Bank took over the Paisley Union Bank in 1838, another joint-stock Paisley Commercial Bank was about to open. Consequently, in the late 1830s, seven joint-stock banks were operating in Paisley, which was absolutely overbanked. Under the circumstances, the directors of the Union Bank were very anxious to avoid bad debts, particularly from the beginning of 1840, and frequently dispatched an accountant of the head office to investigate the Paisley business. In spite of this precaution, the Paisley branch was very vulnerable to bad debts.[64] The result was losses in 1842 and 1843. The overbanked situation resulted in the expenses of the branch management exceeding its revenues.

Severe competition was felt by the Union Bank not only in Paisley but also elsewhere, especially in Glasgow. Prior to 1836, there were three joint-stock banks, including the Union Bank, in the West, where another eight joint-stock banks were added between 1836 and 1844. Six of these newly established banks were based in Glasgow as Table 7 sets out.[65] Glasgow was the most vigorous arena of joint-stock banking. In 1838 when the Clydesdale Bank opened its doors soon establishing a branch in the eastern part of Glasgow, the

TABLE 7

Establishment of Joint-Stock Banks, 1830–44*

	Glasgow a† b‡		Edinburgh a b		West a b		North & East a b		South a b		Total
1830	1	1	0	2	1	1	0	1	0	0	5
1831	0	1	0	2	0	1	0	1	0	0	5
1832	1	2	0	2	0	1	0	1	0	0	6
1833	0	2	0	2	0	1	0	1	0	0	6
1834	0	2	0	2	0	1	1	2	0	0	7
1835	0	2	0	2	0	1	0	2	0	0	7
1836	0	2	0	2	0	1	1	3	0	0	8
1837	0	2	0	2	0	1	0	3	0	0	8
1838	1	3	1	3	1	2	2	5	1	1	14
1839	1	4	0	3	0	2	0	5	0	1	15
1840	0	4	0	3	1	3	0	5	0	1	16
1841	0	4	0	3	0	3	0	5	0	0	15
1842	0	4	0	3	0	3	0	5	0	0	15
1843	3	7	0	3	0	3	0	5	0	0	18
1844	1	4	0	3	0	1	0	5	0	0	13

*excluding the public banks
†a: established
‡b: existing

Source: SGC, 1975, Tables 9 and 11. CWM, 1981 (b).

Union Bank called a special meeting of the board which resolved to erect a more suitable head office building on the former site of the Thistle Bank, already absorbed by the Union Bank, and at the same time decided to open a branch at the old market cross in order to rival the business of the Clydesdale Bank.[66] The competition between the two culminated in a proposal (made by the Union Bank) to withdraw one of the branches, which the Clydesdale Bank rejected. An accountant at the Ayr branch of the Union Bank was also re-employed by the Clydesdale Bank.[67]

Scottish banking, thus, entered the age of amalgamation and competition, under the Glasgow challenge, in which the traditional Edinburgh–Glasgow rivalry disappeared at least in Glasgow in the years of 1840/41 when the Royal Bank resisted the Bank of Scotland's attempt to lower the deposits rate.[68] The Royal Bank, which was doing a larger business in Glasgow than any other Edinburgh bank, had to accept a lower margin. These circumstances meant that the Union Bank entered years of severe trial which, however, it managed to weather successfully.

(b) THE RAPID GROWTH OF ADVANCES AND THE EMERGENCE OF OVERDRAFTS

The deposits of the Union Bank stood at £639,400 in 1837, including the sum transferred from the absorbed Thistle Bank, and further increased to £861,637 in 1838 when the Paisley Union Bank joined the Union Bank. Thereafter, the deposits, excluding those in the hands of Sir William Forbes & Co, decreased for three successive years to £666,832 in 1842. The reduction was almost certainly due to serious competition begun from the late 1830s especially in Glasgow and the West.

The deposits resumed their upward trend in 1843 to £795,099 and jumped remarkably to £4,427,780 in 1844 as a result of the final assimilation of Sir William Forbes & Co and of the amalgamations with Hunters & Co and the Glasgow & Ship Bank in 1843. One result of the increasing amount of deposits was the commencement of a full range of advances.

The amount of each advance greatly increased. Prior to 1836, the directors only rarely sanctioned a credit of more than £1,000. In 1837 the Bank authorised a credit of £20,000 jointly to W & R Orr, J & J Orr & Co and J Donaldson & Co (merchants). In 1838 a credit of £28,000 was allowed to a railway company. From 1840 to 1842, the Bank gave each year an advance of £50,000 to the same railway company. The directors, though increasing the amount of single advances did not forget to hold to the principle of self-liquidating lending. When a large railway company applied for a credit of £100,000 for five years at $3\frac{1}{2}\%$ interest, the Bank declined the proposal on the ground that 'such a length of time at so low a rate'[69] would be dangerous. The Bank of England rate stood at 5% at that time.

As before 1836, advances on discount remained the primary method though the gap between the two became greatly reduced, as Table 8 sets out. Increase in advances on credit accounts was probably due to the emergence of a new method of advance, that is, overdrawing credit account or overdraft.

TABLE 8

Methods of Advances, 1837 and 1844

	Credit Accounts/Overdrafts[†]		Discounts[†]	
1837*	£121,884	(12%)	£924,203	(88%)
1844*	1,939,490	(43%)	2,577,461	(57%)

*date as in April each year
†%: proportion between the two

Source: UBAAB

Overdrafts made their first appearance in provincial banking. In 1829, the Perth Bank allowed a customer to 'overdraw' his account as a temporary advance.[70] Among the Edinburgh banks, the Royal Bank was the first to adopt this method when the directors found by accident in 1832 that several accounts of their customers had been overdrawn without their knowledge.[71] 'Overdrawing or overdraft', thus, became a banking terminology, and, following these examples, the Union Bank allowed its first overdrafts to John Leadbetter, an influential director, in 1841.[72] Overdrafts must have attracted the customers' attention and soon increased because the Union Bank amended its contract in 1843 to the effect that,

> The said Directors are hereby authorized to give credit, on cash accounts, to the Partners of the Company, to the extent, or amount, of one-half of their advanced stock, and to such farther extent as the circumstances of the Company, and the value of the stock may seem to warrant, without any farther or collateral security but that arising from the right of retention competent to the Company, and assignation in security hereinafter contained; but to no other person, or persons, unless with security, real or personal, to their satisfaction, *except for temporary overdrafts sanctioned by a Committee of Direction.*[73] (the italic is in the amendment).

Even under the original clause, the directors could extend the amount of credit beyond the value of one half of the customer's paid up stock, but this extension of advance was, of course, enjoyed only by the shareholders and also secured by the other half of the paid up stock. In this way, advances on cash credit had two limitations which were lifted by overdrafts. These, though they were to be allowed temporarily, were not guaranteed by security at all and could be awarded to parties other than the shareholders, although the Union Bank from time to time proposed to take securities. Indeed, advances on overdraft gave flexibility to short term lending thus responding to the growing and fluctuating demands for credit.[74] It was, thus, very important for the customer whether or not he could enjoy the right to overdraw his account. When he could obtain an overdraft from another bank, he might easily change his bank. In fact, the Union Bank proposed to offer the facility to a customer of another bank and he was given a large overdraft limit to the extent of £40,000.[75]

Overdrafts, on the other hand, had a risky aspect. As they were unsecured advances, the directors regularly and carefully investigated the list of overdrawn accounts.[76] In spite of their caution, the amount of overdrafts tended to increase beyond authorised limit without the knowledge of the directors. The account of Lord Belhaven, owner of coal mines, was a troublesome example. In November, 1845, Lord Belhaven overdrew his account at Edinburgh by more than £10,000 without any arrangement and was, thus, instructed to repay a part of the sum or to offer the Bank stock as security. He was suspected of being in financial difficulty. The Bank had to wait nearly one year to secure repayment. Again later in 1847, the debit in his account amounted to £80,200 chiefly due to overdrafts and his business was eventually forced into liquidation.[77]

Nonetheless, it was obvious that overdrafts gave great flexibility to lending and increased advances on cash account. Along with the emergence of overdrafts, advances on heritable security became usual. The directors also granted a credit even on a life insurance policy.[78] The Bank also started acceptance business in this period whose progress was, however, primarily seen in the following period.[79]

A feature of the emergence of a fuller range of banking services was the appearance of two noteworthy groups of borrowers, heavy industry and railways. Among the heavy industrialists, Lord Belhaven was the most notable as well as the largest borrower as seen by his operation of overdrafts.

From 1841 to 1843, he obtained six credits, with one of which he bought Union Bank stock, so strengthening his borrowing power. In 1843, he proposed to borrow £6,000 on the personal security of himself, W G A Cunningham and Lord Ruthven which was authorised and was twice renewed in the same year.[80] Dunlop of Dunlop, MP, who had already introduced Neilson's hot-blast into his Clyde Iron Works and started another Iron Work at Coatbridge, usually borrowed on a rather moderate scale, from £700 to £1,500. When he applied for a large credit of £10,000, the Bank rejected the proposal.[81] The Bank also supplied funds to the extent of £3,000 to a firm of shipbuilders, J S & W Napier.[82] Thus, the Bank, though timidly, started financing the rising heavy industry.

A remarkable performance was seen in railway financing. The Glasgow, Paisley, Kilmarnock & Ayrshire Railway Co (GPKA) was the most important customer, and in it the Union Bank was represented by three directors, including J Leadbetter, and so were two other banks; the Glasgow & Ship by A Fletcher, T Walrond and J Campbell and Hunters & Co by C D Gairdner.[83] GPKA financing commenced in 1838 when the Union Bank sanctioned two large credits of £28,000 and £37,000. GPKA, still under construction, needing a large amount of money, demanded that its shareholders subscribe a call and also proposed that the Union Bank should advance funds to the shareholders on their GPKA stock. The Bank agreed to advance in this way more than £10,000, limiting the direct advance to £20,000 in the autumn of 1839. The restriction of credits aroused a protest from some of the directors of GPKA who even proposed on their board that they should change their main bank. It is quite probable that the Glasgow & Ship, or Hunters & Co, or the British Linen, in whose directorate a relative of Hunters & Co was represented, were suggested. The information was soon reported by Leadbetter to the Union Bank which immediately took strong action, i.e., making a proposal to withdraw all advances. Eventually, GPKA surrendered to the Union Bank which remained the main bank of the railway company.[84]

From the summer of 1840 to the summer of 1842, the Bank authorised advances on cash accounts and overdrafts to the extent of £50,000 to GPKA and also for the first time on debentures. Thereafter, the Bank changed its policy, starting to buy shares in GPKA from October 1842 to August 1843 when the directors further resolved to increase the holding of GPKA stock up to 2,000 shares.[85] The reason for this resolution is not exactly known, but it might not be inappropriate to say that the Bank was increasingly interested in the business of GPKA. Indeed, the result of this resolution was remarkable because, two days after the resolution, Hunters & Co, one of two other banks involved in GPKA, proposed to make over their business to the Union Bank and, two months afterwards, another, the Glasgow & Ship Bank, also joined the Bank. Consequently, the Union Bank won the battle over GPKA finance taking over two provincial banks in the West. GPKA financing was more than an ordinary banking business. It helped the Union Bank to establish itself firmly in the West.[86]

The financing of the Edinburgh & Glasgow Railway Co (EG) was also important in another respect. EG, which obtained an act in February 1838 and opened 'a new era in the social history of the two cities',[87] made its first appearance as a borrower in September 1838. Leadbetter was a leading spirit in EG taking office as the chairman of the company,[88] through whom EG proposed that the 'Glasgow business of the railway company will as hitherto be given to the Bank'.[89] EG also offered the Edinburgh business to the National Bank. There formed a sort of cartel which the Western Bank tried to enter in October 1841. The Union and National authorising credits for £50,000 and £25,000 respectively, the Western Bank proposed to give an advance of £25,000. EG reported that,

> As the Western Bank of Scotland, in offering also to advance the sum of £25,000 annex to their offer certain conditions in regard to the future banking business of the Company to which the board decline according, it be agreed that the Glasgow Union and National Banks be requested to advance the said sum in the proportion of the respective sums above mentioned and in addition thereto.[90]

The directors of the Union Bank were satisfied with the proposal and the additional credit proposed was immediately given at the Edinburgh office. EG was also one of the customers which was allowed overdrafts.[91]

From the financing of GPKA and EG, we may make two deductions. Firstly, railway business was obviously profitable as well as being a large outlet for the resources of the Scottish banks which were competing very strenuously to obtain business. At the same time, it was also clear that railway financing could be done by the large scale banks, that is, joint-stock. This was the reason why Hunters & Co and the Glasgow & Ship, both provincials with a small number of partners, gave up their independence, making their business over to the joint-stock Union. This fact also supports the argument that Scottish banking was never reluctant to finance railway companies whose vital needs, especially when they were under construction, were met by Scottish credit.[92] Secondly, the Union Bank showed a different attitude towards the banks in the West compared with the Edinburgh banks. Facing the banks in the West, the Union Bank never gave up keen competition. In sharp contrast to this, the Bank showed moderate behaviour towards the Edinburgh banks with which the Union Bank even co-operated. This policy, contrary to that of the Western Bank, was one of the reasons why the Union Bank was more calmly accepted by the Edinburgh banks.

(c) INCREASES IN INVESTMENTS

The problem of the management of surplus funds, which were accumulating as a result of the amalgamations and growth of business, continuously confronted the directors, who required to place their funds not only for the purpose of the reserve but also for profitability. In August 1836, the portfolio of the Union Bank was composed of the Glasgow Gas stock, East India bonds, Bank of England, Bank of Scotland and British Linen stock, the total sum of which stood at £99,100 (7.7% of the total liabilities).[93] Feeling the necessity to diversify the portfolio, the directors considered two unauthorised outlets, investments in the stock of joint-stock companies, not incorporated under a charter or an act of parliament, and foreign securities. As examples of this sort of investment, the directors chose the stock of the Provincial Bank of Ireland and the Bank of Manchester and the bonds of the United States Bank, but the plan was soon abandoned because counsel in Edinburgh, consulted by the Union Bank, replied that these investments were forbidden according to the fifth clause of the contract.[94] Thereafter, the board of directors stayed silent till May 1838 when the purchase of the bonds of the United States Bank was summarily reported by Sir William Forbes & Co who had just joined the Union Bank.[95]

There was indeed a certain connection between the management of surplus funds and the absorption of the firm of Sir William Forbes & Co. After the unfavourable reply of counsel, the sub-committee on investments was repeatedly instructed to 'consider of the best employment of the spare funds',[96] but they could not give any decisive recommendation to the board. It is probably safe to say that the directors were searching for a legal way of making foreign investments without amending the contract and consequently began to contact the firm of Sir William Forbes & Co from the autumn of 1837. Sir William Forbes & Co, though they had lost much of their initiative from the late 1820s, were the most senior private bankers doing a kind of merchant banking and they were well acquainted with foreign investments. It can therefore be argued that the firm of Sir William Forbes & Co was kept separate from the absorbing Union Bank in order to effect foreign investments legally, as will be discussed in the following chapter.

The operation of Sir William Forbes & Co proved to be, to a large extent, instrumental in suggesting profitable outlets to the Glasgow directors. Indeed, following their recommendation, the portfolio of the Bank was gradually diversified including the 'illegal' investments in the bonds of the US Bank as well as the legal securities of English railway companies such as the Birmingham, Eastern Counties and Great Western. Later in 1843, the Union Bank added to its portfolio the bonds of the Royal Bank of Australia,[97] the first Australian connection in Glasgow.[98]

To its inter-bank network, the Union Bank added a Welsh and two English banks, that is, the Monmouth & Glamorgan, the East of England and the Northumberland & Durham Banks. The notice required to call up inter-bank loans was usually eight to ten days.[99]

(d) THE CASE STUDY OF AMALGAMATIONS

A   The Thistle Bank

The Thistle Bank, which was the third Glasgow bank founded in 1761 and whose notes once enthusiastically invaded the North in the latter half of the eighteenth century,[100] had by the early 1830s long lost its initiative, and, indeed, the surplus of assets over liabilities was only £3,532 in 1836 when the Thistle Bank indicated it wished to make over its business to the Union Bank.

The directors of the Union Bank quickly responded to the offer, resolving

within seven days to take it over. The Union Bank agreed to pay the Thistle
Bank the following sums,

Sum stipulated	£5,000
Salaries	900
Loss of interest on price of house, expenses of transferring securities and other charges	600
	£6,500[101]

In addition, the Union Bank promised to take the old notes of the Thistle
Bank for £862 which brought the total expenses to £7,362. Despite these
expenses, the advantages of the take-over were estimated as that,

Deposits £450,000, of which it is supposed two-thirds may be expected to be retained. £300,000 yielding an annual profit of $1\frac{1}{4}\%$,	£3,750
Of the notes in circulation there are £4,350 dated prior to 1817 for which £862 only is allowed, but as in the last three years £135 only of these old notes have come in. The amount still to appear will probably not exceed the interest of the £862 received—the profit on this head may at least be taken at,	£500
Of the remaining £26,000 dated subsequently to 1816 and taken over at their full amount, it seems not too sanguine to estimate a sum never to appear of,	£600
and a profit (at $3\frac{1}{2}\%$) on the circulation of remainder,	£500
Without putting down anything for the probability of unclaimed deposits, these items make an aggregate of,	£5,350[102]

Based on this calculation, the Union Bank would be able to recover over 80%
of the take-over cost in only a year. The anticipated retention of large deposits
was also attractive. It was due to this merit that the Union Bank decided to
take over 'the whole (business) without exception'[103] of the declining Thistle.
The remarkable amalgamation movement of the Union Bank, thus, commenced in the year 1836, a year which also witnessed another amalgamation
between the provincials, the Glasgow Bank and the Ship Bank. The year 1836
was effectively the last days of Glasgow provincial banking.

B Sir William Forbes, James Hunter & Co

Sir William Forbes, James Hunter & Co, who were formerly the partners of
the firm of John Coutts & Co (est. 1724),[104] were undoubtedly the oldest and
finest private bankers in Scotland. The firm prospered especially under the

leadership of Sir William Forbes of Pitsligo (1739–1806), 'the beau ideal of the Edinburgh banker.'[105] He was succeeded in 1806 by his son, Sir William of Edinburgh. His leadership, however, began to witness the decline of private banking and after his death in 1828 the firm lost ground, encountering difficulties in the 1836 crisis during which it experienced a heavy run.[106] It was probably during this crisis that Sir William Forbes & Co were attracted by the idea of junction with another bank. This idea found fruition in a merger with the Union Bank whose problem was how to place funds in profitable investments. Negotiations between Sir William Forbes & Co and the Union Bank, led by J Leadbetter,[107] had thus made good progress by the beginning of 1838.

Although it had suffered losses in the 1836 crisis, the firm of Sir William Forbes & Co could still yield the large profit of £16,000 in 1836, compared to the £16,844 by the Union Bank in the same year. Its liabilities/assets in 1838 amounted to £1,580,000 compared to the £1,711,581 of the Union Bank. Furthermore, the firm of Sir William Forbes & Co was very highly regarded in Scottish banking. Consequently, the Union Bank proposed complex but attractive terms for purchasing the business of Sir William Forbes & Co, which had only six partners. The directors of the Union Bank resolved that,

> By assigning to the partners (of Sir William Forbes & Co) one thousand shares/but not guaranteed/to yield a dividend of £3,000 per annum, and the balance of the two-thirds of profits in annuities on the basis of four partners of Sir William Forbes & Co—Sir John Forbes and Sir John Hay receiving no annuities. The annuities of Messrs G Forbes, D Anderson and A Hay being equal, that of Mr C Forbes of lesser amount, which annuities shall be a debit against the Glasgow Union Bank.[108]

The value of 1,000 shares was £50,000 because half of the £100 share was to be paid. The sum of annuities was not recorded in the minute book, but, according to R S Rait, the amount on aggregate was at least £400 for the four partners. In addition, the Union Bank paid £20,000 for the purchase of the banking premises of Sir William Forbes & Co, who had three branches. The take-over of the firm of Sir William Forbes & Co involved the Union Bank in expending £70,400 in all for the first year of their junction, which was the largest amalgamation cost of the five as Table 9 sets out.

In exchange for this large expense, the four partners of Sir William Forbes & Co were to,

> undertake the personal management in Edinburgh as at present for six years, and during that time they shall have the entire nomination of the clerks and other persons employed under them; and to assist in the Glasgow management for the same period.[109]

Under this agreement, the firm of Sir William Forbes & Co was to exist separate from the Union Bank for six years during which the latter could legally make foreign investments through the former. In order to assist the Glasgow directors, Charles Forbes was to reside in Glasgow. The amalgamated firm of Sir William Forbes & Co was, thus, the direct ancestor of the Edinburgh committee of directors instituted in 1843.

The junction with the firm of Sir William Forbes & Co not only pioneered profitable outlets for investments and set the Union Bank on a firmer footing in Edinburgh, but also brought with it other opportunities for amalgamation. Sir William Forbes & Co were acting as the Edinburgh agents on behalf of at least seven provincial banks.[110] Five of them, that is, the Paisley Union, Hunters & Co, the Glasgow & Ship, the Perth and Aberdeen Banks, afterwards joined the Union Bank. Remarkably, three amalgamations were carried out within the period of the sole management of the Edinburgh business by Sir William Forbes & Co. Although there remains no direct evidence except in the case of Hunters & Co, it might not be unreasonable to suggest that the later amalgamations were pioneered by Sir William Forbes & Co. The annual report of 1838, reported that,

> A junction has been negotiated and concluded, upon terms of mutual advantages, between this company and that of Sir William Forbes, James Hunter & Co, Edinburgh—a firm oldest in point of date, and first in character and connections among the private banking companies in Scotland, with a business about equal to our own, and with gentlemen of perfect honour and distinguished talents in its management.[111]

Although this union was exciting for the rising joint-stock Union Bank, it was true that Sir William Forbes & Co had outlived its usefulness in Scottish banking and that its passing marked the end of the private banks in Scotland.

C   Paisley Union Bank

Established in 1788, the Paisley Union Bank soon opened branches at Glasgow, Beith, Hamilton and Greenock and aggressively invaded the north of England at the end of the 18th century.[112] However, in common with other provincial banks, the Paisley Bank stagnated especially from 1820 and was declining by the late 1830s, though it could still yield profits of £14,472 in 1836; total liabilities fell from £651,395 in 1820 to £447,099 in 1838, capital from £40,489 to £24,000 and note circulation from £107,220 to £87,598.[113] The decline of the Paisley Bank exemplified the fate of provincial banking in the industrial West, where agents of the public and joint-stock banks were established, particularly from the early 1830s, strenuously competing with each other.[114] The Paisley Bank must have been unable to bear the brunt of this competition and made over their business to the Union Bank in June 1838 just after Sir William Forbes & Co.

The Union Bank offered two alternative schemes to the partners of the Paisley Bank, either a single payment of £20,000 or annuities for ten years which would come up to £20,000. The latter proposal was preferred by the remaining three partners, each of whom also bought 50 shares of the Union Bank stock at the market price. The banking premises at Paisley and Glasgow were bought up by the Union Bank at the price of £1,600. The total cost of take-over was thus £21,600. The manager and office of the Paisley Union Bank became the agent and branch at Paisley, through which the Union Bank incurred losses in 1842/43 as already mentioned.

D   Hunters & Co

Hunters & Co came into being in the autumn of 1773 when the Ayr Bank of Douglas, Heron & Co was already in liquidation. In contrast to the enterprising and large scale firm of Douglas, Heron & Co, Hunters & Co started with four partners, one of whom, William Hunter, was the elder brother of James Hunter of the firm of Sir William Forbes & Co. Although their policy was rather conservative as R S Rait suggests, Hunters & Co took over the Kilmarnock Bank (provincial, est. 1802) in 1821 and had seven branches by the early 1840s.[115]

However, the firm of Hunters & Co was among the declining provincial banks which suffered from the wave of joint-stock banking, especially from 1830 when the joint-stock Ayrshire Bank was established under the management of Quintin Kennedy, who used to be a joint-agent of Hunters & Co. Deposits of Hunters & Co diminished from £668,000 in 1829 to £428,000 in 1833.[116] Also in financing the Ayrshire Railway Co, Hunters & Co encountered fierce competition from the Union Bank. Furthermore, they witnessed the hardship of the oldest private bankers, Sir William Forbes & Co in the crisis of 1836/37. In these circumstances, Hunters & Co felt that their time had passed and they began to search for a large bank which would purchase their business. C D Gairdner wrote,

> During the following ten years (since 1821 when he entered Hunters & Co) Joint-Stock Banks were making rapid strides, and they encroached with some severity on the credit of private Banks. I must say for myself that while seldom enervated by such matters I felt annoyed at times in case some foolish story should cause a run upon us, and when a heavy demand came upon Sir William Forbes & Co, some years after, I felt that we also might be placed at disadvantage and that it was really scarcely fair to partners having large independent estates to expose them to any risk whatever. I believe these views guided the Company generally after Mr Coman's death in 1841. I considered that the transfer of our business to another Bank was a mere matter of time. In 1842–43 this subject was often talked of at our private meetings—After much discussion, it was agreed that one partner should be empowered to exhibit privately to the British Linen Company and to the Union Bank an exact state of the extent of our business—that no information should be given to the one Bank more than to the other, and that they should be both requested to give sealed secret offers on a fixed day. As I was the person selected by the Company, I proceeded to Glasgow and Edinburgh, and at interviews with the respective managers I told them that, as the business, if exposed, would greatly injure us, I could not agree to either manager consulting more than one individual director of each Bank. I need not enter on particulars further than that our partners were all highly satisfied with the offer of the Union Bank.[117]

C D Gairdner revealed how anxious provincial bankers were over their weak position in these last days and also that make-over offers on equal conditions were made to the two banks, which the Union Bank won. None the less, the success of the Union Bank might not be due entirely to the better offer it proposed. Perhaps it was Sir William Forbes & Co who suggested Hunters & Co might join them, because Hunters & Co were for 'a long period in confidential communication with Sir William Forbes, James Hunter & Co'.[118] The Union Bank paid £25,000 to Hunters & Co in August 1843, who transferred £0.5m of deposits and seven branches to the Union Bank.

E   Glasgow & Ship Bank

The oldest Glasgow based Ship Bank, set up in 1749, had long lost its initiative since the death of Robin Carrick, in 1821, and thus, joined the small but enterprising Glasgow Bank in 1836, which was itself a creation of Dundee entrepreneurs. The amalgamated Glasgow & Ship, though still a provincial bank, was a substantial concern in all terms of business (see Table 9 below); the paid-up capital, £500,000, equal to that of the Union Bank, note circulation £180,000, large deposits of more than £1.4m and total reserve and profits of more than £100,000 in 1843. Indeed, the Glasgow & Ship was effectively on the scale of joint-stock banking although not of course with an equivalent number of partners.

Naturally, the Glasgow & Ship considered offering their shares to the public as a joint-stock concern in the spring of 1843 and even prepared a new contract of co-partnership as well as new banking premises at the top of Virginia Street, which were completed in 1843.[119] However, the time was not favourable for the Glasgow & Ship to convert itself into an open bank, because Glasgow was already over-banked. In the early 1840s Glasgow banking entered the stage of amalgamation. Consequently, the partners of the Glasgow & Ship Bank, witnessing the make-over of Hunters & Co to the Union Bank, came to the conclusion that,

> In the course of last summer, the longest established and highly respected copartnership of Messrs. Hunters & Co of the Ayr Bank, having resolved to merge their business in that of a Joint-Stock Company, thought proper to make overtures on the subject to the Union Bank and after a short negotiation an agreement was concluded on terms satisfactory to both parties and which the Directors still continue to consider highly advantageous to the Union Bank. . . . (The directors of the Glasgow & Ship) had at last resolved to adopt the new prevailing system of a Joint-Stock Company, when in preparing to do so, it occurred to them that the most eligible way of effecting object would be, instead of attempting to create a new constituency, to connect themselves with this Company, whose accumulated funds, their position and connection would enable them to turn into safe and profitable channels of investments. Upon this idea suggested to the directors—after gradually communicating to each other—both parties came to the conclusion that no two co-partneries could be better suited for forming an Union advantageous to each.[120]

The Union Bank expressed the merits of the amalgamation from its point of view that,

> The general ground upon which it has been proposed to unite the Glasgow and Ship Bank and the Union Bank, are, that the Union Bank from its various junctions with

and assumptions of the business of other banks has acquired a large disposal amount of funds than it can readily employ with profit and safety, whilst the Glasgow and Ship Bank, from its long established business connections has the means of employing this surplus to advantage; and therefore a coalition/by which also a large part of the present annual expense would be saved/would be equally for the advantage of both.[121]

The merits and purposes expressed by the two boards of directors indicated that the two banks encountered difficulty in placing funds more profitably and safely in severe competition, exemplified by railway financing.

The similar size of business of the two banks made it easier for them to unite. The capital stocks were, of course, treated as of equal value making up the total paid-up capital of £1m. No payment was made by either of them. The manager of the Union Bank, J A Anderson, was to be a manager of the united Bank whose business was to be conducted exclusively in premises at the top of Virginia Street, just completed by the Glasgow & Ship Bank.[122] This was a real amalgamation among the five though the Union Bank was a little larger in dimension and the title of the new Bank was that of the Union Bank.

F   First Amalgamation Movement, 1836–43

In addition to this successful amalgamation, the Union Bank had an opportunity to take over the Leith Bank (provincial, est. 1792). Fortunately, the Leith Bank declined the Union's offer and failed in 1842.

Table 9 shows the situation of the assimilated banks at their amalgamations, or at the nearest dates possible, and the money terms of take-overs, from which we could group the five take-overs into three categories. The first consisted of only one case—the Glasgow & Ship Bank—which was an amalgamation in its real sense. No payment was made and all business was regarded as equal by both banks. The second category was the case of Sir William Forbes & Co who were paid a larger sum than that paid to the other three banks. It is certainly true that Sir William Forbes & Co were absorbed by the Union Bank, but it should also be noted that the prestige brought by the highly regarded Edinburgh house was invaluable in raising the status of the Union Bank. It also helped to establish the Union Bank's Edinburgh business and encouraged other amalgamations. As a result of the successful amalgamation with the Glasgow and Ship Bank followed by the take-over of Sir William Forbes & Co, the Union Bank found itself in a much stronger position and more able to dictate terms in the cases of Hunters & Co (who were eager to relinquish business) and Paisley Union Bank. They fell into the third category.

What were the motives for the amalgamations? The assimilating Union Bank had the problem of placing funds more profitably and safely under the circumstances of increasing competition, which was aggravated more especially from the mid-1830s, when the provincial and private banks were also struggling to survive. The assimilated banks, though small and outdated (except the Glasgow & Ship), must have had a long-established network of customers to whom the Union Bank might not have had access until it took

TABLE 9

Amalgamations of the Union Bank of Scotland, 1836–43

	Union Bank April 1836	(1)*Thistle Bank June 1836	(2) Sir William Forbes & Co April 1838	(3) Paisley Union Bank July 1838	(4) Hunters & Co August 1843	(5) Glasgow & Ship Bank November 1843	Union Bank of Scotland April 1844	Abortive Case (6) Leith Bank May 1842
1 Total Liabilities	£1,284,072	£468,604	£1,580,835	£447,099	—	£2,414,665	£6,294,782	—
2 Capital paid	287,050 (22.4)	—	—	24,000†† (5.4)	£18,000§§ (1.9)	500,000 (20.7)	1,000,000 (15.9)	—
3 Deposits	451,583 (35.2)	303,294‖ (64.7)	1,137,860 (72.0)	333,507 (74.6)	500,000 (52.8)	1,414,233 (58.6)	4,427,780 (70.3)	£116,407
4 Notes	338,080 (26.3)	20,980 (4.5)	309,466 (19.6)	87,598 (19.6)	428,387‖‖ (45.3)	179,380 (7.4)	243,152 (3.9)	5,500
5 Advances†	480,812 (37.4)	213,088 (45.5)	824,057** (52.1)	137,233‡‡ (30.7)	—	1,789,799 (74.1)	4,669,414 (74.2)	—
6 Investments	45,336 (3.5)	47,990 (10.2)	434,885 (27.5)	13,707†† (3.1)	118,354 (12.5)	—	973,114 (15.5)	—
7 Reserve	1,344‡ (—)	3,300¶ (0.7)	91,500¶ (5.8)	—	—	50,030 (2.1)	100,000 (1.6)	—
8 Profits	16,844 (1.3)	—	16,000 (1.0)	—	2,620¶¶ (0.3)	55,000 (2.3)	82,623 (1.3)	—
9 Dividend	5%	—	—	—	—	8%	7¼%	—
10 Partners	517§	8	6	3	10	36	29	10
11 Offices	14	—	4	5	8	3	—	4
12 Money Term of Take-over	—	£7,362	—	£21,600	£25,000	equal	—	£5,000

*( ) of each column, % of total liabilities or of the aggregate of available figures
†Discounts and cash advances
‡Contingent account

§December 1835
‖This figure does not agree with that recorded in UBM 21/6/1836. This figure might be transferred to the Union Bank

¶Specie
**Including inter-bank loans
††1836
‡‡Discounts only

§§1830
‖‖1833
¶¶1842

Sources: UB Annual Reports, UBM, UBMGB, UBAAB, UBPJ, UBPL, CIB Minutes of the Board of Directors, NBS Minute of the Board of Directors, C W Boase 1867, J Buchanan 1884, R S Rait 1930, J M Reid 1938, and C W M 1931

over their banks. Accepting offers from the long-established banks, the Union Bank took the opportunity of obtaining new customers.

The motives of the absorbed banks seem to be easily understandable, because they undoubtedly saw the passing of their days of usefulness as C D Gairdner put down that 'the transfer of our business to another Bank was a mere matter of time'. But why did they do so? Advances as a percentage of deposits might provide an answer to this question. The percentages, except that of the Glasgow & Ship, did not exceed 100%; Sir William Forbes & Co 72%, the Thistle 70% and the Paisley Union 41%. Even the largest private bank, Sir William Forbes & Co, whose deposits were larger than those of the Union Bank, lent only less than three quarters of their deposits. The Paisley Union Bank, situated at the centre of keen competition in the West, lent less than half of its deposits. Why could they not lend more? They might have thought that greater lending out of deposits would be risky because they were vulnerable to runs which might happen at any time in a fluctuating economy like the mid-1830s. C D Gairdner certainly deplored the possibility that 'some foolish story should cause a run upon us'. Consequently, it could be argued that only a bank based on a substantial capital stock was capable of lending safely to the growing as well as fluctuating economy. This was the reason why the Glasgow & Ship Bank, which had a large capital of half a million, could lend in excess of its deposits, and considered putting itself on a joint-stock principle.

It must also be stated that the absorbed banks had difficulty in making advances. Some banks must have lost borrowers faster than they lost depositors perhaps because they were only prepared to offer loans insufficient to meet customers' needs. Small scale banking was no longer adequate in Scotland in the 1840s.

Scottish banking as a whole entered the stage of amalgamation in the mid 1830s as Table 10 sets out. In aggregate, seventeen amalgamations were accomplished. Eleven of them were accomplished by the Glasgow banks; five by the Union, four by the Western and two by the Clydesdale. The banks which the Union Bank took over were all provincial and private in comparison to the cases of the Western and Clydesdale Banks. As a result, only three provincials survived the stormy amalgamation movement, that is, the Dundee Bank, the Perth Bank and the Banking Co in Aberdeen (revised as joint-stock in 1839). Among them, the Aberdeen and Perth Banks were eventually taken over by the Union Bank in 1849 and 1857 respectively, as will be discussed in the following chapter.

4 The Emergence of the Union Bank of Scotland as a National Bank in 1844

The years from 1841 to 1844 witnessed the culmination of the controversy over banking and currency. In 1841, a Select Committee on Banks of Issue was appointed, which extended its investigation to Scotland. The Scottish banks

TABLE 10

Joint-Stock Banks and Amalgamations, 1830–44

Bank	Year of Est.	Joint Stock*	Absorbed Banks Provincial & Private†	Remark‡
1 Commercial Bank§	1810		Arbroath Bank (1844)	charter (1831)
2 National Bank	1825	No. 18 (1844)	Commercial Bank of Aberdeen (1833), Perth Union (1836)	charter (1831)
3 Aberdeen Town & County	1825			
4 Union Bank	1830		Thistle (1836), Sir Wm. Forbes (1838), Paisley Union (1838), Hunters (1843), Glasgow & Ship (1843)	
5 Ayrshire Bank	1830	No. 14 (1844)		to No. 6 (1845)
6 Western Bank	1832	No. 5 (1845)	Greenock (1843), Dundee Union (1844).	
7 Central Bank (Perth)	1834			
8 North of Scotland (Aberdeen)	1836			
9 Eastern Bank (Dundee)	1838			
10 Southern Bank (Dumfries)	1838			to No. 13 (1841)
11 Clydesdale Bank	1838	No. 16 (1844), No. 20 (1844)		
12 Caledonian (Inverness)	1838			became No. 21 (1844)
13 Edinburgh & Leith	1838	No. 10 (1841)		to No. 6 (1844)
14 Paisley Commercial Bank	1838			
15 City of Glasgow	1839			
16 Greenock Union	1840			to No. 11 (1844)
17 Glasgow Joint-Stock	1843			became No. 21 (1844)
18 Bank of Glasgow	1843			to No. 2 (1844)
19 Glasgow Banking Co	1843			to No. 6 (1844)
20 Glasgow Bank (No. 2)	1844			to No. 11 (1844)
21 Edinburgh & Glasgow	1844			No. 13 plus No. 17

*Bank symbolised as number in the table ( ); year of amalgamation †( ); year of amalgamation ‡( ); year §absorbed Caithness Bank in 1826

Sources: SGC, 1975, Tables 9 and 11, CWM, 1981 (b)

despatched a delegation, led by Alexander Blair, treasurer of the Bank of Scotland, before which Blair argued for Scottish banking, and for small notes. In spite of his pleading, a Bank Act, which would affect Scottish banking, was thought to be unavoidable.[123]

In these circumstances, the directors of the Union Bank began to consider what changes in their organisation would be necessary in order to obtain a charter. The task of preparation was entrusted to Sir William Forbes & Co, who sounded the opinion of the Lord Advocate and Sir William Rae of the Royal Bank because it was thought that all applications would be referred to them.[124] Despite the effort of Sir William Forbes & Co, the application of the Union Bank was unsuccessful again perhaps because of opposition from the Edinburgh public banks. Changes in the organisation were carried out at the special meeting of the shareholders held in May 1843.

Changes in the copartnery were made in eight articles of the original contract, of which three were important amendments. In the first place, the Bank abandoned the local name 'Glasgow' and styled itself simply as 'the Union Bank of Scotland'. In the second place, the nominal capital stock was decreased from £2.5m to £1m divided into 10,000 shares of £100, of which £50 was to be paid up. In the third place, two head offices were instituted at Glasgow and Edinburgh and the number of directors was increased to twelve, half of whom were to constitute each board of directors at each head office.[125]

Although the change in the Company's form was mainly aimed at obtaining a charter, there were other purposes which are worth mentioning. Firstly, the capital stock, which was raised to £2.5m in 1839, was again changed, being reduced to £1m, which was the same amount as that of the Glasgow & Ship Bank. From this, it could be argued that as early as May 1843 the directors of the Union Bank were expecting amalgamation with the Glasgow & Ship. In addition the directors of the Union Bank endeavoured to increase their small reserve, which had decreased due to the losses caused by the Paisley business, to £50,000 in the course of the business year of 1843/44, which was exactly the same as that of the Glasgow & Ship. Consequently, it is fair to say that the directors, intending to amalgamate with the Glasgow & Ship, were smoothing the way for it. They later commented that the amalgamation was 'much simplified' because of the same amounts of capital and reserve in both.[126]

Secondly, the amended fifteenth article of the contract contained the insertion that,

> George Forbes, David Anderson, Sir Adam Hay, and Charles Forbes, being the acting partners of the late firm of Sir William Forbes, James Hunter & Company, shall be re-eligible as Directors as long as they continue to hold the requisite amount of stock.[127]

The special treatment of these four directors reflects the importance of the Edinburgh management which was regarded as indispensable for the Union Bank as a whole. During the course of discussion on the change of the copartnery, George Forbes expressed the desire for earlier retirement. He was persuaded to remain in the directorate.[128]

However important the Edinburgh directors were, it was the Glasgow directors who led the Union Bank forward. Their energy shown in take-overs was a forerunner of the enterprise of their successors in the late 1840s and 1850s by which the Union Bank again grew rapidly. Among them, John Leadbetter was the most active. As a linen merchant, he was himself a large borrower. He also took over another firm of merchants in 1841.[129] As a director of three railway companies, the Ayrshire, Edinburgh and Glasgow and Dumfries, he was more than able to obtain business for the Bank.[130] Although a conservative in politics, he was never so in banking, being always ready to accept new challenges. When the first westward move of the Bank premises was being discussed in 1832, he supported the proposal despite the opposition of Robert Stewart, the leader in establishing the Union Bank. Although it is not quite true to say that he dominated the Bank, Leadbetter was undoubtedly the most remarkable director in the amalgamation period.

The growing business accompanied by the successful amalgamations also raised the status of the Glasgow manager. The amendment in the copartnery made him an *ex officio* member of both boards of directors at Glasgow and Edinburgh. This was effectively the creation of a general managership though the term was not adopted until the late 1870s. The management of J A Anderson pleased the directors who increased his salary to £1,500 per annum on the consideration of 'the encreased duties and the responsibility devolving on Mr Anderson' in the autumn of 1843 when the last amalgamation was completed.[131]

In establishing their branch network, the directors did not show aggressiveness. From 1836 to 1844, the number of branches increased by 15 to 29, which were chiefly a result of the take-overs of Sir William Forbes & Co and Hunters & Co. The Bank did not always keep open the branches which had been taken over. Save for those taken over, no branches were created between 1841 and 1843. The directors thought that 'the improvement and regulation already established'[132] should be the priority. However, the investigation of branches was carried out only by occasional inspectors to whom members of the staff of the accountant's department of the Glasgow office were usually appointed. It was in the autumn of 1843 when the Bank first appointed a full-time inspector following an increase of seven branches taken over from Hunters & Co. The first inspector was I Stock who was a member of the accountant's department and who had been frequently engaged in the occasional inspections.[133]

During the first fourteen years, the Glasgow head office of the Union Bank moved three times. In 1833, immediately after the setting up of the Western Bank, it moved from 114 Trongate, the old city centre near the Market Cross, to the foot of Virginia Street. In 1838, again following the setting up of another joint-stock bank, the Clydesdale Bank, it moved northward along Virginia Street. Lastly in 1844, it moved into the newly built premises of the Glasgow & Ship Bank, facing south at the top of Virginia Street.[134] The coincidence of the moves along with the creation of new banks suggests that the Union Bank, feeling increasing competition, eagerly wished to move westward, where the Glasgow banking centre was emerging and, therefore, inter-bank relationship and facilities for information could be improved (see Map 2). As a result of the

Map 2

Move of the Glasgow Head Office of the Union Bank and Glasgow Banking Centre in 1844

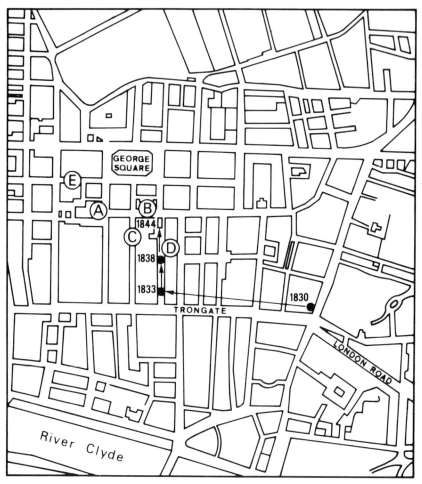

A	Queen Street	D	Virginia Street
	1 Royal Bank		6 Commercial Bank
	2 British Linen		7 National Bank
	3 Clydesdale Bank		8 Union Bank
B	Ingram Street		9 City of Glasgow Bank
	4 Bank of Scotland	E	St Vincent Street
C	Miller Street		10 Edinburgh & Glasgow
	5 Western Bank		Bank

Sources: as Map 1

moves of the Union Bank office, the Glasgow banking centre was basically formed by the mid 1840s.[135]

The first fourteen years of the Union Bank, the first Glasgow based joint-stock, were tremendously successful. The total amount of liabilities jumped up from £0.7m to £6.3m in 1844, which was almost the same as that of the Royal Bank in 1845 and ten times larger than the provincial Dundee Bank in 1844.[136] Thus, the Union Bank of Scotland, primarily owing to the amalgamations, and leading the Glasgow challenge, firmly established itself in the heart of the industrial West.

Chapter 2

Rapid Growth, 1844–1858

The Union Bank of Scotland, a synthesis of the six banks and based on the two cities, entered a period of rapid growth for another fourteen years influenced by the unprecedented development of the British economy. Developing their business, the Union Bank took over another two banks, invading the North and East and establishing itself all over the country. This rapid growth also resulted in great difficulties for the Union Bank.

1 Co-operation and Competition

The emergence of the Union Bank as a national bank, increasingly committing itself to banking affairs, not only in Scotland but in Britain as a whole, resulted in a relationship between the Bank and others which produced two responses, co-operation and competition.

The Union Bank joined other Scottish banks to try to prevent Peel's Bank Act from coming into existence. Note issue was the classic subject of discussion in England well before the nineteenth century. Before the 1840s Scottish banking had not undergone serious restriction though the issue of small notes was endangered in 1825. During the late 1830s when joint-stock banks were rapidly emerging both in England and Scotland and the economy was convulsed by speculation, Sir Robert Peel's government began to consider disciplinary legislation on banks of issue not only in England and Wales but also in Scotland and Ireland. They were believed to favour the principles of the Currency School, which had formulated that both inflation and speculation resulted from the excessive issue of paper notes and therefore that a certain portion of note issues should be backed by bullion.[1]

Confronting this serious situation, the Scottish banks dispatched a delegation, whose chairman was the manager of the Union Bank, J A Anderson, to the Select Committee on Banks of Issue (1841). Before the Select Committee, Alexander Blair, treasurer of the Bank of Scotland, a distinguished banking scholar of his time and a friend of Thomas Tooke, argued for the Scottish case that,

The notes are not held by the public, but are paid into their accounts; in consequence of the rate of interest allowed by the banks, no one in Scotland has any inducement to keep bank notes in his pocket, and the general practice of the country is, to keep the circulation at as low a rate as possible; then the numerous branches which are situated up and down the country are the means of taking notes of their neighbours out of the circle, speedily as possible, and they are transmitted, of course, without delay to Edinburgh to be exchanged;—in fact it (circulation) is at a minimum.[2]

The existence of the system of branch offices, which gave in Scotland one branch per 6,000 people, was instrumental to a great extent in encouraging a speedy return of notes to the issuers. The note exchange was also held twice weekly in Edinburgh, Glasgow and elsewhere. Under this Scottish system, and as Tooke argued against the Currency School, notes were never issued in excess of those needed by the public. Indeed, the proportion of notes to deposits was one to ten. Furthermore, as the Scottish banks did not re-issue discounted bills, there was rarely any anxiety over the abuse of rediscounting which remained an English phenomenon.[3]

Despite strong objection by the Scottish banks, Peel succeeded in legislating the Bank Act of 1844 in England and Wales (7 & 8 Vict. c.32) immediately intimating in the spring of 1845 his willingness to enact the same law in Scotland. The only step which was available for the Scottish banks at this moment was to urge the prime minister to extend the limits of note issues. Indeed, this was the crucial point, but their effort was in vain and the Bank Act of 1845 came into existence in July 1845. The first article of the Act stipulated that,

it shall be lawful for every such banker to continue to issue his own bank notes to the extent of the amount so certificated, and of the amount of gold and silver held by such banker at the head office or principal place of issue of such banker, in the proportion and manner hereinafter mentioned, but not to any further extent; and it shall not be lawful for any banker to make or issue bank notes in Scotland, save and except only such bankers as shall have obtained such certificate from the commissioners of stamps and taxes.[4]

Under this Act, the amount of notes issued by each Scottish bank was to be limited within that of the average circulation over the year preceeding 1 May 1845, and issues in excess of the authorised amount had to be covered in gold or silver. This was the first act that had a serious and substantial effect on Scottish banking. It also became a decisive factor in separating the Scottish system from its English counterpart, making it more difficult for the Scottish banks, which had various as well as different notes from their English counterparts, to invade England.[5]

The effect of the Bank Act was soon felt by the Union Bank, probably in common with other banks. The directors stated in their annual report that,

(The regulations of the Bank Act) had effect of locking up in the coffers of the Bank, a very unnecessary amount of the precious metals—thus rendered totally unproductive.—In the main object of its enactment, it has proved, as already mentioned, signally inefficient.[6]

The Union Bank also joined the unchartered Scottish banks in petitioning for a charter. In spite of the prohibition of new issuing joint-stock banks, stipulated by the Bank Act, the competitive situation was growing among the existing Scottish banks. Under this circumstance, the unchartered banks suffered inconvenience and handicap, compared to the five chartered Edinburgh banks, which the directors of the Union Bank explained, the double object of obtaining a charter—more convenient transmission of heritable property and being enabled to hold certain public and other deposits, directed by law to be limited to chartered banks.[7]

This was the purpose of obtaining a charter, for which the Union Bank had unsuccessfully applied by the early 1840s. After the legislation of the Bank Act, the four Glasgow banks, the Union, Western, Clydesdale and City of Glasgow, together with the Edinburgh & Glasgow Bank, joined forces to urge the government to grant charters under Peel's Act (9 & 10 Vict. c.75). In the spring of 1850, the five banks sent a memorial to the Lord Advocate who opined that,

the banks to forego the benefit of charters rather than subject themselves to the disadvantages which might arise from subjecting to the provisions of the existing act.[8]

It was expected that a charter under Peel's Act would oblige a bank, which would apply for it, to disclose its business. This condition was totally unacceptable to the unchartered banks.

During the first half of the 1850s, the five banks continued their co-operation and in this the Union Bank took the initiative. In February 1851, to amend the Bank Charter Acts, the directors of the Union Bank drew a draft of a bill, which was then delivered to the secretary of the Treasury. Furthermore in January 1854, another memorial was sent to the Treasury, which, eventually, promised to introduce a short bill so as to enable the unincorporated banks to obtain charters under Peel's Act without giving up their common law rights. Peel's Act was thus to be amended (19 & 20 Vict. c.47 and 20 & 21 Vict. c.14) and the directors of the Union Bank declared in the annual meeting of 1856 that a 'charter may now be safely applied for',[9] but application for a charter was not made because the 1857 disaster, in which the Western Bank collapsed, soon followed. Consequently, the first joint action of the Glasgow banks, which the directors of the Union Bank termed 'the charter movement' ceased to exist, and incorporation of the unchartered banks, together with the adoption of limited liability, was not realised until another big and insecure City of Glasgow Bank disappeared in the general crisis of 1878.[10]

So far, co-operation. Scottish banking developed price competition during the middle of the 1840s especially in Glasgow, where there were seven joint-stock banks just before the enactment of the Bank Act and whose lending opportunities had already by the late 1830s overtaken those of Edinburgh.[11] The amalgamations could not mitigate the competition, which was even aggravated by the establishment of exchange companies.[12] In these circumstances, the rate policy of the Edinburgh chartered banks was becoming increasingly inefficient, especially in Glasgow.

As A Blair of the Bank of Scotland put forward before the Select Committee of 1841, it had already been the practice by 1841 that the Scottish bank managers met to 'consider whether any change should be made in the rate of deposit and the rate of discount'.[13] The meeting was usually held at the office of the Bank of Scotland, the senior bank, which was apparently taking the initiative. This situation, which had already started to change in the late 1830s,[14] began to turn totally against the Edinburgh chartered banks in the mid 1840s. In September 1844, Adam Hay of the Edinburgh Board of the Union Bank intimated that a meeting of the bank managers had been held in Edinburgh to consider a reduction in the deposit rate. No agreement being reached, the delegation of the Edinburgh banks arrived in Glasgow a week later to discuss the matter. The meeting again failed to make any resolution.[15] The failure to reach agreement was evidence that the Edinburgh banks found it increasingly difficult to direct the Glasgow banks in the decision on their rates, which put up with a half per cent smaller margin than their Edinburgh counterparts in order to obtain depositors and borrowers thus competing with each other and challenging Edinburgh banking.

At least from 1844 to 1848, the leadership in price competition was taken by the Glasgow banks, especially by the Western Bank which certainly needed an instant change of rates following the alteration of the Bank of England rate because it was doing aggressive business with narrow reserves and was therefore vulnerable to fluctuations in the growing economy. The earliest proposal for changes in rates on the part of the Western Bank appeared in the autumn of 1844, the manager of the Union Bank reporting that,

> The manager, after meeting with Smith of the Western Bank of Scotland, suggesting Edinburgh Committee increase a discount rate of local bill which was approved and suggested any arrangement with the Edinburgh banks would be best made through their Glasgow agents.[16]

The quickest to respond was the City of Glasgow Bank which was followed by the Clydesdale and the Edinburgh & Glasgow Banks. The Union Bank was the most reluctant among them. In February 1847 when the Western Bank together with the City of Glasgow Bank raised their rates on deposits, the Union Bank delayed the increase on the recommendation of A Hay, Edinburgh director, and C D Gairdner, Kilmarnock agent, though it was forced to raise its rate two weeks afterwards.[17]

In this severe price competition, the role of the Union Bank was special in one respect. As suggested in the record of the minutes of the Union Bank quoted above, the directors did not neglect to make arrangements with the Edinburgh banks before their decision was made. Also in November 1845 and in November 1847 when the Bank of England rate was altered and the Glasgow banks, excluding the Union Bank, instantly changed their rates, communication was made by the Union Bank to the Edinburgh banks.[18] In this way, the Union Bank was standing in the middle between Edinburgh and Glasgow banking. This attitude, it was hoped, might counteract the rivalry between the two cities. This behaviour was certainly due to the existence of the former partners of Sir William Forbes & Co in the Edinburgh directorate.

Whatever its attitude might be, it was also true that the Union Bank was competing with others. In February 1847 when the Western Bank increased the rates of interest to $3\frac{1}{2}\%$ on current account and to 4% on more permanent account, the directors of the Union Bank, though resolving to have a single rate on both kinds of deposits, approved that,

> The manager had written them (agents) to say to any depositors that might enquire, that the same rate would be allowed to them as had been advertised by the Western and City Banks.[19]

Also in July 1850 when the Bank of England rate was as low as $2\frac{1}{2}\%$, the directors of the Union Bank gave the manager a discretionary power to charge a lower discount rate to certain customers as,

> various rates of discount which at present prevail among the different Banks in town. The manager was desired to exercise such discretionary power in regard to the rates of approved bills as he thought calculated to meet the existing competition.[20]

The price competition continued unabated at least until 1854 when the Glasgow banks began to follow conjointly changes in the Bank of England rate.[21] Over the next decade, Scottish banking as a whole ceased to compete in rates, at least on the surface.[22]

During this phase of co-operation and competition, the Union Bank developed its business as Table 11 sets out. The Bank grew by 140% in terms of total liabilities, which was, however, not easily achieved. From 1844 to 1847, the Bank grew steadily, increasing the dividend from $7\frac{1}{2}$ to 8% in 1847 which was declared by the directors to be 'permanently maintained',[23] though they also warned the shareholders of a hidden danger of catastrophe. Indeed, the 1847 crisis incurred for the Bank a loss of more than £12,000.[24] The amount of

TABLE 11

Growth of Liabilities, 1844–1858

	Liabilities	Growth Index; 1844:100
1844*	£6,294,781	100.0
1845	6,642,512	105.5
1846	6,695,188	106.4
1847	6,753,233	107.3
1848	6,221,661	98.8
1849	6,062,090	96.3
1850	7,741,526	123.0
1851	8,150,622	129.5
1852	7,915,409	125.7
1853	8,661,280	137.6
1854	8,728,187	138.7
1855	8,289,758	131.7
1856	8,159,896	129.6
1857	8,775,532	139.4
1858	8,827,550	140.2

*date April each year

Sources: UB *Annual Reports*

liabilities decreased in the two successive years of 1848 and 1849 and the reserve had to be depleted in order to maintain an 8% dividend.

The downward trend was stopped by the amalgamation with the Banking Co in Aberdeen in the autumn of 1849 and, as a result, the Bank entered an upward trend from 1850 to 1854, though the Bank sustained a large loss of more than £20,000 by the failure of Alexander Russell & Sons (iron founders, Kirkcaldy) in 1850 and another loss at Glasgow in 1852. These losses must have resulted in the decrease of liabilities between 1851 and 1852.

From 1854 to 1858, the amount of liabilities moved V-shaped. In 1856 when the amount decreased by £130,000, the directors raised a dividend to 9% assuring the shareholders that the 'most careful consideration to the present and future prospects of the Bank'[25] had been made. In May 1857, the Bank, again anticipating an approaching catastrophe, added £40,000 to the reserve which amounted to £200,000. The difficulties in the 1857 crisis were unprecedented in the Bank's history, but the Union Bank increased its liabilities in the course of the crisis which reached the highest point in 1858. This increase in difficulty was mainly the result of the take-over of the Perth Bank in the summer of 1857, which had nearly £0.9m of total liabilities.[26]

The development of the Union Bank in this period, though substantial, was thus fluctuating. The decrease of business was relieved twice by amalgamations. Indeed, the Union Bank, which was in a sense literally a synthesis of six banks when it entered this period, was apparently only able to develop as long as it was taking over others.

2   Business in the Railway Age

(a) THE INNOVATION OF A NEW METHOD OF ADVANCES AND AN INCREASE OF ACCEPTANCE BUSINESS

In this period, advances on credit account for the first time constantly ranked with those on discount as Table 12 shows. Between 1845 and 1858, the amount of credit accounts even overtook that of discounts four times in 1850, 52, 56 and 58. From this, the claim of Professor Cameron that,

> Cash accounts remained an important lending device of the Scottish banks until at least the second quarter of the nineteenth century,[27]

should be revised at least in the case of the Union Bank as, that credit accounts were increasing in the mid nineteenth century and from time to time gained the position of the primary method of advances.

Table 12 also suggests that there was a correlation between the growth rate of total liabilities and the volume of advances on discount. Excluding 1855 and 1858, the growth of liabilities correlated absolutely with the increase in discounts. On the other hand, credit accounts tended to increase when the growth of liabilities lost ground as in the years of 1849, 52, 55 and 56, to which the year 1858 could be added because the increase in liabilities at that time was probably due to the amalgamation with the Perth Bank. From these correlations, we may conclude that discounts were one of the main factors of the development of the joint-stock bank. This subject will be re-examined in the following chapters.

TABLE 12

Methods of Advances, 1845–1858

	Credit Account /Overdrafts	%*	Discount	%*	Growth of Liabilities 1845:100
1845†	£1,818,307	40	£2,750,613	60	100
1846	2,021,701	40	3,079,863	60	101
1847	1,914,583	38	3,153,728	62	102
1848	2,051,694	49	2,170,620	51	94
1849	1,973,440	50	1,939,315	50	91
1850	2,702,287	55	2,214,676	45	117
1851	2,419,019	48	2,609,908	52	123
1852	2,671,662	53	2,349,459	47	119
1853	2,449,094	49	2,589,154	51	130
1854	2,778,919	48	2,981,467	52	131
1855	3,053,549	50	3,058,939	50	125
1856	3,073,734	51	2,908,441	49	123
1857	3,128,235	47	3,522,086	53	132
1858	3,858,501	54	3,277,996	46	133
Average	—	48	—	52	—

*%: proportion between the two methods
†Date as in April each year, except 1858 whose figure is as in May

Sources: UB *Annual Report*, 13/5/1858. UBAAB

Along with the development of ordinary advances, the Bank innovated an unusual method of lending, that is, loans of 'railway company stock'. In all, the Bank lent railway stock for £150,000, two thirds of which were borrowed by J & A Dennistoun & Co (merchants at London and Glasgow). The term of the loan was thus,

1   That the promissory note of the firm be granted at three months for the present value the stock being about £102,000 with discount added at the rate of 6% per annum,

2   That the same amount of the London & North Western stock be replaced in the Bank's name within three months from the first of November, failing Messrs. Dennistoun doing so, the Bank reserves power to buy in the stock, any loss arising on the operation to be borne by Messrs Dennistoun.[28]

1853 was just a year after the hectic period of railway investments, in which the Union Bank was involved, holding a large amount of railway stock. What advantage the Bank could gain from loans of railway stock is not exactly clear. The motive might have been simply to make use of the hoarded stock.

Therefore, this sort of lending was not repeated because the hectic years of railway investments passed very quickly as will be discussed in the following section.

Already, prior to 1844, the Union Bank started acceptance business, but it was in the post 1844 period when British foreign trade was rapidly developing that this commission business made remarkable progress. Bills of exchange, which were the most useful as well as popular method of payment especially in foreign trade, had to be guaranteed by the drawee to the effect that the payment would be made on maturity. Originally, this guarantee was made by the drawee himself.[29] In consequence of the development of foreign trade, especially from as far away as East India, America and Australia, it became increasingly difficult for the drawer of bills of exchange to obtain accurate information on the creditworthiness and financial situation of the drawee, that is, the payer. In order to overcome this inconvenience, a person or firm in a financial and commercial centre began to guarantee the payment on behalf of the drawee. This guarantor was termed acceptor or accepting house during the hectic years of Anglo–American trade in the 1830s.[30]

Before entering the operation of acceptance business, two essential arrangements had to be made between the acceptor, or the bank, and the drawer and drawee, or the bank's customer. In the first place, the bank issued the customer the open or clean letter of credit which promised acceptance of bills drawn and this had to be produced to the correspondent of the bank. The open letter of credit was often termed simply 'open credit'. In the second place, the extent to which the bank would guarantee had to be determined. It was usually arranged that the limit of acceptance would be renewed when the payment was effected at maturity, and, therefore, the acceptance allowed on this arrangement was often termed 'running or revolving credit'.[31] Consequently, the acceptance business of the Union Bank was termed acceptance, open credit, running credit and also issue of credit. From time to time, the bank proposed to take security, but there was a large number of unsecured authorisations, many cases of which were in the Union Bank and which were called 'uncovered credit'.

By the early 1850s the directors of the Bank were well acquainted with the acceptance business whose development primarily resulted from the progress of the American and Australian trade in which J & A Dennistoun & Co were especially active. A detailed example can be shown by the arrangement made between the Union Bank and Jaffray & Co (merchants, London) that,

The credit to be a running one, terminable after four months' warning from either party, each advance to be payable at the expiration of six months from the date of deposit by bills of exchange endorsed by their New York House drawn by (first) Dennistoun, Wood & Co, or A Dennistoun & Co, or the Liverpool Borough Bank, (second) by Bank of British North America, (third) Brown Brothers & Co, or Brown, Shipley & Co, (fourth) M Morgan or Overend, Gurney & Co, (fifth) by Duncan Sherman & Co or George Peabody & Co or Union Bank of London or such others as shall from time to time be approved of by the Bank, their bills deposited being returned to them on the bills of exchange being placed in the hands of the Bank's agents.[32]

In this case, it is not really clear whether or not the Bank directly accepted bills. More usually Glyn & Co, London correspondents of the Bank, accepted bills on behalf of the Bank. In such case, the minutes recorded as 'running credit— upon Glyn & Co to be available by drafts at 30 to 60 days'.[33] Commissions for acceptances were ordinarily from $\frac{1}{4}$ to $\frac{3}{4}\%$.

Acceptance business also developed the relationship of the Union Bank and international banking as the arrangement with Jaffray & Co suggests. The houses of Brown, Morgan and Peabody were already famous merchant bankers. On the other hand, there was a latent risk in this business as it was often unsecured and employed in distant foreign trade which was vulnerable to price fluctuation as well as the political situation of foreign countries and colonies. Indeed, Dennistoun & Co suffered losses caused by their trade to America where the 1857 crisis originated and, thus, involved the Union Bank in great trouble.[34]

Facing the expanding economy, the Union Bank was giving greater financing to two sectors other than railways, that is, the trade and the iron and steel industry. Large borrowers in the trade sector were those engaged in foreign trade, such as Dennistoun in the American and Australian trades, Kelsall & Co (London) and Finlay, Campbell & Co (Liverpool) both in the East India trade. They operated mainly on discounts and acceptances, together with cash credits. In October 1853, the account of Dennistoun stood at nearly £400,000. Through their business, the Union Bank also obtained new customers with whom Dennistoun's had business relations.[35] The business of Dennistoun's was indeed one of the main factors in the development of the Bank.

In the sector of the iron and steel industry, there were two groups of customers. One group was composed of the industrialists such as Dunlop & Co, the Monkland Iron & Steel Co and the West of Scotland Malleable Iron Co. Each advance to these industrialists was quite large, exceeding £50,000, which was usually allowed on discounts or credit accounts. Except the Monkland Iron & Steel, which was suspected of being in trouble during the early 1850s,[36] the others were profitable and large outlets for the Bank's resources. Dunlop & Co were supplied with funds which enabled them to take over other works, expanding their capability of production around 1850. West of Scotland Malleable, which had been a customer of the Western Bank, transferred its account in the autumn of 1848 to the Union Bank, soon obtaining a large credit of £100,000.[37]

Another group in this sector was iron dealers who might be included in the sector of trade. However, they could be safely grouped into this sector because they seem to have specialised in the iron trade and also Glasgow was famous for its large iron market.[38] Notable borrowers were J G Hamilton and T Walrond who were allowed advances on discount, cash credit and overdraft to the extent of £30,000 between the late 1840s and early 1850s. In granting credits, the Bank usually took personal bonds or railway stock as security. It was not until the early 1850s that the directors allowed iron warrants or scrips as security.[39]

Otherwise, there was no perceivable characteristic in the sectoral lending of the Union Bank. One thing to be noted was that the Union Bank for the first time awarded a credit of £20,000 to J & G Thomson, shipbuilders, in May 1855, whose debits gradually increased over the next ten years, resulting eventually in financial difficulties during the early 1880s.[40]

(b) RAILWAY FINANCING

There was a similarity between railway lending and investments. When an advance was made on railway stock or debentures, the result was the same as investments to the effect that the bank was in possession of railway securities. However, there was a basic difference between the two businesses. When the bank lent to a railway company, or any other customer, on railway stock, a margin of 15 to 20% as to the amount to be repaid was always claimed by the bank by which any loss arising from depreciation of the market price of railway shares could be covered. Therefore, lending on railway stock was much less speculative and risky than direct investments.

Already, prior to 1844, railway lending was quite important as well as profitable for the Union Bank which was competing with other Scottish banks to do railway business. Also in this period, the Union Bank was very anxious to obtain railway business, often forming a cartel with other Scottish banks as they did in the previous years, so that,

> The chairman and secretary of the latter (Edinburgh & Glasgow Railway) when calling to arrange this payment stated that they now propose doing half of their business with this Bank and other half with the branch of the Commercial Bank and was informed by the manager in reply to enquiries by them that he thought the Bank would not object to their overdrawing their account to the extent of £15,000 or £20,000 if required, which was approved.[41]

Cartel lending, formed with four other Scottish banks, was also made to the Edinburgh, Perth & Dundee Railway for £128,000 on aggregate at $5\frac{1}{2}\%$ in February 1850 and to the Monkland Railway for £50,000 at $4\frac{1}{2}\%$ in January 1851.[42] Cartel lending in railway financing was thus very common among the Scottish banks which obviously sought to spread their risks.

In advancing to the Scottish railway companies, the Union Bank preferred personal bonds to railway stock even after February 1849 when the manager was authorised to increase advances on railway stock to £200,000.[43] Nearly half of railway lending was made on personal bonds in this period. Why the Union Bank preferred them is not exactly known. We might speculate that inter-directorates between the Union Bank and railway companies, exemplified by John Leadbetter, resulted in this selection, or that the marketable quality of the Scottish railway stock or any situation of the Scottish stock exchange had an effect. The length of time for advances was usually less than twelve months and sometimes only a few weeks. Consequently, Scottish railway lending by the Union Bank was no longer than for its ordinary advances. The principal borrowers in addition to the three mentioned above were the Glasgow & South Western (the amalgamated version of Ayrshire Railway), North British, Caledonian and Great Northern.

The Union Bank lent to the English railway companies chiefly through Glyn & Co. Large scale lending commenced according to the resolution of February 1849. As the advances were mainly made through the London correspondents, they were granted entirely on railway stock or debentures and no authorisation was made on personal security. The margins were from 10 to 25%. The Bank preferred larger companies like the London & North Western, South Eastern, Great Western and Midland. Length of loan tended to be longer than the Scottish case, being mainly six months and in some cases two to three years. English railway lending was, thus, closer to investments.

Even before 1847, 'the great railway construction peak',[44] the Union Bank made investments in railway securities such as the Ayrshire, London & Birmingham, Northern & Eastern, Eastern Counties and Midland Counties.[45] But it might also be true, as George Kinnear, manager of the Glasgow Commercial Exchange Co (est. 1845), put forward,[46] that the Scottish banks as a whole were rather reluctant to invest in railway securities which must have been thought by them as against their principle of self-liquidating credits. This attitude of Scottish banking resulted in the proliferation of exchange companies. In the two years of 1844 and 1845, more than nine exchange companies were created, of which at least eight were operating in Glasgow.[47] Their business was conducted in the way that;

> to lend no money in Scotland or on Scottish lines; to select for securities 10 or 12 work lines in whose shares there was (sic) daily transactions in the London market; not rely on personal security but solely on the margin in the value of the stock beyond the sum advanced; and to sell promptly and peremptorily whenever that margin was not maintained.[48]

Through this operation, which was no more than stock-broking, depriving Scotland of resources, the exchange companies could earn a margin of some $2\frac{1}{2}\%$ though they offered a much higher deposit rate than the Scottish banks.[49]

This profitable business attracted the interest of the Scottish banks, but they avoided taking to this business independently. Instead, the Scottish banks joined forces in 1847 to establish 'an association among the Banks for the purpose of facilitating the investment of money by the Banks and other Public Bodies in loans upon Railway Stock',[50] and this was the first joint scheme of business by the Scottish banks. The initiative came from the Royal Bank and the Bank of Scotland which drew a plan to take over the British Trust Co.[51] Five banks, including the Union Bank, were to join and a detailed scheme was prepared, in which the Union Bank was to take 250 shares in the Company.[52] So far, so good. However, when the take-over bid was about to be made, the Bank of Scotland dropped out on the ground of 'some difficulty to take shares in British Trust Co in their corporate capacity'.[53] This excuse seems to be odd; surely the directors of the Bank of Scotland had earlier considered their legal position? They might perhaps have perceived a certain danger in railway investments. The initiator, the Royal Bank, too, soon withdrew. The first joint scheme of the Scottish banks was, thus, abandoned within four weeks in March 1847. Perhaps the Jeremiahs of the banking world felt themselves justified for the 1847 crisis, which burst the railway mania, followed in only seven months.

After the 1847 crisis, the Scottish banks had to pursue railway investments separately. In the summer of 1848 when British banking was entering the cheap money era, the Union Bank encountered an increasing problem in employing funds more profitably and the directors began to reconsider railway investments. At this time, the most active Glasgow Commercial Exchange Co, which had an account with the Union Bank,[54] was anxious to make over their business because of increasingly difficult prospects. The Union Bank took the opportunity to purchase in June 1848 the whole business of the Exchange Co whose scale is unfortunately unknown.[55] However, the directors did not proceed further with the business already undertaken. They rejected a proposal raised by the shareholders in the annual meeting of 1850 to increase railway investments.[56]

In the spring of 1852 when the Bank of England rate was further reduced to 2% which was the lowest since its establishment in 1694,[57] the directors of the Union Bank were finally forced to change their policy declaring that,

> Since then (May 1850) directors' opinion of railway security and property have undergone a considerable change and they now think that it may be safe as well as advantageous to the Bank to employ a certain portion of their fund in such investments.[58]

The large scale investments, thus, commenced in May 1852 and amounted to £530,000 in August 1852,[59] but almost ended in the same month as Table 13 sets out. As early as October of that year, the Union Bank began to dispose of railway securities. The change in policy was probably due to increases in the Bank of England rate, which was raised six times in 1853, reaching 5% in September, and to yields of Consols, which were also gradually recovering.[60] Indeed, the Bank placed the proceeds of railway stock in Consols and short term loans such as in the hands of Overend, Gurney & Co at the beginning of 1853.[61] The railway mania of the Union Bank ceased in only four months and the directors never repeated this scale of railway investments.

(c) 'ILLEGAL' FOREIGN INVESTMENTS AND THE PURCHASE OF UNION BANK STOCK

In December 1850 when the directors of the Bank were still hesitant in embarking upon railway investments, they could not see their way to place surplus funds in foreign investments, which were still illegal according to the contract. Nevertheless, the Bank ordered Overend, Gurney & Co, through the Edinburgh committee, to purchase Canadian bonds, but the offer of sale did not appear. However, from 1853 to 1858, when the Bank was getting rid of large railway investments, they were in possession of, at least, two foreign securities, that is, Turkish and Canadian bonds, the latter amounting to £22,000 in February 1853.[62] 'Foreign investments' were talked about only in the Edinburgh boardroom, and the records of their holdings were kept secret

TABLE 13

Main Railway Investments, 1852

Date	Railway Security*	Amount
May 5	Lancaster & Carlisle	£50,000
May 5	Lancashire & Yorkshire	10,000
May 26	South Eastern	10,000
June 23	Clydesdale Junction	30,000
June 23	Glasgow, Paisley & Greenock	630
June 23	Barrhead & Neilston	1,120
June 23	Garnkirk & Glasgow	1,758
June 23	Glasgow & South Western	6,700
July 14	London & North Western	11,450
July 14	York, Newcastle & Berwick	26,250
July 14	London & South Western	10,000
July 28	London & North Western	30,000
August 4	same	30,000
August 11	same	10,000
August 11	Glasgow, Paisley & Greenock	11,000
August 18	London & North Western	20,000
November 4	Garnkirk & Glasgow	3,031
November 4	Glasgow, Paisley & Greenock	3,875
December 15	Caledonian†	30,000
Total		£295,814

*Otherwise mentioned, stock
†Debentures
Sources: UBM as at dates

TABLE 14

Investments, 1845–1852

	Union Bank Stock	Glasgow Gas Stock	Glasgow Water Stock	Exchequer Bill	Consols	East India Bond
1845*	£63,450	£11,055	£5,536	—	—	—
1846	55,273	11,324	6,332	—	—	—
1847	78,016	3,490	5,499	£50,131	—	—
1848	73,798	2,486	3,685	25,500	—	—
1849	91,777	2,617	2,925	39,877	£18,400	£12,275
1850	105,509	15,863	7,691	71,932	38,450	—
1851	130,425	—	9,709	30,810	38,900	23,715
1852	123,205	—	5,250	—	—	—

*Date as in April each year

Sources: UBMGB as at 20 April each year except 1845 and 1851 whose dates are as at 19 April

in the private journal at the Edinburgh office.[63] If the contract had been amended so as to enable the Bank to invest abroad, there probably would have been large foreign investments, say, securities of stable foreign governments, instead of railway securities.

The 'formal' portfolio of the Union Bank's investments, excluding railway securities, is shown in Table 14. Surprisingly, a not inconsiderable amount of funds was constantly placed in Union Bank stock. There were two ways by which the Bank gained possession of its own stock. Firstly, the directors were authorised by the contract to buy the Bank stock as ordinary investment. If this power was used to a great degree, the directors could improve the market price of their shares. Secondly, the twenty-seventh article of the contract stipulated that,

> an offer of the share or shares shall be first made—to the Directors,—shall have full power to accept, and three lawful days shall be allowed them to consider of the same—after the lapse thereof, the Partner making the offer shall be entitled to make a sale, or sales. . . .[64]

When the offer was accepted by the directors, the offered share was in possession of the Bank or transferred to other shareholders. It is not known how this was working between 1845 and 1852, but no matter what, a large holding of its own stock undoubtedly supported the market price of the Union Bank share. Indeed, the minute book itself confessed that the directors resolved,

> to buy Bank shares under £95 when the purchaser were not found.[65]

Consequently, a large premium, say, 54% in 1848,[66] might be the result of this large holding, and probably this happened with other Scottish bank shares.

The directors of the Union Bank did not seem to have attached great importance to government securities, especially Consols, up to the late 1840s. The constant holding of Consols was seldom seen after the 1847 crisis and even disappeared in 1852. This might be due to the imperfection of available material from which we could know where surplus funds of the Bank were going. However, it is fairly reasonable to say that the directors had not yet built up an idea of holding, at least, Consols as safe investments or so called 'secondary reserve'.

(d) THE LONDON CORRESPONDENTS AND THE INTERNATIONAL BANKING CONNECTION

As J A Anderson, the manager, suggested before the Select Committee of 1841, the Union Bank tended to move the surplus funds among other banks in search for higher returns in the 1830s.[67] This kind of inter-bank loan was reported only in three cases; the East of England and Monmouth & Glamorgan Banks in 1846 and the Northumberland & Durham District Bank in 1848.[68] The reduction of this sort of operation was probably due to rates of interest being gradually unified in the British Isles.

Instead, London became the place where the Union Bank increasingly and constantly placed its funds. In London, there were three firms of correspondents. Glyn & Co were the principal correspondents doing business with many Scottish banks, and their relationship with the Union Bank was further strengthened by the take-over of the Banking Co in Aberdeen which had an account with them. Glyn & Co continuously increased their business with the Union Bank which awarded them a commission of the London broker's rate up to £60,000 and $\frac{1}{2}\%$ on sums beyond £60,000 to £100,000.[69] Another two firms of correspondents were Overend, Gurney & Co and Coutts & Co who were doing business chiefly with the Edinburgh office.[70] Money was usually placed in the hands of these correspondents at very short notice, like seven to ten days,[71] which was clearly 'secondary reserve' in its nature.

It was also in this period that the Union Bank opened an account with the Bank of England, which also suggests that the Union Bank was building up a reserve policy against its small holding of Consols. In the spring of 1848 when the Union Bank was struggling with the surplus funds accumulated in the wake of the 1847 crisis, the Edinburgh directors strongly recommended that an account with the Bank of England should be,

a respectable thing itself and giving easy access to the Bank of England.[72]

The reserve policy of the Union Bank, which emerged, at least, as short term deposits placed in the hands of London correspondents and the Bank of England, was of vital importance to its survival in the 1857 crisis as will be discussed later. In this respect, the Edinburgh directors repeatedly proved themselves a cornerstone of the Union Bank.

As the Union Bank increasingly committed itself to foreign trade financing, exemplified by the business of Dennistouns,[73] its international banking connection widened. Firstly, in the autumn of 1844, the Rothschilds, Paris, were introduced by Sir Adam Hay, Edinburgh director.[74] Secondly, at the beginning of 1845, the Union Bank opened an account with King & Co, New York, who were the agents of Dennistoun & Co.[75] Thirdly, in the summer of 1846, the Bank started business with the Agra Bank of India.[76] Lastly in 1852, the Union Bank of Australia joined the network of correspondents.[77] Thus, by the early 1850s, a network of the Union Bank's correspondents was established on the main continents, whose development might result in increasing the business of the London correspondents because the acceptance business of the Union Bank was mainly done by them, especially Glyn & Co.

A risky situation was also developing with regard to the Union Bank's relationship with Dennistoun's who were trading aggressively with America and Australia, as well as borrowing from the Liverpool Borough Bank which also owed money to the Union Bank. The opening of 'double accounts', were doubly dangerous and could as a contemporary banker argued[78] easily be used to produce 'a kite'. Indeed, the triangular relationship between the three was destroyed in the 1857 crisis, as will be discussed later.

3   The Reorganisation of the Board of Directors and the Expansion of the Branch Network

(a) THE DUAL-BOARD SYSTEM

There were two Scottish banks which had two boards of directors along with two head offices. The Edinburgh & Glasgow Bank, which was the product of the amalgamation of the Edinburgh & Leith and Glasgow Joint Stock Banks in 1843, instituted two boards, one in Edinburgh and one in Glasgow. Almost from the outset of the amalgamated Bank, there was deep-rooted conflict between the two boards of directors who even refused to communicate their minutes to one another, indulging themselves in their own gains and also following the risky business of railway investments as exchange companies did. The result was heavy losses incurred in the 1847 and 1857 crises from which the Bank was not able to recover and eventually in 1858 it was obliged to make its business over to the Clydesdale Bank.[79] The dual-board system of the Edinburgh & Glasgow Bank was unsuccessful. Another bicameral system was in operation at the Union Bank of Scotland. How did this come about?

Before the establishment of a head office at Edinburgh, a local committee, instituted at the outset when the Edinburgh branch opened in 1830, was responsible for the conduct of business there and this was succeeded by the personal management of Sir William Forbes & Co, amalgamated with the Union Bank in 1838. By the amendment of the contract in 1843, the managing directors at Edinburgh formed the new board exclusively at the new Edinburgh head office, formally called 'Committee of Directors for Edinburgh'. Under an agreement, the four Edinburgh directors were entirely reponsible for the management at the new head office between 1843 and 1846, during which the firm of 'Sir William Forbes & Co' still remained in the Scottish scene and no managership was instituted. In May 1846 when the transition period expired and the grand old firm of Sir William Forbes was about to disappear, the general board of directors expressed in the annual meeting that,

> The directors would deeply regret the change in the Edinburgh management, if they apprehended that it would lead to the withdrawal of the interest and influence of the former partners of Sir William Forbes & Co—the prosperity of the Edinburgh business so essentially depends on (their services).[80]

Under the management of the Edinburgh directors, the special character of the Edinburgh business had been emerging as Table 15 sets out. The amount of business done at Edinburgh was quite large reaching 25% of the total liabilities of the Union Bank as a whole. 'Cash chest' literally contained gold and silver coins. 'Bank account' was supposed to be money deposited with other banks. 'London account' must have been the sum of funds placed in the hands of London correspondents. Both advances made on these two accounts were at very short term. Consequently, the aggregate of bullion, short term loan and government securities, which were the main constituent of banking reserve, was £1,053,184 which was nearly two-thirds of the Edinburgh business.

TABLE 15

Edinburgh Balance Sheet, June 1846

Liabilities		Assets	
Current Accounts	£803,156	Current Accounts	£343,138
Deposit Money	338,149	Cash Chest	132,809
Notes Payable	1,532	Bonds Payable	28,017
Bank Account	88,369	Bank Account	386,235
London Account	19,058	London Account	210,390
General Account	29,307	General Account	145,733
Bank Notes	183,820	Government Securities	84,005
Bank Notes of Union Bank	194,000	Bills Discounted	87,318
		Balance of Cash	239,746
Total	£1,657,391		£1,657,391

Source: UBM, 30/6/1846

The special position of the Edinburgh business was strengthened as a result of the legislation of the Bank Act of 1845 which obliged the Scottish banks to hold gold and silver to the extent of the circulation in excess of their authorised amounts. Intending to make use of the hoarded gold, the directors resolved in the autumn of 1845 that,

> It was the opinion of the meeting that the present system of exchanging by means of Exchequer bills should be discontinued and that if gold be used instead the principal stock of it held by the Bank should be kept in Edinburgh.[81]

The task of adjusting a proportion between gold and Exchequer bills was to be carried out by the Edinburgh directors. However, it is very doubtful that this operation actually came into existence, because no other evidence supports its existence and the Union Bank purchased a large amount of Exchequer bills for £100,000 in the first half of 1847.[82] Whatever the motive might be, the idea of clearing balances by gold must have been rather unrealistic considering its expense and risk.

The Edinburgh office was, indeed, the safe of the Union Bank, where the Edinburgh directors were carefully watching the position of the Bank reserve. This duty must have been executed most suitably by such persons as the late partners of Sir William Forbes & Co whose existence in the directorate was also indispensable in another respect.

In the autumn of 1843 when the Union Bank merged with the Glasgow & Ship Bank, two directors of the Bank, including John Leadbetter, a leading figure in the amalgamation period, retired and their places were filled by two partners from the Glasgow & Ship. Thereafter, the Glasgow board of directors was seemingly 'taken over' by the former partners of the Glasgow & Ship Bank. The active directors in this period were all from the Glasgow & Ship; Alexander Dennistoun (merchant), John Tennant (chemical industrialist), Theodore Walrond (iron merchant) and John Young whose business is not known. Another person, John Fergus (textile manufacturer, Kirkcaldy), joined the Edinburgh board from 1850. Of these, A Dennistoun, aggressive trader to America and Australia and one of the largest shareholders,[83] was causing a stir in the boardroom.

In spite of the large holding of Bank stock, his business was outgrowing his capacity to borrow on stock, and, thus, he raised twice, in 1845, the subject of increasing the Bank capital. This suggestion was discarded by the other directors.[84] Furthermore, Dennistoun asked the Bank to adopt a new kind of advance, that is, loan of railway stock, which he obtained.[85] He was also a borrower who very frequently demanded additional credit. Besides Dennistoun, there were another two directors' firms at risk both of which were the outcome of the amalgamation with the Glasgow & Ship Bank; Michael Rowand, Dunlop & Co (merchants, Glasgow) and Monkland Iron & Steel Co both of which stopped payment in 1848 and 1861 respectively.[86]

It was in these circumstances that the Edinburgh directors stepped in to obviate any doubtful business by their Glasgow counterparts. In the middle of the 1847 crisis, Sir Adam Hay laid on the table two motions,

1. That all advances from this time shall be restricted as much as possible until the Bank holds a sum of about £500,000 in government stock, Exchequer bills, or with Messrs. Overend & Co,
2. that the Bank shall not purchase its own stock in future, and only acquire shares in cases of bankruptcy where thought advisable.[87]

Also at this meeting, a special warning was given to A Dennistoun that,

Mr Anderson having been asked whether Mr Dennistoun was acting on the understanding with him, in regard to his transaction with the Bank. Mr Anderson answered that he was.[88]

The first motion was carried and, as a result, restricted the conduct of the Bank for nearly one year, during which the Edinburgh directors continued to keep a close watch on their Glasgow counterparts as the minute of the general board recorded that,

Motion 1—was called attention by Sir Adam Hay; who requested the continued attention of the Glasgow directors and manager to its fulfilment.[89]

Nevertheless, it is doubtful whether this motion was adhered to; the holding of government securities did not notably increase as is shown in Table 14. However, it could be argued that at least the Edinburgh directors had perceived the importance of a reserve policy.

The second motion was rejected. The majority of the directors thought that the market price of the Bank shares should be supported by purchases made by the Bank itself especially when the price was falling sharply from £95 to £78 in the aftermath of the 1847 crisis.[90] During this period, the Bank bought a substantial amount of its own stock, the result of which was the large holding from 1848 to 1852 as has been mentioned. If the directors had not purchased

these shares, the market value would have fallen more drastically. Why did the
Edinburgh directors raise such a motion which could adversely affect the
situation of the Bank? There is no evidence to suggest their motive for this
motion, but it might be argued that they were simply displeased to see the
manipulated support of the market price of the Bank stock. This idea, we may
suppose, might originate from the sort of principles which were believed to
have motivated that 'beau-ideal of the Edinburgh banker', Sir William Forbes
of Pitsligo.

There was, thus, an apparent difference of banking policy between the two
boards of the Union Bank. The Glasgow directors were obviously expansionists. However, excluding the case of Dennistoun's financing, no serious
conflict existed. In aggregate, the conduct of the Union Bank could keep an
even balance, due to the two boards of Edinburgh and Glasgow directors, who
preferred policies of stability and growth respectively. As long as the balance
could be maintained, the Union Bank was able to grow steadily. The Union
Bank was under trial during the hectic years of British economic growth in the
1850s during which the equilibrium was seemingly lost. The result was the
tremendous difficulties in the 1857 crisis as will be discussed later.

(b) THE EXPANSION OF THE BRANCH NETWORK

It is unexpectedly difficult to assess accurately the number of branches
between 1844 and 1858. The difficulty is due to the fact that the Union Bank
was establishing some as well as withdrawing others of its branches, especially
in the late 1840s.[91] This was one of the effects of the Bank Act of 1845 which
obliged the Scottish banks to hold bullion against amounts in excess of their
authorised note issues. The Union Bank, intent on counteracting the
increased cost of holding larger reserves of gold, discontinued some of its
branches which had been created only for the purpose of pushing its
circulation.[92] Therefore, Table 16 shows only the outline of the branch
network. However, even from this incomplete table, one point comes out—

TABLE 16

Number of branches in the 1840s and 1850s

1841	22
1844	29
1848	31
1849	48*
1856	73
1857	96
1858	99

*Simple addition of the 17 offices of the Banking Co in Aberdeen amalgamated with the Union
Bank in 1849 to the existing 31

Sources: Select Committee, 1841. Edinburgh Almanac, 1849, 1857, 1858. Table 9. UB *List of
Branches 1858*

that the directors were careful in establishing branches till 1848 when the Union Bank stood the sixth in the ranking of the Scottish banks (see Table 17).

Compared to the above period, a great increase was made over the next ten years. Twenty-nine of the extra branches were the result of the take-overs of the Banking Co in Aberdeen in 1849 and Perth Bank in 1857. At the time of the closure of the Western Bank in 1857 the Union Bank took over two branches and three agents of the former.[93] In addition, more than the number of the taken-over branches was created by the Bank itself. From the mid 1840s the Union Bank apparently changed its policy of branch establishment. This rapid extension of the branch network was undoubtedly accelerated by the new manager, James Robertson, who succeeded J A Anderson in 1852. The Glasgow directors approved, recommending that,

> The manager mentioned that there were several towns in Peebleshire, Wigtonshire and the Stewartry of Kirkcudbright at which he thought branches might be established with advantage to the Bank. He was requested to go to Peebles and Innerleithen and to make arrangements if he saw it expedient for opening branches at both of these places.[94]

The Peebles and Innerleithen branches were soon followed by two more at Maryhill (Glasgow) and Tarbert. The creation of a new town branch at George Street, Edinburgh, in 1856 was also Robertson's idea.[95] By 1857, the Union Bank topped the league table with more branches than any other Scottish bank (see Table 17).

Usually, selected branches of the bank were inspected each month. If any irregularity was found, a stricter or special investigation was ordered. If the investigation resulted in a change of agent, cash, bills and vouchers in the hands of the dismissed agent were immediately taken over by the inspector. If the appointment of a new agent was delayed, the inspector remained in temporary charge of the branch.[96]

Between 1844 and 1848 when the only branch in the East or the North was at Lerwick (formerly that of Sir William Forbes & Co), troubles happened exclusively in the West and South, that is, at Thornhill, Stranraer and Stewarton. At Thornhill and Stewarton, the agents were dismissed and inspectors took temporary charge of both branches. The trouble at Stranraer was caused by a difference of opinion between the joint agents, one of whom was discharged. But there were no great losses.[97]

The expansion of branches into the North and East did bring troubles in their wake. Branches under the direct supervision of the Aberdeen local committee (instituted in 1849), caused especial anxiety to the directors, who were still wondering in January 1851, fifteen months after the take-over, how inspections there should be carried out by the cashier of the Aberdeen office.[98] There was some doubt expressed also as to the location of the branches in the North East, as the manager explained,

> We have a branch bank where you may say there is no town at all; there are only a church and two or three houses; but there is a rich district round them; I refer to Aberdeenshire.[99]

In addition, the Aberdeen committee frequently ignored instructions from the head office. In the winter of 1853, the general board of directors twice had to send letters of warning to the Aberdeen committee which had granted a large credit on railway stock without knowledge of the board. The second letter was quite clear,

> While the general board are desirous that local board in Aberdeen should continue to supply the commercial and agricultural wants of their friends in the same liberal and judicious manner they have hitherto done since their connection with the Union Bank, they wish it to be understood that the consent of the general board of directors must first be obtained before transactions of such magnitude as that of MacKenzie's can finally be agreed to.[100]

This letter suggests that the Aberdeen committee favoured particular customers, who were probably former partners of the Aberdeen Bank. Despite a repitition of this warning, the Aberdeen committee tended to ignore the regulations of the copartnery.[101]

Another troublesome office was that at Kirkcaldy which was set up in 1843 as a result of the amalgamation with the Glasgow & Ship Bank. The agent was George Anderson who had been in charge since 1833. In January 1848, it was discovered that an accountant at Kirkcaldy had deliberately allowed overdrafts without Anderson's knowledge. The Kirkcaldy branch was, as a result, put under the close supervision of the Edinburgh board.[102]

In May 1850, shortly before the annual meeting, Alexander Russell & Sons (ironmongers, Kirkcaldy) failed, owing the Bank a large sum. The investigation proved that the credits to Russell & Sons had been made on fraudulent statements on securities over the years. The losses were expected to exceed £20,000 which was far larger than those incurred in the 1847 crisis. It was also revealed that the fraud resulted from 'the neglect of duty on the part of agent and his disregard of the rules of the Bank during a long course of years'.[103] The directors demanded that Anderson bear half the loss, that is £10,000, although the usual liability of agents on losses was one quarter.[104] Anderson pleaded with the board for a reduction of the penalty and J Fergus, who was an influential director as well as one of the largest borrowers at Kirkcaldy, argued for him. Eventually the liability was reduced to £5,000, that is one quarter of the loss, 'on the condition of his remaining unconnected with banking business in Kirkcaldy'.[105]

During the rapid expansion of the branch network there were many irregularities especially in the North. The directors made no change in their system of investigation which was still carried out by only three inspectors. There is no record that the directors themselves joined their inspectors. Even the Glasgow manager, despite his former career as inspector in the service of the British Linen Co,[106] did not seem to have inspected branches himself, either. This circumstance of entrusting only three officers with inspection was, indeed, foolhardy at a time when in the late 1850s the Union Bank had nearly one hundred branches. Consequently, the system of inspection underwent a great change in the post-1857 crisis period.

TABLE 17

Number of Branches of Scottish Banks: Ranking in 1848, 1856 and 1857

1848

	Bank	
1	Western Bank	60
2	Commercial Bank	47
3	British Linen	43
4	National Bank	38
5	N. of Scotland	33
6	Bank of Scotland	31
6	Union Bank	31
8	Edinburgh & Glasgow	20
9	Banking Co in Aberdeen	16
10	City of Glasgow	13
11	Clydesdale Bank	12
11	Aberdeen Town & County	12
13	Caledonian Bank	8
14	Royal Bank	6
15	Central Bank	5
16	Eastern Bank	3
16	Perth Bank	3
18	Dundee Bank	1
	Total	382

1856

	Bank	
1	Western Bank	98
2	City of Glasgow	97
3	Union Bank	73
4	Commercial Bank	61
5	National Bank	49
6	British Linen	48
7	Bank of Scotland	35
7	Royal Bank	35
9	N. of Scotland	30
10	Edinburgh & Glasgow	23
11	Aberdeen Town & County	20
12	Clydesdale Bank	13
13	Caledonian Bank	10
13	Perth Bank	10
15	Central Bank	8
16	Eastern Bank	4
17	Dundee Bank	1
	Total	615

1857

	Bank	
1	Union Bank	96
2	City of Glasgow	92
3	Commercial Bank	64
4	National Bank	61
5	Royal Bank	60
6	British Linen	49
7	Bank of Scotland	42
8	N. of Scotland	32
9	Aberdeen Town & County	27
10	Edinburgh & Glasgow	26
11	Clydesdale Bank	24
12	Caledonian Bank	11
13	Central Bank	9
14	Eastern Bank	5
15	Dundee Bank	4
	Total	602

Source: Edinburgh Almanac, 1849, 1857, 1858

(c) THE EMERGENCE OF A HIERARCHY IN STAFF ORGANISATION

As the business of the Union Bank developed, so did the organisation. The number of the Bank staff was already increasing and a staff hierarchy emerging.

In 1846 when the firm of Sir William Forbes & Co was finally assimilated with the Bank, another managership was instituted at the Edinburgh office. The Glasgow manager remained senior, being almost similar to a general manager, although there was no formal difference between the two managers' contracts. Indeed, the Union Bank was represented at the Select Committee of 1858 by the Glasgow manager, J Robertson, who explained the authority of his office that,

> (What authority have you to act without the consent of the directors?) By special powers contained in the contract, I conduct the business of the bank in all departments, reporting to them from time to time what takes place; every week they see the whole proceedings. (Have you an unlimited authority to make advances without the consent of the directors?) If there was anything extraordinary, I would take the directors along with me; I would not presume to make any large advance without consulting the directors.[107]

The manager was required to offer securities for no less than £10,000 and to hold more than 30 shares of the Bank.

As the second officer, the cashier was requested to attend meetings of the board of directors and sign formal documents in the absence of the manager. Outside the two head offices, the cashiership was instituted at Aberdeen and Perth as a result of the amalgamation with the Aberdeen and Perth Banks. They were all required to offer securities for more than £8,000 and to hold more than 20 shares in the Bank.

Under the two officers at the Glasgow head office, a hierarchy of the staff organisation emerged as Table 18 sets out. Though the figures in the table are very incomplete and unfortunately the salary of the cashier is unknown, a discrimination in salaries is distinguishable, that is, a great gap is evident between those of the officials—composed of the manager, cashier, secretary, accountant and inspectors—and others. In 1843, the salary of the manager was thirty times larger than that of the most junior clerk, though the average amount of the clerks' salaries was increased from £71 in 1843 to £163 in 1853. At the top of the hierarchy the importance of two officials was increasing. Between 1843 and 1853, the secretary was allowed the greatest rise of salary among the officials. This was undoubtedly due to the increased pressure as the business developed. The office of the secretary, which the contract did not define in any way, might have overtaken that of the cashier, ranking effectively second to the manager in this period. Another official was the inspector. No. 5 and no. 6 in the table, enjoyed large rises. This was obviously due to the expansion of the branch network especially in the 1850s.

The decision on salaries was, of course, within the authority of the board of directors. Responding to applications for increases, the directors usually appointed a sub-committee to consider them or trusted the subject to the sub-committee on establishment. There was, as yet, no special scale of salaries. On the part of the staff, excluding the manager, an *ex officio* member of the board, applications for increases were separately made in the 1840s. At the beginning of the 1850s, the staff started to make jointly 'general application for increased salaries'.[108] Although it is not known whether the general application continued, this case might be a very early example of collective bargaining of bank staff and certainly led the directors to consider their salaries annually, usually every May or June. In salary rises, the officials enjoyed five to ten times larger increases than the lower staff—which must have contributed to the making of the hierarchy.

TABLE 18

Glasgow Head Office Staff and Salaries in the 1840s and 1850s

Officer	1843	1844	1845	1850	1852	1853	1858
1 Manager	£1,500	£1,500	£1,500	£1,500	£1,500	£1,500	£1,500
2 Cashier	—*	—	—	—	—	—	—
3 Secretary	250	300	—	400	500	600	—
4 Accountant	250	300	—	—	400	550	—
5 Inspector	150	160	200	250	250	320	600
6 Inspector	150	160	200	—	300	350	600
7 Inspector	120	130	200				—
8 Clerk	80	90	100		—		—
9 Clerk	80	90	100		—		—
10 Clerk	80	90	100		—		—
11 Clerk	80	90	100		—		—
12 Clerk	70	80	90	929	—	2,600	—
13 Clerk	60	70	80		—		—
14 Clerk	60	70	80		—		—
15 Clerk	50	60	70		—		—
16 Clerk	80	90	100		—		—
17 Clerk			120		—		—
18 Clerk				200	—		—
19 Clerk				200	—		—
20 Clerk				200	—		—
21 Clerk					—		—
22 Clerk					—		—
23 Clerk					—		—
Total	£3,060	£3,280	£3,040	£3,679	—	£5,920	—

*no data

Sources: UBM, 11/6/1844, 6/5/1845, 5/6/1850, 13/4/1853, 30/6/1858

The salaries of agents together with those of the head office staff, also began to be considered annually by the directors from the early 1850s. Their salaries must have been decided according to their volume of business, though no evidence remains. Salaries of some agents were far below those of the clerks at the head office, ranging from £100 to £140.[109]

4   The Last Two Take-overs; Invasion of the North and East

(a) THE TAKE-OVER OF THE BANKING COMPANY IN ABERDEEN, 1849

In 1844 when Westminster was preparing for the legislation of a bank act which would restrict Scottish banking, the Banking Co in Aberdeen, established in 1767 and reorganised as joint-stock in 1839, began to search for a larger concern which would take it over. However, an offer made to the National Bank in that year was rejected probably because of their poor financial situation.[110] Indeed, the dividends of the Aberdeen Bank were reduced to $2\frac{1}{2}$ and $3\frac{3}{4}\%$ on the old and new stocks respectively in 1843. Although it had 477 shareholders and 16 branches, the actual capital sum had diminished to only a little more than £7,000. The Bank was also involved in bad debts. Despite the gradual growth of the economy in Aberdeenshire, including shipbuilding and engineering and fishing and agriculture,[111] there was no bright future for the Aberdeen Bank which, however, renewed its contract of copartnery in January 1849. A few months afterwards, the Union Bank proposed to take over the business of the Aberdeen Bank and immediately entered into negotiations. The agreement was reached in June 1849 that,

1.   The purchase of the 35,000 shares of the Aberdeen Bank stock at 30 shillings per share—£52,500. Also the call of 20 shillings per share due today—£35,000. Which sum of £87,500 would be paid in the Union Bank stock valued at £80 per share.
2.   The Union Bank would open a contingent account in name of trustees for the Aberdeen Bank for which on the junction would be credited with the remaining capital of that Bank, amounting to £7,047 and for a period of five years afterwards at each balance of the Aberdeen Bank's books after deduction of all expenses, losses, etc., a sum of £6,000 would first be carried to the credit of the Union Bank and the remainder of profits to the credit of the contingent account; the whole amount of which would be held as a guarantee for realisation of the assets of the Aberdeen Bank.[112]

The institution of the contingent account was obviously due to the bad debts of the Aberdeen Bank which became the owner of a cotton mill as a result of the failure of Thomas Bannerman & Co. Despite this device, an objection was raised by a shareholder of the Union Bank who was strongly against the take-over 'if it involved the purchase or working of any cotton factory'.[113] Responding to the objection, the directors made further investigation of the books of the Aberdeen Bank, re-estimating the value of the cotton mill and instructing the Aberdeen Bank to close the account of Bannerman & Co. On the other hand, the shareholders of the Aberdeen Bank claimed that the payment to them was insufficient. The directors of the Union Bank willingly agreed to this demand, increasing their offer to £2 each on the 35,000 shares.

The negotiations took five months during which the directors of the Union Bank conceded the demands of the shareholders of both banks, thus successfully invading the North.

(b) THE TAKE-OVER OF THE PERTH BANK, 1857

The Union Bank made its first take-over bid in 1849 for the Perth Bank, which rejected the offer and showed its independence, by renewing its contract of copartnery in the same year. However, in the late 1850s, the Perth Bank was compelled to take account of growing pressure by joint-stock banks whose branches were making their appearance in Perth.[114] In this circumstance, the Union Bank made the second take-over bid to which the Perth Bank favourably replied,

> It seemed to them (the directors) that the recent extraordinary multiplication of bank branches throughout the country and the consequent competition for business which these engendered threatened results of a character which by and by could scarcely fail in producing disaster—Feeling strongly that the best interests of the community, and of the banks themselves, would be promoted by a judicious consolidation and amalgamation of some of the existing banks rather than by the keen competition and rivalry which had for some time existed— the directors were led to entertain favourably overtures for a junction which reached them from one of the most influential and prosperous banks in Scotland.[115]

In strong contrast to those words of C D Gairdner,[116] the Perth Bank seems to have still been confident in itself. Indeed, the market price of its shares stood at £200 (£10 paid) in 1857 compared to £100 (£50 paid) of the Union Bank shares and the amount of total liabilities was increasing during the 1850s.[117] However, it was also true that the age of the provincial banks had passed. The amount of their liabilities, though growing, was as small as 10% of that of the absorbing Union Bank. Thus, the Perth Bank, one of the two remaining provincial banks, sold its business for £100,050 to the Union Bank. It disappeared from the Scottish banking scene just before the disaster of 1857 which the Perth directors had anticipated.

(c) THE SECOND AMALGAMATION MOVEMENT

From 1849 to 1857, the Union Bank made six take-over bids for four Scottish banks; one each for the Aberdeen Bank in 1849 and the Dundee Bank (provincial, est. 1763) and two each for the Perth Bank in 1849 and 1857 and the Caledonian Bank (joint-stock based in Inverness, est. 1838) in 1851 and 1856.[118] Among them, two were successful, and the financial situation at the dates of amalgamation and the terms of take-over, together with those of the unsuccessful cases, are set out in Table 19. The Union Bank also took over the Dunblane Savings Bank in February 1857, details of this are unknown.

From the bids, both successful and unsuccessful, all made to the banks in the North and East, it is quite clear that the Union Bank was aiming at the expansion of business into these districts where its branch network had not yet been established. However, there might have been a slight difference between the bids made in the years of 1849/51 and of 1856/57. The years of 1849/51, when the Union Bank made three bids, witnessed cheap money, during which the Bank of England rate stood at $2\frac{1}{2}$ to 3% and the surplus funds of the Union

TABLE 19

Amalgamations of the Union Bank of Scotland in 1849 and 1857

	Union Bank April 1848	(1)* Aberdeen Bank October 1849	(2) Perth Bank May 1857	Union Bank April 1858	(3) Abortive Cases Caledonian Bank December 1856	(4) Dundee Bank February 1857
1 Total Liabilities	£6,221,661	£1,115,883	£866,290	£8,827,550	—	£835,910
2 Capital paid	1,000,000 (16.1)	7,047 (0.6)	100,050 (11.5)	1,000,000 (11.3)	£125,000	60,000 (7.2)
3 Deposits	3,884,829 (62.4)	820,568 (73.5)	588,605 (67.9)	6,544,064 (74.1)	—	686,605 (82.1)
4 Notes	598,664 (9.6)	269,653 (24.2)	101,977 (11.8)	598,087 (6.8)	69,450	41,906 (5.0)
5 Advances†	4,222,314 (67.9)	694,681 (62.2)	464,867 (53.7)	6,624,274 (75.0)	—	698,429 (83.5)
6 Investments	377,505 (6.1)	182,659‡ (16.4)	252,391 (29.1)	1,047,761 (11.9)	—	29,220 (3.5)
7 Reserve	133,320 (2.1)	—	56,000 (6.5)	200,000 (2.3)	—	30,000 (3.6)
8 Profits	48,000 (0.8)	—	56,043 (6.5)	98,224 (1.1)	—	15,764 (1.9)
9 Dividend	8%	6%§	10%‖	9%	8%	10%
10 Number of Partners	592	477§	200‖	1,113	803	79
11 Number of Offices	33	17	11	101	11	2
12 Term of Take-over	—	£105,000	£100,050	—	—	£126,000

*( ) of columns 2-8; % in total liabilities   †Discounts and credit accounts including overdrafts   ‡Including cash balance   §1848   ‖1856

Sources: UBM, UBMGB, UBAAB, UBPL, Perth Bank *Minute of Board of Directors,* C W Boase, 1867, R S Rait, 1930 and CWM, 1981

Bank accumulated, probably in common with other Scottish banks. Therefore, the motive of amalgamation might be to place their funds more profitably in the North where the economy was obviously developing. In contrast, the Bank of England rate was fairly high in the years of 1856/57, when another three bids were offered, standing at 7% in November 1856. The motive might have been to increase their resources. Anyway, as R S Rait argued,[119] the Union Bank established its business in the North and East, not as an invader but as 'one of the most influential and prosperous banks in Scotland'.

Although two-thirds of the take-over bids were unsuccessful, there was no doubt, except for that one case of the Perth Bank in 1849, that the four banks were anxious to make their business over to the Union Bank. Indeed, in the case of the Dundee Bank only the objection of two partners prevented the amalgamation. The contract stipulated that nothing could be done without 100 per cent approval of the partners.[120] Their willingness to sell their business was certainly due to the fact that the economy outgrew their ability. Even the Caledonian joint-stock bank, and largest of the four in terms of number of shareholders, had only about 10% of the capital of the Union Bank. It could be argued that even the joint-stock bank, if based on only a small amount of capital, was not able to survive, or at least could not make progress in, the growing and fluctuating economy.

The Union Bank developed its business in all respects between 1848, a year before the take-over of the Aberdeen Bank, and 1858, a year after that of the Perth Bank; total liabilities grew by 142%, deposits by 168%, advances by 157% and investments by 277%. But how far the growth was due to the amalgamations is not really clear because the Bank itself was making rapid strides in the same period. However, one important development definitely resulted from the amalgamations, that is, the wide network of 28 branches in the North and East. It can be argued that the business of the Union Bank for the first time covered the whole country in this period. The creation of branches in the North and East was particularly necessary for gathering deposits. Indeed, if the Perth Bank, whose deposits were £0.6m, had not merged with the Union Bank, the deposits might have decreased in the course of the 1857 crisis because the amount of deposits of the Bank increased only by £0.13m between April 1857 and April 1858, and a tremendous money flow from the North and East to the West certainly resulted from these amalgamations.[121]

5   The Crises of 1847 and 1857

There were two major crises between 1844 and 1858. The 1847 crisis damaged the business of the Western Bank and the Edinburgh & Glasgow bank, both of which had to ask the Bank of England for assistance, and also effectively terminated the operation of exchange companies. Other Scottish banks did not suffer from such heavy losses. The following decade witnessed the rapid

growth of Scottish banking, which primarily resulted from the energetic
business of the Glasgow banks, and ended in the disaster of 1857, in which the
Western Bank finally closed its doors, the City of Glasgow Bank temporarily
stopped payment and the quasi-Glasgow-based Edinburgh & Glasgow Bank
was fatally damaged. What happened to the Union Bank of Scotland? Is it
right to say with R S Rait that 'the storm was safely and even brilliantly
weathered'?[122] If this is correct, it should then be queried— what caused 'the
storm' and how 'brilliantly' did the directors manage to survive it?

(a) THE 1847 CRISIS

In May 1847 deputations of English bankers met the Chancellor of the
Exchequer to urge him to suspend the Bank Act of 1844. In Scotland, bankers
were anxious. The directors of the Union Bank began to examine the accounts
of doubtful borrowers, making a list as Table 20 sets out. The concern of the
directors turned out to be justified. In September 1847, J & A Denny (no. 12 in
Table 20, grain merchants, Glasgow) failed, owing the Union Bank a large
debt which was fortunately covered by security.[123] There followed failures of
at least six firms, all the Bank's customers till January 1848. In one of these D
Lamb & Co (no. 13 in Table 20) were involved.[124]

TABLE 20

Doubtful Borrowers in 1847

	Borrower	Debts
1	H Taylor & Son	£8,880
2	R Scott & Son	12,520
3	M Wotherspoon	2,115
4	J Miller	1,500
5	A Miller & Co	7,600
6	J Lamb	2,345
7	Anderson & Halden	2,720
8	E T Bald & Co	2,625
9	R A C Currie	7,187
10	R Cowan	15,875
11	J Currie	8,071
12	J & A Denny	75,640
13	D Lamb & Co	13,960
14	R Neil & Co	2,781
	Total	£163,819

Source: UBM Scroll Book, 21/5/1847

There were apparently another three doubtful borrowers who worried the
directors in the course of the 1847/48 crisis, that is, Lord Belhaven, J & A
Dennistoun & Co and Rowand, Dunlop & Co. Lord Belhaven, a large as well
as a troublesome borrower, failed to procure a loan from the Bank, which was

to be applied to the repayment of his debt, in arrears, and eventually his business of coal mining went into liquidation in August 1847.[125] Dennistoun & Co, who were suspected to be in certain difficulties, asked the directors for an emergency retirement of their bills for £86,000 just before the crisis.[126] Rowand, Dunlop & Co, encountering difficulties, were allowed an overdraft to the extent of £30,000 which, however, could not stop the deterioration of their business, and they stopped payment in August 1848. Their debts were covered by the security of a large estate in Glasgow.

The total loss, which the Union Bank incurred in the 1847 crisis, was £12,125 which was less than that sustained by the Kirkcaldy branch in 1850. There was no especial danger to the Union Bank, though the doubtful business with regard to Dennistoun's had already begun to worry the directors.

(b) THE 1857 CRISIS

In the nine years from 1848 to 1856, the Glasgow banks appeared stronger, especially in terms of number of branches, which increased from 136 in 1848 to 304 in 1856, nearly half of the total Scottish branches (see Table 22). Among the Glasgow banks, the Clydesdale Bank added only one branch to its network. the extra 164 branches were made by three banks; the Western created 38, the City of Glasgow 84 and the Union 42. In addition to their keen lending policy in the 1850s, their tremendous network of branches must have involved all three in heavy running costs and bad debts. Thus, the three banks, which were first, second and third in the ranking of number of branches (see Table 17) just before the crisis, faced unprecedented hardship in the autumn of 1857.

At this moment, the Edinburgh banks took the opportunity to eliminate the risky as well as formidable Western Bank, as Professor R H Campbell has suggested[127] and as A Blair, the treasurer of the Bank of Scotland, really intended, saying that,

> their system of business (the Western Bank) has been more like that of a pawn-broker than of a banker . . . This can be effected by an arrangement to wind up the affairs of the Bank failing any other proposition securing the community from a further repetition of the same misconvenience and danger.[128]

The Edinburgh banks, led by Blair, thus, 'organised attempt to overthrow'[129] the Western Bank and naturally delayed taking any action during the crucial negotiations of the emergency loan asked by the Western Bank. Firstly on 17 October 1857, the Western Bank deputed one of the directors to ask the Bank of Scotland for assistance. But there was no answer. The second delegation of the Western Bank was despatched on 21 October. The Bank of Scotland did not make any move, suggesting that the delegation seek assistance from the Bank of England on the ground that,

> the action of the Bank Charter Acts throws important cases like the present very much under the consideration of the Governor and the Bank of England.[130]

The opinion of the Bank of Scotland, effectively that of Blair, was confirmed by the Edinburgh banks.[131]

On 26 October when the Western Bank failed to obtain assistance from the Bank of England and Union Bank of London, the Edinburgh banks first resolved that,

> Upon consideration of the proposal of the Western Bank for an advance to that bank of £500,000, that the advance be given in equal portions by the banks, coupled with the condition that the directors of the Western Bank shall dissolve and wind up the Company, and also that the whole advance shall be covered by a deposit of satisfactory commercial bills, not less than £750,000 and that the directors, or a sufficient number of the shareholders, to the satisfaction of the banks, undertake personal responsibility by bill or bond for the advance.[132]

The clause of the compulsory winding-up, the intention of A Blair but impossible under the contemporary laws, was eliminated by the effort of the managers of fellow Glasgow banks, but time ran out because *The Times* (London) disclosed the crucial point of the negotiations and, as a result, there was a sudden heavy run on the Western Bank, which closed its doors on Monday 9 November 1857. That most go-ahead Western Bank, condemned as 'a pawn-broker' by Blair, thus, disappeared from the Scottish scene as indeed the Edinburgh banks intended.

During the crucial negotiations between the Western Bank and others, the Union Bank joined the Edinburgh banks and the manager signed under the headline of 'Minute of the Edinburgh banks'. Was the situation of the Union Bank safe and sound? The real situation of the Bank cannot be decided by the figures in its balance sheet which even showed increases from 1857 to 1858. 'The ordeal of a run'[133] was to be a very real experience for the Union Bank.

The directors of the Union Bank first felt strain at the beginning of September 1857 when Carr, Josling & Co (merchants, London) failed, leaving debts of £300,000 in which two of the Union Bank's customers were involved. One of the two applied for a relief credit which the directors refused. There followed a large number of failures which involved the Bank in bad debts to a very large extent; the Liverpool Borough Bank stopped payment on 27 October, Dennistoun & Co, who had large stakes in the Liverpool Bank, on 7 November, and the Northumberland & Durham District Bank on 25 November. The liabilities of Dennistoun & Co—a leading member of whose firm was Alexander Dennistoun who was a director of the Union Bank—were the largest among those merchants whose business had collapsed in the autumn of 1857, amounting to more than £2.1m,[134] though their stoppage was claimed by a contemporary writer to have been rather 'artificial'.[135]

Two days after the stoppage of Dennistoun & Co, the Union Bank itself experienced the heaviest run,[136] and the directors instructed the manager,

> to transmit the London bills due in February and March to Messrs. Glyn & Co. with directions to discount the same and remit the proceeds in gold. Should there not be time to accomplish this tomorrow, £150,000 to be sent in gold. The manager was desired to forward various railway stocks, Consols &c—to London and suggest Glyn & Co. to convert the same into cash.[137]

Meanwhile the Bank strengthened the holding of gold at the Edinburgh office, £50,000 of which was brought up from London and Newcastle.[138] However, the run on the Bank, particularly in the West, was increasing, and, thus, the Glasgow directors resolved to send a delegate to Edinburgh in order to raise a loan on local bills for £2,000,000. The resolution was objected to by the Edinburgh directors who were afraid that measures for securing such a large loan on local bills in Edinburgh could expose the Bank to greater risks. The last resort was London, and the delegation, composed of Sir Adam Hay, John Fergus, both Edinburgh directors, and G Somervell, a Glasgow director, was dispatched to negotiate with the Bank of England. On returning from London, Somervell reported the successful result of negotiations and the directors seriously resolved that,

> (Somervell) conjunction with Sir Adam Hay and Fergus arranged through Glyn to discount direct with the Bank of England the bills taken up by him and those transferred from Edinburgh/£2,000,000/. A cursory view of the financial position of the Bank with a prospective view of its affairs having been taken, it was considered and it appeared necessary that the business of the Bank should be diminished as much as possible without pressing too hard on its customers. With this view, it was resolved to look over the accounts of those parties having overdrawn accounts and large discounts, and to urge them to curtail their business as much as possible.[139]

Glyn & Co, whose role was of vital importance in negotiating with the Bank of England, also provided £200,000 in cash.[140] In sharp contrast to the case of the Western Bank, the Union Bank was given generous support by its fellow Scottish banks; the Clydesdale Bank lent £35,000 in gold[141] and three Edinburgh banks, the Bank of Scotland, the British Linen and the Commercial Bank, assisted by refraining from presenting Union Bank bills for £400,000 to Glyn & Co.[142]

In the meantime, serious reports were pouring into the head offices. On 11 November, the Edinburgh manager reported that,

> We have had a crowded day, but scarcely amounting to a run, though it was both the term and market day. We have had about £40,000 taken from us in gold and a good deal otherwise. We had to give £10,000 in gold to Dundee.[143]

The Greenock agent reported on the same day that the run was slighter than on the previous day, adding that,

> here and at our branches we still hold £8,500 of gold.[144]

The most remarkable report came from the Aberdeen cashier that,

> For two hours yesterday the crush was terrible, being met, however, in the way it was, it gradually died away. . . . The dead set was at first on us, the City of Glasgow Bank being the next door to us, but the run went over the whole banks, and was greater or less in proportion to the extent of their business, the North of Scotland Bank and ourselves bearing the greatest weight. Gold has been flowing back in some cases. . . . Unless at one or two branches, things are equally good. The cause of these

exceptions is one of the most scandalous things that probably ever took place. . . . The Great North of Scotland Railway Co telegraphed, early on the morning of the panic here, to every Stationmaster on the line to Keith and on that to Turriff, 'not to take any of the notes of the Union Bank of Scotland or Western Bank'. The Officials at some places went into shops and inns and circulated this official order. You may conceive what we had, along with our agents, to contend against that trying day.[145]

The reports indicate that the public was aware of the real situation of the Union Bank. Indeed, an offer of stock was burst upon the directors from 14 November 1857 when 268 shares were laid on the table of the boardroom and transferred to other shareholders at the prices between £82 and £100. The price of offered stock continuously dropped, touching the lowest price of £70 on 30 December 1857. The large scale offer of stock did not cease until the end of January 1858 when a sign of recovery in the market price could just be seen. Consequently, in three and a half months from November 1857, more than 1,400 shares were offered.[146] The falling rate of the market price of the Union Bank share was 32% which was the largest among the surviving Scottish banks. Even the share of the tottering Edinburgh & Glasgow Bank was reduced in price only by 28%.

What really caused this trouble for the Union Bank? The direct cause of runs upon the Union Bank was the closure of the Western Bank which gave rise to anxiety in the public over any banks, especially those based in Glasgow. This was no more than a general circumstance which would occur in a banking crisis. A particular and basic factor which involved the Union Bank in great difficulties was heavy commitment in one particular firm, that is, J & A Dennistoun & Co whom we have already mentioned.

Earlier in 1846, the firm of Dennistoun & Co was specially authorised to borrow £75 per share, which was three times larger than the ordinary amount of cash credit.[147] This was really the commencement of heavy involvement in this firm. A year after the authorisation of special credits, Dennistoun & Co again asked the Bank for special treatment and the directors,

agree to retire for Dennistoun £86,000 extra bills in London this month being the portion that should have been retired by the Borough of Liverpool—a number of London bills due in June and July to be rediscounted by Messrs Glyn & Co if necessary, to fill at the account and Mr Dennistoun to be requested to refrain from asking such a thing again.[148]

The only objection to this resolution was raised by the Edinburgh directors who strongly contended that,

advances so extensive could not in future be made to them or any other individual house.[149]

None the less, a sentence 'if possible' was afterwards added to the resolution of the Glasgow board. The equilibrium between the two boards was for the first time at stake.

The energetic business of Dennistoun & Co, which must have developed tremendously in the hectic years of the British economy during the 1850s, led the board of directors, of which A Dennistoun himself was a member, to make an unreasonable resolution in 1853 that,

> they (Dennistoun & Co) should have a fixed credit of £280,000 on security of Stock on condition that never less than £150,000 is drawn—at all events that usual cash credit rate of interest be charged on £150,000—London acceptances up to £1,000,000 and when the transactions exceed that amount 1/8% can be charged on the excess.[150]

The tremendous amount of credits for more than £1.2m to one firm was sanctioned at the general board of directors which the Edinburgh directors, of course, attended. The equilibrium between the two boards was eventually lost. The advance of £1.2m to one concern might have had an even worse result than the case of the Western Bank whose stoppage was caused by £1.2m credits to three firms.[151] The swollen business of Dennistoun & Co undoubtedly became vulnerable to any small change in its trade. Indeed, ten days after the failure of the Liverpool Borough Bank, Dennistoun & Co were forced to stop payment on account of a slight delay of remittance from America. The result was the difficulties in the autumn of 1857. Consequently, it could be argued that the real situation of the Union Bank was not very different from that of the collapsed Western Bank. If the Western Bank could be blamed as 'a pawn-broker', should the Union Bank be also? It should then be queried as to why and how the Union Bank could survive this critical situation.

The first question is why the Bank of England and the Edinburgh banks, both of which refused the plea of the Western Bank, helped out the Union Bank. There might be three reasons. Firstly, the third stoppage of a large joint-stock bank following the failure of the Western Bank and the temporary closure of the City of Glasgow Bank had to be prevented because the effect of such an incident would be far-reaching. Secondly, the Union Bank had never given offence to the Edinburgh banks, while the Western Bank had been notorious for its risky business and aggressiveness, especially directed at the Edinburgh banks. Moreover, the Union Bank was seemingly accepted as a member of the Edinburgh banks the manager of which signed under the headline of the Edinburgh banks. Thirdly, the Union, unlike the Western, had a reserve policy on the suggestion of the Edinburgh directors. In these last two respects, the existence of the Edinburgh directors, that is, the three surviving partners of the late firm of Sir William Forbes & Co, was extremely important. The crucial negotiations with the Bank of England were obviously led by Sir Adam Hay who was a corner stone of the Edinburgh board as well as of the Union Bank as a whole.

The second question is whether the Union Bank had built in an element which could help itself. The branch network might provide a key. In terms of number of branches in 1856 (see Table 17), the Union Bank ranked third, following the Western Bank and the City of Glasgow Bank. If we look into the patterns of the branch network of the Union Bank and the Western Bank, an absolute difference can be found, as Table 21 sets out. Although the Western Bank claimed to have the largest number of branches, 70% of their branches were located in the West and South of Scotland. It had no branches further

North than Tayside. The Western Bank was, thus, literally, the bank of the West. On the contrary, almost half of the Union Bank branches were situated in the North and East, especially in the Grampian area. The branch network of the Union Bank was, thus, well balanced between the West and the North and East, having a character of national coverage with its shareholders distributed all over the country. This pattern of branch network might help the Union Bank in two ways. In the first place, the Union Bank could transfer its resources in the North and East to the West where the heavy runs were occurring. This kind of transfer was made, particularly between the head offices, that is, from Edinburgh to Glasgow. In the second place, the national coverage of business might help to encourage the Bank of England in giving assistance to the Union Bank, because a collapse of the bank on such a scale would have had a disastrous effect on the whole country. Indeed, the situation of the Union Bank in the autumn of 1857 roused fears in the Chancellor.[152] In building up the branch network on this pattern, the take-overs of the Aberdeen and Perth Banks, without whose branch network the Union Bank might have succumbed to the storm, were invaluable.

TABLE 21

Pattern of Branch network in the late 1850s

	Union Bank (Dec. 1857)	Western Bank (Dec. 1856)
Strathclyde	27	52
Dumfries & Galloway	9	14
Borders	3	4
Lothian	3	12
Central	8	2
Fife	6	6
Tayside	16	8
Grampian	21	0
Highlands	1	0
Orkney	1	0
Shetland	1	0
Total	96	98

Source: Edinburgh Almanac, 1857, 1858

The 1857 disaster had a great effect on Glasgow banking as Table 22 clearly shows. The dropping out of the large as well as aggressive Western Bank itself caused a great diminution of the Glasgow share in Scottish banking and a loss of Glasgow initiative. Thus, in terms of capital and number of branches, Glasgow-controlled banking was overtaken by its Edinburgh counterpart. Even including the Edinburgh & Glasgow Bank, the Glasgow share in the total Scottish banking capital became reduced to a little more than one-third. As far as Glasgow-Edinburgh rivalry is concerned, Glasgow-controlled banking was in retreat. In this climate of Glasgow banking, the Union Bank, which had narrowly escaped disaster, began to make a great change in its conduct of management.

TABLE 22

Dimensions of Glasgow, Edinburgh and North & East Based Banks, 1848, 1856 and 1857

	1848*		1856*		1857*	
Capital						
Glasgow†	£5,515,830	46.3%	£5,307,380	45.3%	£3,807,380	37.6%
Edinburgh	5,100,000	42.8%	5,600,000	47.8%	5,600,000	55.3%
North & East	1,296,300	10.9%	818,890	6.9%	718,840	7.1%
Total	£11,912,130	100.0%	£11,726,270	100.0%	£10,126,220	100.0%
Partners						
Glasgow†	5,772	40.5%	6,439	46.0%	(Not available)	
Edinburgh	3,816	26.8%	3,698	26.4%		
North & East	4,647	32.7%	3,854	27.6%		
Total	14,235	100.0%	13,991	100.0%		
Branches						
Glasgow†	136	35.6%	304	49.4%	238	39.6%
Edinburgh	165	43.2%	228	37.1%	276	45.8%
North & East	81	21.2%	83	13.5%	88	14.6%
Total	382	100.0%	615	100.0%	602	100.0%

*Date as in December each year
†Edinburgh & Glasgow Bank included in the Glasgow banks

Source: Edinburgh Almanac, 1849, 1857, 1858

Chapter 3

The Union Bank of Scotland at its Zenith, 1858–1865

The years from 1858 to 1865 were another period of increasing prosperity for the Union Bank of Scotland. None the less, in the aftermath of the 1857 crisis and two successive failures of large borrowers in the early 1860s, the Union Bank was forced to make a great change in its conduct of management and the result was the appointment of Charles Gairdner, a young accountant, as joint manager. When the great change in its policy was going on, the Union Bank was approaching its zenith.

1 The Appointment of Charles Gairdner[1] as Joint Manager in 1862

In the aftermath of the 1857 crisis, the Union Bank was still suffering from bad debts which were caused by two large customers in Aberdeen and Glasgow.

Blackie & Son, who were mentioned by the directors in their annual report as 'a firm of such high repute'[2] in Aberdeen, failed in 1860. Blackie's financial situation had already caused worry for the directors in April 1859 when the firm violated the agreement made with the Bank. The board gave them a warning through the Aberdeen cashier, stating that,

> With reference to the Aberdeen minutes of 14th, the manager was desired to write to Mr Wyllie (Aberdeen cashier) to express the regret of the directors that Messrs Blackie had violated the arrangement made with them under which they undertook not to overdraw their operative account and to inform him that while they approve of the plan adopted for obtaining repayment, he is to intimate Messrs Blackie that no overdraft will be again permitted.[3]

In spite of this precaution, the Bank could not escape the bad debts of Blackie & Son because of whom the Bank incurred a loss of £30,638. The loss debited the reserve in two successive years.

The situation of the Monkland Iron & Steel Co was also disturbing the directors nearly three years before the failure. In the autumn of 1858, when the usual investigation on cash and overdrawn accounts at the Glasgow head office was made, they instructed the manager,

> to get executed whatever deeds the law agent may consider necessary for keeping the Bank's security in order in consequence of the death of Mr Murray (general manager of the Company).[4]

At the same time the directors gave an instruction to the accountant to draw up a report which would investigate 'the state of Monkland's affairs'.[5] In spite of these steps, the failure of Monkland Co in July 1861 resulted in another great loss for the Union Bank.

These two successive failures of large borrowers, following the difficulties in 1857, eventually led the directors to have doubts about the whole conduct of their business and to make a serious investigation of all accounts, which was carried out from the end of 1861 to the spring of 1862.[6] In carrying out the investigation, the directors did not entrust the Glasgow manager, J Robertson, with the duty and appointed an outsider, Charles Gairdner, a chartered accountant and one of the liquidators of the Western Bank of Scotland. He revealed that the Union Bank was in possession of bad debts for £140,000 in all, including the loss sustained from the failure of the Monkland Co.[7] Why was the manager omitted?

According to the annual report, the circumstances of Gairdner's appointment were that,

> The extended business of the Bank has for some time forced upon the attention of the directors the necessity of increasing the staff of the establishment at Glasgow; and while the subject was under consideration, Mr Robertson the manager of the Bank having been strongly recommended by his medical advisers to abstain for a time from business, the directors were induced to make such arrangements as would relieve him of a portion of his duties. This they have done by the appointment of Mr Charles Gairdner to be joint manager along with Mr Robertson.[8]

Two reasons were given for the appointment of Gairdner. One was 'the extended business' which was not borne out by the figures in the balance sheets. In all terms of total liabilities, deposits, advances and profits, the business of the Bank considerably diminished from 1861 to 1862 (see Table 32). The second reason, 'illness of the manager', must have been diplomatic, because Robertson was still active in his new dock company business after the discharge of his managership.[9] From the two unsatisfactory explanations given in the report, with regard to his omission from the inspection and the reduction of his salary from £2,000 to £1,750 in 1863,[10] we may infer that Robertson, along with the secretary, was blamed for the accumulation of bad debts and was nearly 'dismissed'.

However, the change of the Glasgow manager was no more than the visible peak of an iceberg. In the aftermath of the 1857 crisis, the Edinburgh directors re-enforced their authority over the Glasgow directors whose expansionist policy was clearly accountable for the difficulties. In this situation, the Edinburgh directors spoke out. In the first place, they were not satisfied with the system of inspection of branches hitherto executed and sent their resolution to their Glasgow counterparts earlier in August 1858 that,

> The subject of inspecting the branches under this department having been mentioned, it was suggested that with a view to the introduction of a uniform and systematic mode of inspecting and reporting upon all the branches, it might be expedient that the inspector for the Glasgow department with his assistant should

receive charge of the whole. . . . It was resolved to bring this matter before the general board.[11]

Soon after their resolution, the Edinburgh directors independently appointed an inspector of book-keeping at the Edinburgh office.[12] However, their opinion in favour of a 'uniform and systematic mode of' inspection did not immediately result in any decision and was soon followed by the two successive failures of Blackie & Son and the Monkland Co. Thus, it seems that the Edinburgh directors, especially Sir Adam Hay and D Anderson both of whom were the partners of the late firm of Sir William Forbes & Co, disciplined their Glasgow counterparts and demanded the removal of the Glasgow manager who was ultimately responsible for strict inspection.

In the second place, it was the Edinburgh directors who from time to time raised objections to the large credits of Dennistoun & Co who were still causing trouble in the course of repaying their debts to the Bank. In order to effect the repayment, Dennistoun & Co frequently proposed the sale of their large amount of Union Bank stock and this was rejected by the directors.[13] Eventually in August 1860, the Dennistouns were specially requested to attend the Edinburgh committee, at which Sir Adam Hay, D Anderson and a Glasgow director, Colin Campbell, were present. As the minute recorded,

A conversation took place with Messrs A & J Dennistoun/who had come to attend this meeting/respecting their obligations to the Bank. They mentioned that they had looked to the sale of shares of the Bank to meet Messrs J Dennistoun & Co's note for £18,196 9s. 3d. due on the 19th instant, but since receipt of the late letters from the manager (Edinburgh) they had to consider other modes of doing so and proposed to transfer to the Bank mortgage notes due at periods of three and five years on estate sold at New Orleans, as security for the ultimate payment of said note. The directors decline accepting this security. . . . Messrs Dennistouns intimated their determination to realise the mill property, the proceeds to be applied to the instalment notes of Messrs J Dennistoun & Co, Mr John D (*sic*) undertook to realise the property of Alex Fletcher & Co either by sale of the mill or otherwise in all 1861 and to extinguish the debt due to the Bank on the said amount. Messrs D (*sic*) farther undertook to place 500 shares of the Bank on the market at once to be sold as opportunities offer but in the mode least calculated to injure their or the Bank's interest.[14]

Despite allowance for the sale of the Bank stock and the promise to 'extinguish the debt', the repayment was not effected in 1861. Besides their own debts, another firm, A Fletcher & Co (flax spinners, Glasgow), in which John Dennistoun was a partner, was asking the Bank for credits, becoming one of the large borrowers.[15] In order to get rid of Dennistoun financing, an extraordinary step, say, an appointment of a new manager of strong personality, was essential.

Charles Gairdner was, thus, apparently the choice of the Edinburgh directors, who were doing business with Gairdner as stock broker,[16] and they must have appreciated his ability. Indeed, their selection proved to be right. Against the claim of the senior manager, Robertson, that the outsider would not be able to investigate the bank business,[17] Gairdner discovered a large amount of bad debts. The branch inspection was systematically and energetically executed as will be discussed later. The Bank also saw a prospect of getting rid of the bad debts of Dennistoun & Co in October 1863 when Gairdner reported that,

> in reference to A & J Dennistoun joint bill of £199,500 now reduced to £184,739 would come to an end in January.[18]

Charles Gairdner started his joint managership with every appearance of success. His salary for the first year was £1,750 which was equal to that of the senior manager. Immediately in the wake of his appointment, Gairdner recommended, as a new Glasgow secretary, James Syme, who was an agent of the Bank of Scotland and he became the first assistant manager of the Union Bank in 1865 when Gairdner took over the sole managership. There was no special vote of thanks for the services of J Robertson and the out-going secretary. The appointment of Gairdner was a major change. Under the new regime, the Union Bank was to become the most cautious of institutions.

2   Business in Search for Stability

(a) CANNINESS IN LENDING

Cash credits and discounts remained the main methods of advances of the Union Bank. In this period, however, discounts constantly exceeded cash credits and again absolutely correlated with the growth of total liabilities as Table 23 shows. Discounts were really a major factor in the growth of the Union Bank.

Along with the increases in transactions of bills of exchange, the Union Bank introduced a curious method into the system, which was termed

TABLE 23

Methods of Advances, 1859–65

	Credit Accounts/ Overdrafts		Discounts		Growth Rate of Liabilities: 1859: 100
1859*	£2,865,405	46% †	£3,312,421	54%	100
1860	2,881,786	43%	3,773,084	57%	105
1861	3,037,039	45%	3,728,607	55%	102
1862	2,772,309	45%	3,374,845	55%	99
1863	2,526,720	42%	3,557,576	58%	100
1864	3,074,167	46%	3,619,780	54%	105
1865	3,121,894	44%	4,010,252	56%	111
Average		44%		56%	

*Date as in April each year
†%; proportion between the two

Sources: UBAAB

'marginal credit'. This method made its first appearance in the end of 1863 as the minute recorded that,

> It was agreed to issue to Messrs Finlay, Campbell & Co, merchants, London, for negotiation in Melbourne by Messrs McCulloch, Sellars & Co, marginal credit bills for £60,000, £10,000 of which have now been issued, and a like sum to be issued during each of the ensuing five months; all against six promissory notes to the Bank, payable on demand, amounting to £60,000, by Finlay, Campbell & Co, and L Inglis & Co together with letter from the former firm explanatory of the reason for which they have been granted.[19]

The unusual term 'marginal' was,

> so named because on the margin of the actual bill form to be used is a letter detailing the terms of drawing and acceptance, and authorising the person to whom it is addressed 'to draw the annexed bill . . .' This letter must not be detached from the bill portion of the document.[20]

The marginal credit was expected by the Bank to help to avoid the acceptance of accommodation, or fictitious, bills which had undoubtedly swollen in the 1850s. Indeed, it was based on the real bill doctrine of Adam Smith and was also a forerunner of documentary bills.

In operating this method, the Bank was careful to demand a large guarantee deposit,

> First: promissory notes . . . £85,000.
> Second: deposit in cash £21,250 . . . being 25% on the amount of credit. $\frac{1}{2}$% commission to be paid on all drafts against said credit, it being in the option of the Bank to put an end to the credit at any time on giving 12 months notice.[21]

Marginal credit first made its appearance in the balance sheet of 1864, the amount of which was, however, only less than 1.2% of the total liabilities. Judging from the date of its appearance, it seems likely that Charles Gairdner was the initiator. He also introduced in 1864 a systematic 'opinion book' which recorded both outgoing and incoming correspondence regarding credit-worthiness of customers.[22] Furthermore, he himself put down in his confidential note-book detailed information on his customers. He was a very careful banker. Under his managership, the Union Bank became a canny lender.

It is difficult, or almost impossible, to establish an exact distribution of the Bank's sectoral lending. However, if we ignore small advances, say, less than £10,000, there emerge two sectors which the Union Bank seemingly preferred, that is, trade and railway. Two-thirds of the large advances exceeding £10,000 were given to these two sectors. The iron and steel sector, which was one of the two favourite borrowers up to 1858, dropped out of the top rankings. In the trade sector, there were well-known, enterprising merchants such as James Morton, John Pender, James Scott and James Nicol Fleming, all of whom were allowed overdrafts and marginal credits. The firm of Pender, Scott & Fleming obtained a large credit of £100,000 on the security of iron warrants, which was the largest lump sum of credit sanctioned to this sector.[23] This authorisation also suggests that iron warrants had become good securities for a bank loan.[24] J Morton was, at this moment, striving to create a market in Scotland for a whole range of colonial products, the business of which was afterwards incorporated into the New Zealand & Australia Land Co.[25] Notably, all of these large borrowers were also customers of the City of Glasgow Bank in which J N Fleming was even a director. However, the Union Bank did not deepen its involvement further in any one particular firm of this sector. The lesson of dangerous Dennistoun financing was certainly learnt.

As in the previous period, the Union Bank took a different attitude towards the Scottish railway companies and their English, Irish and Welsh counterparts. The Scottish railways continued to be ordinary customers and were allowed advances mainly on overdrafts and promissory notes. In the circumstances of increasing competition among the Scottish railways, exemplified by the North British and Caledonian Railways,[26] cartel lending was continued in order to distribute risks. In October 1860 when the North British took a large loan of £120,000, the Union Bank lent one third and the rest was supplied by the Royal and National Banks.[27] From time to time, the Union Bank supplied funds to railway companies to enable them 'to pay their dividend warrants',[28] relieving them of lack of short-term liquidities. The number of customers dropped (because of amalgamations) and the principal borrowers were three—the North British, Glasgow & South Western and City of Glasgow Union Railways.

The English, Irish and Welsh railway financing was almost entirely made by transfers of Consols, which were used by them as Parliamentary deposits. The terms of the loans of Consols were usually six months at 3 to 5% as Table 24 sets out. Loans of Consols were said to be allowed on a very favourable basis because the Bank of England rate was standing at 5 to 9% in this period, but the Union Bank, too, made use of Consols which were increasing in its portfolio in this period. It is not clear whether or not the English banks did this business on behalf of their railway customers.

TABLE 24

The Transfer of Consols, 1862–65

	Amount	Rate of Interest	Length	Remarks
December 1862	£1,229,452	—	—	English contractors
January 1863	140,000	3%	—	1 English railway
December 1863	265,000	—	6m	1 English and 1 Irish railway
January 1864	439,480	4–5%	—	same
July 1864	265,000	—	—	continuation of Dec 1863
January 1865	1,453,280	4%	6m	28 English, 2 Welsh and 2 sewage cos.
January 1865	126,160	—	—	5 Scottish railways

Sources: UBM, 17/12/1862, 13/1/1863, 2, 6, 23/12/1863, 22/1/1864, 27/7/1864, 11, 18/1/1865. UBPJ

(b) CONSOLS AS THE MAIN OUTLET FOR INVESTMENTS

In the balance sheets attached to the annual reports, it is not revealed what the real portfolio of the Bank investments was. They only show the aggregate sum of various investments, excluding those made in the Bank premises. However, fortunately, the annual abstract balance, from which the balance sheet was produced, reveals the real situation of the investments in this period and this is set out in Table 25.

Excluding 1859 when the Union Bank held an extraordinary amount of its own stock to support its market price from the end of 1857 to 1858, the average proportion of the aggregate sum of the three main investments in the whole portfolio was over 80%. Among them, the government securities, primarily Consols, were overwhelmingly large, reaching more than 77% on the average of the total in this period. Consols became the main item of investments, and the Union Bank certainly established the idea of regarding Consols as a part of the reserve in this period.

At the other end of the scale railway investments declined to below 1% in 1863 and disappeared thereafter. There is evidence that the Bank was still willing to make railway investments in 1862 when the Glasgow secretary sent letters to five English railway companies asking,

> We would be glad to know if you are open at present to borrow on debentures for one year, and if so, at what rate?[29]

The replies and results are not known. The directors were searching for outlets for their surplus funds during one of the most notable cheap money periods when the Bank of England rate was reduced to only 2% in the middle of 1862.

The disposal of over £200,000 of Bank stock held in 1859 also remains a mystery. Was there a suspicion of 'window-dressing'? But the Union Bank ceased to buy its own stock, at least on a large scale, in the middle of the 1860s.

(c) THE SCHEME OF A 'JOINT LONDON OFFICE'

The network of correspondents of the Union Bank was well developed by the end of the 1850s as Table 26 shows. The Bank developed relationships with correspondents through Newcastle, Carlisle and Whitehaven to Lancashire, Yorkshire, the Midlands and Nottinghamshire. There was also connections with banks in Ireland and with Rothschilds in Paris. Although the pattern of the network of correspondents was basically similar to that of the 1830s,[30] the development into the industrial Lancashire, Yorkshire and Midlands made excellent progress, which must have been due to the increasing business of the Bank customers with these districts.

Further progress was seen in the increase of the number of London correspondents, which were composed of three private banking houses, one joint-stock bank and one discount house. The amount of London accounts in the annual balance was negligible—around 4% of the total assets in this period—but the total turnover of their business was substantial. For example,

TABLE 25

Main Investments, 1859–65

	Government Securities	(a)†	(b)‡	Railway Securities	(a)	(b)	Union Bank Stock	(a)	(b)
1859*	£914,914	77.8%	10.3%	£86,308	7.3%	1.0%	£213,926	18.2%§	2.4%
1860	546,910	70.5%	6.0%	55,220	7.1%	0.6%	14,426	1.9%	0.2%
1861	837,634	79.5%	9.2%	39,440	4.2%	0.4%	14,109	1.3%	0.2%
1862	1,042,532	85.5%	11.9%	17,997	1.5%	0.2%	14,109	1.2%	0.2%
1863	1,176,867	74.9%	13.2%	5,795	0.4%	0.1%	14,109	0.9%	0.2%
1864	1,064,065	76.5%	11.4%	—	—	—	16,618	1.2%	0.2%
1865	1,040,023	79.0%	10.6%	—	—	—	16,618	1.3%	0.2%

*Date; as in April each year
†(a); % of total investments
‡(b); % of total liabilities
§The aggregate sum of government securities, railway securities and the Union Bank stock exceeds the total amount of investments (see Table 32).
The holding of its own stock was clearly excluded from the item of investments in the balance sheet of 1859.

Source: UBAAB, UB *Annual Reports*

Glyn & Co, the largest London correspondents of the Union Bank, turned over more than £6.5m in their operation in 1862.[31] The London business became the most important inter-bank operation of the Union Bank probably in common with other Scottish banks. Indeed, the Glasgow manager went frequently to London, sometimes twice a month.[32]

TABLE 26

Correspondents in the British Isles and on the Continent, 1858–65

1 Carlisle City & District Bank	11 Birmingham Bkg Co
2 Whitehaven Joint Stock Bkg Co	12 Warwick & Leamington Bkg Co
3 Lambton & Co, Newcastle	13 Provincial Bank of Ireland
4 Manchester & Liverpool District Bank	14 Belfast Bkg Co
	15 Glyn & Co, London
5 Manchester & Salford Bank	16 Coutts & Co, London
6 Huddersfield Bkg Co	17 Smith, Payne & Smith, London
7 Yorkshire Bkg Co	18 National Bank of England, London
8 Beckett & Co, Leeds	
9 Sheffield Bkg Co	19 Overend, Gurney & Co, London
10 Moore & Robinson, Nottingham	20 Rothschild & Son, Paris

Sources: UBAAB *Edinburgh Almanac, 1858*

From these circumstances, the second joint scheme of the Scottish banks emerged. In July 1864, two months after the opening of the London office by the National Bank of Scotland, three banks, the Bank of Scotland, Clydesdale and Union Banks, joined forces to try to establish their joint office in London. There was anxiety that the English non-issuing banks would oppose such an institution, which was certainly expected to be strong in gathering deposits and competing with them. Indeed, they had already objected to the office of the note-issuing National Bank of Scotland opening in London. Accordingly, the plan was carefully conducted under the initiative of the Bank of Scotland, which had considered a London office earlier in 1832,[33] as the minute of the board of the Bank of Scotland explained that,

> The treasurer informed the court that some communication had taken place between himself and the managers of the Union and Clydesdale Banks upon the subject of the establishment in London of a Joint Stock Bank with limited liability. . . . The court accordingly authorised the treasurer to continue his communication with the managers of the Union and Clydesdale Banks and to enter with them into negotiations with the private banking house referred to, or with any other of high respectability and importance. . . . The court were of opinion that it might be desirable to embrace another Scottish bank in the undertakings.[34]

The private bank in London was Glyn & Co, with whom the three Scottish banks had large business.[35] Following the suggestion of the directors of the Bank of Scotland, another Scottish bank, the British Linen, which was also doing business with Glyn & Co, was included in the scheme.

The detailed prospectus containing sixteen clauses was drawn up by the end of 1865. The title of a new bank was to be designated 'Glyn's Bank'.[36] The first clause of the prospectus stipulated that the capital was to be £3 million in shares of £100 of which £20 was to be paid. 20,000 shares were to be allotted equally among the four Scottish banks and 5,000 to Glyn & Co. The £0.6m paid-up capital was not small, compared to £1m paid-up capital of the biggest joint-stock counterparts, the London & Westminster and London Joint Stock Banks, and, therefore, it could have a substantial effect on the London money market. There was a certain conflict among the partners of Glyn & Co, one of whom opposed the conversion of their firm into a joint-stock concern,[37] but an Anglo–Scottish bank was about to open its doors in the summer of 1866. The initiative of the Scottish banks intent on challenging the English joint-stock banks on their home ground in London was, however, effectively stopped by the deepening commercial crisis of 1866 which engulfed Overend, Gurney & Co. This was the second abortive joint scheme of the Scottish banks.[38]

(d) CARTEL ON INTEREST RATES

Although co-operation outside Scotland had been unsuccessful, the Scottish cartel on interest rates definitely made its appearance, following the earlier examples of Irish banking in 1839.[39] In making changes in various rates of interest, the Scottish managers had already co-operated from the early 1840s,[40] trying to reach agreements which were frequently not adhered to because of the existence of severe competition. The most notorious offender was the Western Bank whose failure in 1857, therefore, made it easier for the surviving Scottish banks to agree on the matter. In December 1860, only three years after the disappearance of the Western Bank, a meeting of the managers resolved to follow automatically changes in the Bank of England rate and jointly announced that,

In order to obviate an inconvenience which had been hitherto felt, the Banks have thought it necessary to issue following instructions as to the course to be pursued at their Head Offices and Branches, on the occasion of the Bank of England making a change in their Discount Rates, and I have to request your strict adherence thereto;
I. ON THE OCCASION OF A RISE IN THE BANK OF ENGLAND RATES—
Immediately on the intelligence reaching you, either by public telegram or otherwise, you will make a corresponding advance in your rates for all kinds of Bills, provided such change shall not have the effect of raising your Minimum Rate above 8%. And you will continue to charge the increased rates until you receive instructions from us on the subject.
II. ON THE OCCASION OF A FALL IN THE BANK OF ENGLAND RATES—
Immediately on the intelligence reaching you as above, you will make a corresponding reduction in your rates for all kinds of Bills, provided such change shall not have the effect of reducing your Minimum Rate below 4%. You will make no change until you receive instructions from us.[41]

In general, following this resolution, the Scottish banks allowed the same rates on deposits and charged the same on advances, though there were occasional exceptions.[42] Under agreements, bills were grouped, in terms of length, into three categories; three months to run, four months and over four months. The description of bills, whether drawn on London or other towns, was first not taken into consideration until September 1861 when a favourable difference of $\frac{1}{2}\%$ was given to the London bills.[43] Overdrafts were charged at $\frac{1}{2}\%$ higher than usual in credit accounts.

Regarding deposits, the Scottish banks were allowing a uniform rate on all kinds of deposits by November 1863 when the following circular was issued,

> Any holder of a Current Account, on giving notice, to have the option of receiving, from the date of such notice, Interest at the Deposit Receipt rate, calculated monthly on the smallest sum at his credit at the close of any day, during each calendar month.[44]

The difference between rates on deposit receipts and current accounts was usually from $\frac{1}{2}$ to 1% though this from time to time disappeared.[45] The Scottish banks conjointly devised a detailed method of allowing different rates on the short and long term deposits which was not yet deliberately adopted by the English counterparts.[46] This system was undoubtedly instrumental in gathering a large amount of deposits, as a contemporary economist argued.[47] The agreement on rates resulted in the disappearance of vigorous price competition, at least, from the surface of Scottish banking.

(e) THE CONSOLIDATION OF THE BRANCH NETWORK

In 1858, the Union Bank had 99 branches. There were no increases between 1858 and 1865.[48] Charles Gairdner wrote,

> I think the feeling of our directors here is not in favour of extending our branches further unless it be necessary for the protection of what we already have. My own feeling is certainly in this character.[49]

From this point of view, he also objected to a proposed amalgamation with the Caledonian Bank which would have resulted in an expansion of the branch network.[50] Indeed, the commencement of Gairdner's management marked the end of the amalgamation movement by which the Union Bank had developed.

Before May 1862, the inspection of branches was, of course, regularly carried out, but no special inspections of any larger scale than usual were executed. The direct supervision of branches was, seemingly, almost entirely left in the hands of the inspectors at the Glasgow head office, and local committees at Aberdeen and Perth and their cashiers. When an irregularity was found in a certain branch under the charge of the Perth office, a special report was requested by the directors who, however, took no action.[51] The directors might have hesitated to make further investigation of branches under the direct supervision of the late partners of the amalgamated bank. It also seems probable that the directors and manager in Glasgow tended to neglect inspections of more remote branches. Indeed, in January 1862 when the unsatisfactory situation of the Kirkcaldy branch was reported, the subject of further inquiry was 'remitted to Edinburgh under whom the Branch is'.[52]

Gairdner started to investigate the situation of branches as early as in the summer of 1862. His first inspection was made to branches in Perthshire from July to September 1862.[53] Thereafter, when the close supervision had continued for one year by September 1863, Gairdner visited the Perth office and reported that,

no losses were likely to arise.[54]

A more remarkable inspection was executed in the North during August 1862 when unsatisfactory conduct in business was found in the branches at Ballater, Banchory and Brechin. There was a special report on the Brechin agent which stated that,

Such irregularity must be avoided in future and instruction left at the Branch strictly adhered to; otherwise, the directors would have no other alternative than to close the Branch.[55]

Despite the warning, the annual inspection, held in April 1863, revealed that 10 of 22 branches in the North 'still require special attention',[56] and, as a result, the Aberdeen cashier was called up to attend a meeting of the board of directors who,

had gone over a memorandum recently issued by Mr Gairdner to Mr Norwell (inspector) for the purpose of bringing under the special notice of the inspectors the chief irregularities. Mr Wyllie (the Aberdeen cashier) had expressed his cordial approval of the instructions . . ., thereafter Mr Gairdner had gone over into some detail with Mr Wyllie in pointing out the particular accounts objected to.[57]

The situation of the Aberdeen branches were put on a satisfactory footing eventually in June 1863 when Gairdner visited the Aberdeen office and reported that,

no serious loss was likely to arise.[58]

Meanwhile, another four special inspections were made to branches at Alloa, Helensburgh, Lochgilphead and Strathaven. The Strathaven agent was forced to resign.[59] The unprecedentedly thorough and detailed inspections were thus carried out by Gairdner alone. The senior manager, J Robertson, did not join him.

Gairdner frequently visited not only the chief offices at Aberdeen and Perth but also their branches spread over the North, instructing the cashiers and agents so that any doubtful accounts were eliminated.[60] His status as a liquidator of the Western Bank, made his authority unchallengeable. He did actually discover a large amount of bad accounts amounting to £140,000. It

seems likely that this programme of energetic bank inspection in his first year
in office enabled Gairdner to establish an authority which served him well for
the thirty three years he served as General Manager.

Gairdner's branch scrutiny also resulted in the establishment of the
inspectors' department, which though experimental, was first instituted in
November 1863. The directors appointed A B Henderson the head of the
department and he became one of Gairdner's right-hand men during his
managership. Three assistant inspectors were also appointed. This became
one of Gairdner's contributions to the consolidation and modernisation of the
Union Bank.

3   Money Flow of the Union Bank of Scotland

From 1860 to 1865 when the direct supervision of business in Perthshire was
still placed in the hands of the Perth local committee, the ledger of the annual
abstract balance of the Union Bank at the Glasgow head office kept records
separately on the amounts of advances and deposits of four regions;
Aberdeenshire and the North, Perthshire, Edinburgh, and the rest which was
under the direct charge of the Glasgow head office. There were 22 branches
under the Aberdeen office, 11 under the Perth office, 4 under the Edinburgh
head office including branches at Lerwick and Kirkcaldy and 57 under the
Glasgow head office. The regional distribution of advances and deposits
together with the annual balance of the London correspondents accounts is
set out in Table 27.

The proportions of advances and deposits among the four regions (see
Tables 28 and 29) indicate that the business under the supervision of the
Glasgow head office increased in both absolute and relative terms.
Remarkably, more than three-quarters of the whole advances were made in
the offices under the charge of the Glasgow head office though they gathered
less than two-thirds of the total deposits. On the opposite side of the scale fell
the offices in the North and Perthshire, where deposits were static and
advances diminishing. The sharpest decline occurred in the North whose
proportion of advances showed a reduction of more than one third from 1860
to 1865. This tendency can be more clearly confirmed by advances as
percentages of deposits, as Table 30 shows.

From these figures, it is perfectly clear that the Union Bank was moving
resources away from the North and East and supplying them to the industrial
West. Moreover, the Bank further transferred them to the London correspondents, whose average annual balance, £0.36m, was far larger than the
average amount of advances made in Perthshire. This money flow was
happening while the ability to gather deposits in the North and East did not
show any substantial decline (Table 31). Consequently, we can conclude that
the Glasgow based Union Bank depended considerably on the resources in the
North and East and even began to transfer not insubstantial sums beyond the
border to London.[61]

It should then be queried as to whether this kind of money flow was

TABLE 27

Regional Distribution of Advances and Deposits, 1860–65

Perth

	Advances	Deposits
1860*	£224,392	£727,843
1861	234,955	714,955
1862	224,345	701,096
1863	229,596	664,980
1864	266,424	664,170
1865	190,204	710,668

Aberdeen

	Advances	Deposits
1860*	£661,203	£1,101,443
1861	612,329	1,058,646
1862	661,176	987,784
1863	501,162	1,036,071
1864	433,804	1,004,095
1865	463,565	1,059,525

Aberdeen

Perth

Edinburgh

Glasgow

Edinburgh

	Advances	Deposits
1860*	£845,553	£1,332,057
1861	922,663	1,241,864
1862	789,511	1,248,208
1863	798,153	1,256,092
1864	721,021	1,208,024
1865	765,666	1,253,989

Glasgow

	Advances	Deposits
1860	£4,923,717	£3,853,853
1861	4,995,698	3,712,646
1862	4,522,118	3,642,033
1863	4,555,383	3,981,503
1864	5,272,695	4,421,277
1865	5,712,708	4,589,055

London

1860*	£549,974
1861	201,281
1862	423,633
1863	440,030
1864	325,607
1865	238,080

*Date as in April each year

Source: UBAAB

deliberately pursued by the Union Bank. A positive answer is probable. Irrefutable evidence is the intensive inspection itself which was made, almost exclusively, to branches in the North and Perthshire, as we have already seen. In executing investigations, Gairdner and the directors attached special importance to putting a stop to losses which had arisen from advances,[62] and this undoubtedly resulted in agents there being chary of pushing loans. Therefore, although there remains no record of Gairdner and the directors announcing their intention of depriving the North and East of resources, it is fairly reasonable to say that they regarded their branches there as a reservoir.

The money flow of the Union Bank can be paralleled by an English example which was explained by Thomas Richardson—London bill broker in the early nineteenth century and quoted by Sir Walter Bagehot in his *Lombard Street*,—who said that,

> I receive bills to a considerable amount from Lancashire in particular, and remit them to Norfolk, Suffolk &c, where the bankers have large lodgement, and much surplus money to advance on bills for discounts.[63]

According to Bagehot, the example suggested by Richardson was still prevalent in England during the 1870s, and, therefore, the money flow from an agricultural area such as Aberdeenshire to an industrial area such as

TABLE 28

Advances per Total: Regional Pattern, 1860–65: %

	Glasgow	Edinburgh	Aberdeen	Perth
1860	74.0	12.7	10.0	3.3
1861	73.8	13.6	9.0	3.6
1862	73.6	12.8	10.0	3.6
1863	74.9	13.1	8.2	3.8
1864	78.8	10.8	6.5	3.9
1865	80.1	10.7	6.5	2.7
Average	75.9	12.3	8.4	3.4

Note and source: as of Table 27

TABLE 29

Deposits per Total: Regional Pattern, 1860–65: %

	Glasgow	Edinburgh	Aberdeen	Perth
1860	54.9	19.0	15.7	10.4
1861	55.2	18.5	15.7	10.6
1862	55.4	19.0	15.0	10.6
1863	57.3	18.1	15.0	9.6
1864	60.6	16.6	13.8	9.0
1865	60.3	16.5	14.0	9.2
Average	57.3	17.9	14.8	10.0

Note and source: as of Table 27

TABLE 30

Advances as Percentages of Deposits: Regional Pattern, 1860–65

	Glasgow	Edinburgh	Aberdeen	Perth
1860	127.8	63.5	60.0	30.8
1861	134.6	74.3	57.8	32.9
1862	124.2	63.3	66.9	32.0
1863	114.4	63.5	48.4	34.5
1864	119.3	60.0	43.2	40.1
1865	124.5	61.1	43.8	26.8
Average	124.1	64.3	53.4	32.9

Note and source: as of Table 27

TABLE 31

Average Deposits per Office: Regional Pattern, 1860–65

	Glasgow	Edinburgh	Aberdeen	Perth
1860	£66,445	£26,641	£47,888	£60,653
1861	64,011	34,837	46,028	59,579
1862	62,793	24,964	42,947	58,424
1863	68,646	25,121	45,046	55,415
1864	76,228	24,160	43,656	55,347
1865	77,780	25,079	46,066	59,222

Source: as of Table 27

Lanarkshire is a natural result of a banking business which acts as intermediary between the areas of surplus and of deficit money. It was the system of branch banking which enabled Scottish banks to develop credit flow between saving and spending areas. This feature of Scottish banking, on the scale here exemplified in the case of the Union Bank, was at this time special to Scotland. This sort of money flow, at least on a large scale, was still beyond the capacity of their English counterparts, which had not yet established nationwide branch networks.[64]

4   The Union Bank of Scotland at its Zenith

Making drastic changes in its management, the Union Bank of Scotland was approaching its zenith in this period which can be divided into two phases.

A sharp decline of the total liabilities, deposits, advances and profits was seen in 1862 when all figures fell below those of 1859 as Table 32 shows. The business of the Union Bank was apparently damaged by the accumulation of bad debts such as those of Blackie & Son and the Monkland Iron & Steel Co and was also, probably, influenced by the outbreak of the American Civil War. Facing this situation, the directors for the first time in their history

TABLE 32

Main Items of Balance Sheets, 1859–65

	(1) Total Liabilities	(2) Deposits	(3) Reserve	(4) Advances	(5) Acceptances by London Agents and Marginal Credit	(6) Investments	(7) Other Liquid Assets	(8) Profits
1859	£8,890,290	£6,676,626	£200,000	£6,727,589	—	£1,175,300	£838,716	£104,447
	100%	75.1%	2.2%	75.7%		13.2%	9.4%	1.2%
1860	9,289,667	7,015,196	200,000	7,051,103	—	776,206	1,299,616	110,768
	105%	75.5%	2.2%	75.9%		8.4%	14.0%	1.2%
1861	9,096,257	6,728,111	200,000	6,926,637	—	1,053,302	952,008	122,998
	102%	74.0%	2.2%	76.1%		11.6%	10.5%	1.4%
1862	8,763,680	6,579,121	200,000	6,341,895	—	1,218,859	1,039,555	102,864
	99%	75.1%	2.3%	72.3%		13.9%	11.9%	1.2%
1863	8,914,890	6,938,646	67,864	6,107,950	—	1,570,288	1,069,363	95,292
	100%	77.8%	0.8%	68.5%		17.6%	12.0%	1.1%
1864	9,374,455	7,297,566	78,156	6,771,186	£110,704	1,390,573	1,039,334	118,168
	105%	77.8%	0.8%	72.2%	1.2%	14.8%	11.1%	1.3%
1865	9,834,605	7,613,237	109,368	7,507,748	231,022	1,317,647	842,726	143,028
	111%	77.4%	1.1%	76.3%	2.3%	13.4%	8.6%	1.5%

*Date as in May each year
% of column 1; growth rate
% of columns 2–8; of total liabilities

Sources: UB *Annual Reports.* UBAAB

reduced their dividend in 1863, which remained at 8% till 1865. The reserve also diminished in 1863 to a little more than one third of that in 1862. The result was the major change in the management.

TABLE 33

Advances and Investments as Percentages of Deposits, 1859–65

	Advances, %	Investments, %
1859	100.8	17.6
1860	100.5	11.1
1861	103.0	15.7
1862	96.4	18.5
1863	88.0	22.6
1864	92.8	19.1
1865	98.6	17.3

Source: Table 32

'A special revision of the securities',[65] carried out by Charles Gairdner, led the Union Bank to change its assets management in which investments, primarily Consols, began to be preferred, as Table 33 indicates. Under the management of Gairdner, the Union Bank, consolidating its wide branch network, developed from 1863 to 1865 when it stood only second to the Royal Bank of Scotland in terms of total liabilities, deposits and advances. This was the zenith of the Union Bank of Scotland and this position was never regained.

Chapter 4

Years of Difficulty, 1865–1879

Between 1866 and 1879, the Union Bank of Scotland fell continuously in ranking among the Scottish banks in terms of total liabilities, deposits and advances. The Bank became more and more careful about making advances and reluctant to expand its branch network. This policy was deliberately pursued by Charles Gairdner who was at the same time emerging as the most powerful person inside the boardroom. The policy of canniness was reinforced by two incidents, that is, failure of London firms in 1866 and 1875.

1   The Failure of Two London Firms

Overend, Gurney & Co, who had their origin earlier in the 1810s, converted themselves in July 1865 into a limited company with £1.5m paid up capital in order to provide additional funds to be applied to their expanded financing of foreign trade. Following the collapse of a discount house, Gurney & Co was exposed to heavy speculation on the London Stock Exchange in the spring of 1866. The Bank of England, which had been hostile to them, refused to assist them. In May 1866, Gurney & Co stopped payment, leaving net losses of over £5m and pulling down nine banking and financial concerns.[1]

A telegram from a director of the Union Bank that 'Our friends at the Corner have stopped'[2] reached the manager, Gairdner, and the fellow directors, who were taken by surprise for they had but lately increased their business with Gurney & Co. The Bank had placed funds there for £250,000 in January 1866 and £100,000 in April.[3] Through the business with Gurney & Co, the Union Bank, in common with the Bank of Scotland and City of Glasgow Bank, was in possession of bills of James Morton & Co, which were discounted by Gurney & Co and pledged with the Union Bank. Gairdner and the directors were forced to support the firm of J Morton & Co, soon arranging with the other banks that

> the manager made a statement of the position of the accounts of James Morton & Co with special reference to the stoppage of Overend, Gurney & Co, Limited, with whom they had a discount account and it was agreed to discount for Messrs Morton & Co during the next four weeks in equal proportion with the Bank of Scotland and City of Glasgow Bank, bills to the account of those falling due in the hands of Overend, Gurney & Co, Ltd, . . . this Bank's share of said discounts not to exceed £26,000.[4]

The extent of the Union Bank's responsibility was seemingly not large. As a result of the trustees of Gurney & Co surrendering sufficient securities in

94

November 1867, the Bank could get rid of further commitment to the bad debts, though past-due bills of Gurney & Co still stood at £5,257 in April 1868. In general, Scottish banking did not suffer greatly from this incident, but it was the City of Glasgow Bank upon which the whole onus of financial support of the aggressive Morton & Co fell. Thus, the City Bank started to falsify its balance sheets in the aftermath of Gurney's failure.[5]

The failure of Alexander Collie & Co, one of the largest firms of East India merchants, had a serious effect on the Union Bank. There was no sign of their dangerous situation until 16 June 1875 when the news of their collapse with liabilities of £3m reached the Bank.[6] This was the greatest surprise which Charles Gairdner ever had since his commencement of the managership.[7] The first detailed account appeared in *The Economist,* which reported that,

> On Tuesday afternoon an event occurred, the suspension of Messrs Alex Collie & Co of Manchester and London, with liabilities estimated at 3,000,000 l, which has produced a large crop of suspensions, including one firm of bill brokers. . . . The failures have occurred much more suddenly than those connected with Messrs Sanderson's suspension (in 1857).[8]

The Economist was highly critical of Collies, explaining that,

> extensive system of accommodation bills . . . the greatest offender being Alex Collie & Co . . . the plan of this house, it appears, was to affiliate with it a large group of houses upon whom it drew bills, which were made to bear every appearance of ordinary trade bills; and it then passed off their bills to the discount brokers by whom they were deposited as security for advances, mainly with Joint Stock Banks.[9]

Among 'Joint Stock Banks' was the Union Bank. The Collie's case was, thus, one of the largest systematised 'kite-flying' in the history of British banking, which instantly pulled down 22 concerns including the London Joint Stock Bank and eventually involved 80 merchant houses, six London banks and two discount companies in great difficulty.[10]

The Union Bank was the only Scottish bank directly involved in the Collie fraud. Its relationship with Alexander Collie commenced in 1872 when one of the directors introduced him to Gairdner.[11] Collie was a native of Scotland and a merchant of 'high respect'.[12] Gairdner and the directors did not seem to have suspected that they were at great risk. Collie, an organiser of drawing accommodation bills, was so cunning that he left no evidence in the hands of Gairdner, which could have proved the fraud. Indeed, the negotiations between Gairdner and Collie, surprisingly, proceeded 'so much upon conversations'.[13] Gairdner had ignored the basic caution of a banker, accepting at face value the introduction to Collie. The unhappy directors were forced to decide that,

> dissupported by documentary evidence, it is not expedient that the Bank should proceed criminally as proposed,[14]

and watched the course of prosecution instituted by the London &

DIAGRAM 1

Growth Rates of Total Liabilities: Union Bank and Scottish Total, 1866–79

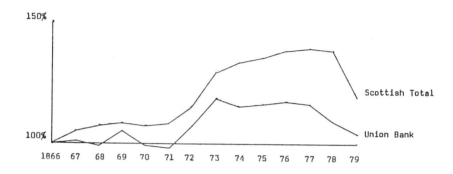

Source: SGC and A B MacDonald, 1973

DIAGRAM 2

Union Bank: Growth Rates of Deposits, Advances, Investments and Profits, 1866–79

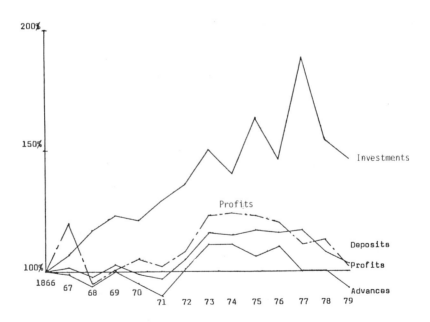

Source: as of Diagram 1

DIAGRAM 3

Scottish Total: Growth Rates of Deposits, Advances, Investments and Profits, 1866–79

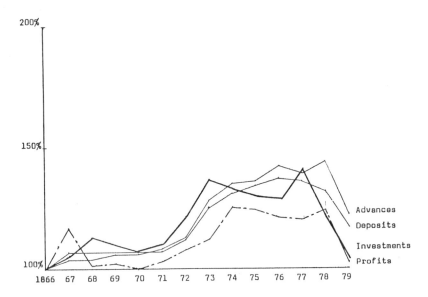

Source: as of Diagram 1

Westminster Bank. There was no recourse. Alexander Collie disappeared and died in New York in 1895.[15] The Collie fraud also involved the customers of the Union Bank; Dennistoun, Cross & Co, Finlay Campbell & Co and Smith, Fleming & Co. The main bank of Smith, Fleming & Co was the City of Glasgow Bank and this must have further aggravated its financial situation.[16]

The losses of the Union Bank amounted to £150,000.[17] To meet them, the Bank had to deplete the reserve by £120,000 and also transfer £33,000 from the profits of 1876. The reserve of the Bank became the smallest among the major Scottish banks in 1876 being only a little more than two thirds of that of the rival, but medium sized, Clydesdale Bank which had total liabilities of £9.5m in comparison with £12.4m of the Union Bank. Only a few years before the general crisis of 1878, the Union Bank had thus been seriously damaged by the Collie fraud in respect of both business and public image.

From 1866 to 1879, the total liabilities of the Union Bank increased from £10.6m to £11.0m. The growth rate was only 3.7% which was far below that of the Scottish total (19%). Especially after 1873, when the British economy was shifting from 'boom' to the so-called 'Great Depression', the gap between the Union Bank and the Scottish total was widening remarkably as diagram 1 clearly shows. The Union Bank was apparently being left behind.

Taking some main items of the liabilities/assets into consideration, a remarkable performance by the Union Bank can be seen (Diagrams 2 and 3).

Two major elements of banking business, that is, deposits and advances, which made similar movements during the whole period as Diagram 2 exhibits, did not grow strongly except in the mid 1870s. The poor performance was particularly obvious with regard to advances which even fell below those of 1866 in the years of 1867/71 and were again slipping down from 1876. At the opposite end of scale of performance rose investments which increased continuously from 1866 to 1873 when their growth rate touched 150% and were strengthening even further, approaching 190% in 1877. The rapid growth of investments was the most remarkable feature of the Union Bank in Scottish banking. The sharp increase in, or need to increase, investments, which might be the result of the general economic climate, the so called 'Great Depression', eventually forced the Bank to change the contract of co-partnery in the mid 1870s as will be discussed later.

There seems little doubt that Gairdner and the directors of the Union Bank were thoroughly scared by the 1866 and 1875 failures. As a result, they reduced their advances, especially on bills, preferring the greater safety of government investments. Their greater caution, however, did reduce their overall business.

2   Business In Difficulty

(a) THE DECREASE OF THE GLASGOW BUSINESS AND THE EMERGENCE OF SECTORAL PREFERENCE

Details of advances by the Union Bank are not known from its balance sheets in this period which only show the aggregate sum of 'Bills of Exchange, Local and Country, Cash Credits and Other Advances'. Fortunately, there remains evidence of business done at the Glasgow head office, which is set out in Table 34 and Diagram 4.

The most favoured method of advance was discounting of bills, with local bills, payable in the towns of Scotland,[18] preferred. Except for the two years of 1875 and 1876, the fluctuation of the amount of discounts corresponded with that of the total liabilities. The most sensitive element was bills of exchange, which were payable in London. In 1875 when the amounts of two other bills, together with other methods, diminished, bills of exchange increased, thus supporting the growth of the Union Bank. From this, though the available figures are limited to those of the Glasgow head office, it might be argued that one of the main factors of the growth of the Bank was not discounts in general but those of bills of exchange in particular. In this respect, the significance of the failures of London firms, especially that of Collie & Co, was so great that Gairdner and the directors learned the lesson that bills of exchange, particularly those arisen from foreign trade and almost exclusively payable in London, were risky and should be avoided. Indeed, after the Collie fraud, the amount of bills of exchange continuously diminished being eventually surpassed by that of 'bills from branches'.

TABLE 34

Business at Glasgow Head Office, 1866–79*

Sources: UB Annual Reports; UBPJ

	(1) Credit Accounts	(2) Loan on Rail & Other Securities	(3) Local Bills	(4) Bills of Exchange	(5) Bills from Branches	(6) 3 + 4 + 5	(7) 1 + 2 + 6	(8) Deposits	(9) 7/8	(10) Growth Rate of Total Liabilities
1866	£1,507,968 27.4%	£167,556 3.0%	£1,984,790 36.0%	£1,431,924 26.0%	£417,075 7.6%	£3,833,789 69.6%	£5,509,313 67.5%	£1,392,024 16.9%	396%	100.0%
1867	1,595,075 28.3	127,626 2.3	2,074,492 36.7	1,380,031 24.4	465,916 8.3	3,920,439 69.4	5,643,140 69.6	1,318,243 15.7	428	100.9
1868	1,723,988 32.5	122,401 2.3	1,996,438 37.7	861,750 16.3	592,460 11.2	3,450,648 65.2	5,297,037 69.3	1,290,616 16.0	410	98.5
1869	1,609,718 29.4	285,992 5.3	1,915,032 35.0	1,037,484 19.0	619,058 11.3	3,571,574 65.3	5,467,284 66.9	1,489,993 17.6	367	104.6
1870	1,701,829 31.9	413,679 7.7	1,555,293 29.1	1,030,894 19.3	639,699 12.0	3,225,886 60.4	5,341,394 68.8	1,289,628 15.9	414	98.8
1871	1,379,703 27.3	543,800 10.8	1,536,356 30.4	998,030 19.8	591,321 11.7	3,125,707 61.9	5,049,210 68.9	1,149,418 14.5	439	97.5
1872	1,334,192 23.8	901,693 16.1	1,641,510 29.3	965,067 17.2	758,645 13.6	3,365,222 60.1	5,601,107 68.3	1,210,853 14.2	463	107.2
1873	940,986 15.9	660,441 11.2	1,702,646 28.9	1,616,858 27.4	980,414 16.6	4,299,918 72.9	5,901,345 65.4	1,263,816 13.3	467	117.7
1874	997,491 16.7	849,605 14.2	1,586,772 26.6	1,413,040 23.7	1,120,848 18.8	4,120,660 69.1	5,967,756 66.1	1,188,561 12.6	502	115.3
1875	771,641 14.1	794,309 14.5	1,509,441 27.5	1,545,758 28.2	867,201 15.7	3,922,400 71.4	5,488,350 63.5	918,495 9.6	598	116.3
1876	978,451 18.4	947,242 17.8	1,334,711 25.0	1,242,903 23.3	827,742 15.5	3,405,356 63.8	5,331,049 58.9	814,640 8.4	654	116.5
1877	951,891 21.3	477,159 10.7	1,194,081 26.7	1,099,978 24.6	747,057 16.7	3,041,116 68.0	4,470,166 55.0	1,068,369 11.1	418	116.2
1878	1,208,871 29.2	387,310 9.4	903,194 21.8	924,825 22.3	715,278 17.3	2,543,297 61.4	4,139,478 50.8	768,401 8.6	539	109.3
1879	925,921 27.8	337,570 10.2	823,138 24.8	615,059 18.5	621,013 18.7	2,059,210 62.0	3,322,701 44.4	937,878 10.9	354	103.7
Average	24.6%	9.7%	29.7%	22.1%	13.9%	65.8%	63.1%	13.2%	461%	

*Date as in April each year. % in columns 1–6 as of column 7. % in columns 7 & 8 as of the total advances and deposits of the Bank. The amounts of deposits seem to be too small for those of the head office because an examination of accounts held in May 1879 revealed that the head office had deposits for £2.8m (UBM, 15/5/1879). Unfortunately, there remains no material which could reconcile the gap.

DIAGRAM 4

Total Liabilities and Advances and Proportions among Methods of Advances at Glasgow Head Office, 1866–79

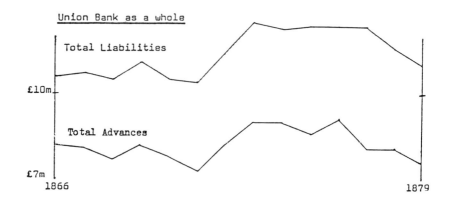

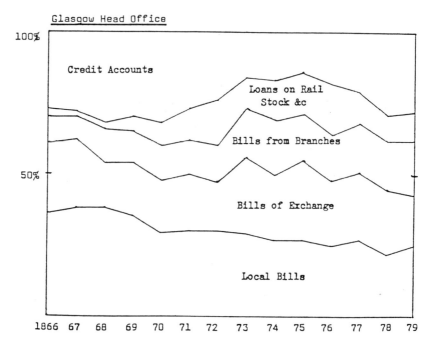

Sources: as of Table 34

Credit accounts, which in the previous periods tended to increase when the total liabilities and discounts decreased, ceased to be the sole alternative method to discounts. Loans on railway and other securities emerged as the third main method of lending in the early 1870s and supported the growth in the mid 1870s. The relative decline of credit accounts suggests that Gairdner and the directors even attempted to reduce unsecured overdrafts which were allowed on credit accounts. The lending policy of the Union Bank displayed, indeed, every appearance of over caution.

Table 34 also emphasises the importance of the head office business of the bank. Up to 1875 when the Union Bank was still pushing advances (Diagram 2), those made at the Glasgow head office constantly amounted to two-thirds of the total and were four to six times larger than its deposits. After 1876, the advances at head office lost ground, being reduced to less than half of the total in 1879, and the total liabilities followed the same course. It could be argued that the whole business of the Union Bank, though it had one hundred branches and a second head office, depended substantially on the activities of the Glasgow head office. Indeed, the business of the head office, directly under the control of the directors and general manager reflected the true state of the bank as a whole.

As caution set in, those sectors which the management of the Union Bank favoured for loans, became clear. As initiative was lost the bank tended to concentrate its advances on certain sectors with which it had already been well acquainted. Of some 175 'special advances' of £10,000 and over, nearly 90% was given to six sectors as are set out in Table 35. Save for the chemical industry, there is an absolute correlation between the number of authorisations and average amount of advances. The methods and purposes of advances made to the upper-ranking three sectors, whose number of authorisations was nearly two-thirds of the special advances and whose business was clearly given the priority, should be worth detailing.

TABLE 35

Sectoral Preference, 1866–79

	Sector	Number	Average Amount
1	Railway	61	£56,129
2	Trade	28	32,019
3	Shipbuilding & Engineering	24	28,816
4	Iron & Coal	20	28,650
5	Textile	14	22,571
6	Chemical	8	28,125
		155	

Sources: UBM, *passim*

In terms of both number and average amount of authorisations, railway companies were preferred customers of the Union Bank. The three main borrowers were, the North British (NB), Glasgow & South Western (GSW) and City of Glasgow Union (CGU). Financing the three companies, the bank allowed NB advances chiefly on its debentures and GSW and CGU credits on overdrafts.[19] CGU, which was engaged in building railway lines, was the most frequent applicant, being awarded at least fourteen special advances in this period. CGU's credits were from time to time guaranteed by the senior NB and GSW.[20] NB and GSW sometimes asked the Bank to sanction credits to enable them to pay off their dividends as they did in the previous years. In one case, the Bank granted a large overdraft of £155,000 for this purpose to GSW.[21] Railway financing for the purpose of dividend payments was, thus, not extraordinary business for the Union Bank, or indeed for other major Scottish banks.[22]

Transfers of Consols, which made their appearance in 1863, were still going on mainly with the English railway companies. From 1865 to the end of 1871, when British railway building was making remarkable progress,[23] the cumulative sum of £1.7m of Consols was transferred to forty-two companies.[24] On behalf of the Scottish railway companies, the Bank allowed transfers of their deposit receipts as parliamentary deposits,[25] the amount of which was far smaller than transfers of Consols to their English counterparts. The transfer of deposit receipts might be a forerunner of the negotiable CD of the twentieth century.

In the sector of trade, there were two sorts of borrowers, that is, private firms of merchants and trading companies of limited liabilities. Among the private firms, Dennistoun & Co were still considerable customers, obtaining a large credit for £100,000 on behalf of the London firm of Dennistoun, Cross & Co.[26] Otherwise, the Bank decreased their advances, in both terms of number and amount, to Dennistoun & Co whose main business had already changed from trade to house building.[27] Another notable borrower, J N Fleming, was authorised to draw on the Union Bank to the extent of £50,000, in 1866.[28] His credit was guaranteed by various entrepreneurial merchants, including William MacKinnon. Both Fleming and MacKinnon were directors of the City of Glasgow Bank.[29] Business with the City Bank's customers did not further develop. The Union Bank apparently began to avoid aggressive firms of merchants, engaged especially in foreign trade, which had caused them so much difficulty during the 1850s. This attitude resulted in the decrease of advances on bills of exchange and the stagnation of acceptance business which was as low as 1.8% on average and far below the Scottish average (7.1%) in 1872.[30]

The Union Bank, thus, obviously preferred large trading companies to private firms of merchants, and then two limited companies appeared as large borrowers, that is, the New Zealand & Australia Land Co (NZAL) and the Haputale Coffee Co. NZAL was the reorganised Canterbury & Otago Association Ltd and was promoted by an aggressive merchant, James Morton, but it soon outgrew his interest involving the Edinburgh banks, Union Bank and particularly City of Glasgow Bank. There seems to have been no particular danger for the Union Bank because NZAL financing was a joint venture of the Scottish banks including the public banks, though the City

Bank failure in 1878 forced the rest of the Scottish banks to bear the whole financial support of NZAL.[31] The Union Bank allowed NZAL advances primarily on debentures and overdrafts.[32]

The Haputale Coffee Co (London), trading to Ceylon, first obtained a large credit of £70,000 in the autumn of 1878 at the newly opened London office.[33] As it was the concern of a director of the Bank, F Pitman, Haputale financing fell exclusively upon the Bank which greatly involved itself in the business of Haputale Co in the following period.[34] Consequently, it seems fairly certain that the Union Bank preferred incorporated trading companies, especially towards the end of the 1870s, which might be considered by Gairdner to be safer than unlimited firms of merchants.

In the shipbuilding and engineering sector, there were two notable borrowers, i.e., Dobie & Co (Govan) and J & G Thomson (Finnieston). Credits authorised to Dobie & Co were entirely operated by overdrafts, ranging from £7,000 to £15,000. Authorisations were usually renewed every four to six months. The Bank never gave Dobie & Co credit in excess of £15,000.

In the case of Thomson's, the Union Bank gradually increased advances on credit accounts, primarily overdrafts, as Table 36 sets out. The funds supplied by the Bank amounted to more than one fifth of the total liabilities/assets of Thomson in 1876.[35] Although the amount of their credits was not the largest among the Bank's loans, this was a dangerous involvement in one customer, any small accidents in whose business could force the bank to make further advances, thus damaging the latter. Indeed, the Union Bank had to undergo a testing time which was really caused by two accidents in connection with the Thomson firm.[36]

TABLE 36

Thomson Financing, 1865–78

Date	Amount
10 May 1865	£40,000
23 August 1871	60,000
7 August 1872	60,000
30 June 1873	65,000
19 January 1876	90,000
8 August 1877	110,000
30 June 1878	92,000

Sources: UB (Glasgow), *Charles Gairdner's Note Book*, 30/6/1873. UBM, as at date excluding 30/6/1873

(b) THE COMMENCEMENT OF FOREIGN INVESTMENTS

Consols, which had become a main constituent of the portfolio of the investments prior to 1865, continued to be the largest outlet for investments by the Union Bank as Table 37 sets out. The constant holding of Consols with more than £1m indicates that they became the central part of the Union Bank reserve. The gap between the columns 2 and 3 of Table 37 was caused by the proportion of other investments which was increasingly noticeably in the early 1870s. This suggests that the Union Bank began to search for other outlets for investments besides British government securities. Thus, the need to increase investments encountered an obstacle in the stipulation in the contract of copartnery which was eventually lifted in May 1874 stating that,

> the Bank, without prejudice to their existing powers of investment, may take investments in the Public Funds, Stocks, Shares, Debentures, or Mortgages, of the Government of India, or of any British Colony, or of the United States of America, and any Funds, Stocks, Shares, Debentures, or Mortgages guaranteed by any such Government; and may purchase, acquire, and dispose of Real Estate in any parts of the United Kingdom, or may lend on security of such Real Estate.[37]

TABLE 37

Investments, 1866–74 †

	(1) *Government Securities*	(2) *Govt. Securities as % of Total Liabilities*	(3) *Total Investments as % of Total Liabilities*	(4) *3—2*
1866*	£1,002,737	9.4	9.3	−1.0‡
1867	1,001,024	9.3	10.0	0.7
1868	1,600,171	15.3	11.1	−4.2‡
1869	1,001,024	9.0	11.0	2.0
1870	1,001,024	9.5	10.9	1.4
1871	1,001,024	9.7	12.4	2.7
1872	1,001,024	8.8	11.9	3.1
1873	1.001,024	8.0	12.0	4.0
1874	1,001,024	8.2	11.3	3.1

*Date; as in April each year.
† Details are not known from the annual reports of 1869/79, and therefore we must rely on the annual abstract balance.
‡Inconsistent figures are probably due to the dates at which the abstract balance and annual report were made.

Sources: UB *Annual Reports.* UBAAB

Immediately from the summer of 1874, the Union Bank commenced foreign investments, especially the United States bonds whose yields were well over those on Consols.[38]

There was another benefit which could be obtained by making investments in the US bonds as,

> Mr Gairdner recommending that prepayment of all instalments thereof should now be made subject to rebate of 2% interest, being the highest rate that could be obtained; approved . . . instructed further . . . tender now be made of prepayment of the instalments in the Bank's new allotment of $1,500,000 of $4\frac{1}{2}\%$ funded bonds under the same rebate.[39]

The offer of 2% rebate in addition to $4\frac{1}{2}\%$ interest must have been attractive to

TABLE 38

US Investments in the mid 1870s

	(1) Amount of Purchase	(2) Purchase Price	(3) Amount of Sale	(4) Sale Price	(5) Foreign Exchange rate
17 June 1874	$262,500	104¾/105¼	—	—	—
	75,000	111/111¼	—	—	—
24 June 1874	107,500	105	—	—	£:4.6
	500,000	104$\frac{13}{16}$/104$\frac{15}{16}$	—	107	—
15 Sept 1876	500,000	—	$500,000	—	—
21 Sept 1876	1,500,000*	—	1,500,000*	—	£:4.6
24 Jan 1877	—	—	445,000	109¼	—
	—	—	75,000	110¼	—
	—	—	370,000	—	—
19 Apr 1877	500,000	104	—	—	£:4.7
	3,500,000	—	—	—	—

*Conversion

Sources: UBM, as at dates

the directors because the Bank of England rate fell to only 2% from April 1876.[40]

The amount of the US bonds investments jumped up from £109,000 (£: $4.6) in June 1874 to £745,000 (£:$4.7) in April 1877 as Table 38 sets out. The large amount of the US investments, more details of which are, unfortunately, not clear, was admittedly a principal factor in the rapid growth of the total investments, which was the most noteworthy performance of the Union Bank in Scottish banking during the 1870s (see Diagram 2).

As the recommendation to take full advantage of high returns suggests, Gairdner was very keen to push the US investments, assuming leadership in the boardroom. As the minute book again recorded,

> as immediate reply was requested by Mr Morgan (merchant banker, London), the manager, after consulting with those directors who could be seen, accepted the proposals.[41]

As a result of this resolution, the sales and purchase in January 1877 were effected. It could be argued that increases in investments were the idea of Gairdner who preferred safe investments to advances especially on bills of exchange, particularly after the Collie fraud.

Transactions of Consols and foreign investments were operated in London. The holding of Consols, which was the largest constituent of Union Bank investments in common with the custom of the major Scottish banks, was actually kept in the books of the Bank of England. Therefore, the manager of any bank which was situated outside London, had to go to London to check with the books of the Bank of England.[42] The bank, situated outwith London, also had to communicate with the stock broker and merchant banker who were really engaged in transacting the issued stocks and shares and underwriting the new issues of securities on the London Stock Exchange. Indeed, the Union Bank was doing business with eight firms of stock brokers and merchant bankers including N M Rothschild & Son and J Morgan & Co.[43] The rapid growth of investments certainly necessitated the opening of a London office, earlier rather than later.

(c) THE SCOTTISH INVASION OF ENGLAND AND THE LONDON OFFICE OF THE UNION BANK

By 1874, three Scottish banks had opened London offices; the National Bank in 1864, the Bank of Scotland in 1867 and the Royal Bank in 1874. The London business became indispensable as well as attractive for Scottish banking because all payments of international trade were centred there by the mid 1860s, transactions of large scale investments were operated and at the same time substantial amounts of deposits were expected.[44] The Union Bank could not remain an exception.

In addition to the increase in investments, there was another factor with regard to the Union Bank which necessitated the establishment of a London branch. Following the opening of the overseas cable, the Bank, together with other British banks, began to remit by telegram to foreign and colonial correspondents. The Bank informed its customers that,

> this Bank is prepared to make remittance to Australia and New Zealand by telegram at a charge of one per cent in addition to the cost of telegram, which is from £9 6s. 6d. to £9 16s. 6d. according to Colonial Port.[45]

Although the Union Bank's acceptances and drafts on London was the smallest among the major Scottish banks,[46] it was also true that the Bank was increasing these transactions as Table 39 sets out and Gairdner reported in 1873 that,

> Mr Currie (a partner of Glyn & Co) brought under his notice that the very large increase in the business transacted for the Bank by the firm of Glyn, Mills, Currie & Co, and in consideration thereof it was agreed; remuneration to them be advanced from £2,000 to £2,500 per annum.[47]

Furthermore, the number of the London correspondents increased in the mid 1870s, when another large joint-stock, the Alliance Bank, joined the network. As a result, the Union Bank had 25 London correspondents in 1875; 12 joint-stock and 13 private bankers.[48] Eventually in April 1875, the Bank changed the contract so that,

> The Bank may carry on the business of Banking in any part of the United Kingdom, and the powers of the Directors are hereby extended to such business accordingly.[49]

Despite the adjustment of the contract, the Union Bank did not proceed forthwith to establish its London office. There might be two reasons. Firstly, the Collie fraud, which soon followed the amendment of the contract, might have made Gairdner and the directors more careful and, at least for a while, reluctant to embark upon the London business.

Secondly, and more importantly, there emerged a renewed conflict between Scottish and English banking, which resulted from the aggressiveness of the medium-sized Clydesdale Bank. As long as the Scottish invasion of England was confined to London, it was unlikely that much serious objection would be raised by their English counterparts, especially their country components, because the London business of the Scottish banks probably concentrated on transactions with stock and bill brokers and the London joint-stock banks were strong enough to compete with their Scottish counterparts.

Attitudes hardened when the Clydesdale Bank opened three branches in northern England in 1874.[50] Facing the Scottish invasion, the English country banks, which were obviously inferior to the Scottish joint-stock banks in terms of capital, deposits and branch network, must have been afraid that the Scottish banks would deprive them of their banking business. Indeed, the Clydesdale invasion of Cumbria took place because of its need to finance the iron trade which was developing between the West and South West of Scotland and Cumberland.[51] Naturally, the English country banks joined

forces to raise strong objections and held 'a very large meeting of English
Country Bankers from every part of the country'.[52] Moreover, the English
banks proceeded to put pressure on George Goschen, the Chancellor of the
Exchequer, who was forced to introduce a bill which would deprive these
Scottish banks which opened branches in England, of their note issues. The
disclosure of Scottish balance sheets, begun in 1865, made it easier for the
English banks to see how greatly Scottish notes were increasing especially in

TABLE 39

Growth of Acceptances and London Drafts, 1866–77*

	Amount	Growth Rate: 1866; 100
1866	£340,791	100
1867	145,980	43
1868	353,297	104
1869	380,013	112
1870	246,744	72
1871	182,720	54
1872	328,693	97
1873	445,951	131
1874	284,151	83
1875	346,826	102
1876	426,594	125
1877	387,504	114

*Figures for 1878 and 1879 are not available

Source: UB *Annual Reports*

TABLE 40

Growth Rate of Note Issue: Scottish Total and Union Bank, 1866–79: 1866; 100

	Scottish Total	Union Bank
1866	100	100
1867	102	109
1868	104	107
1869	100	118
1870	102	91
1871	103	101
1872	113	129
1873	134	138
1874	132	130
1875	125	113
1876	124	109
1877	120	122
1878	118	115
1879	107	111

Sources: SGC, 1975, Table 44. UB *Annual Reports*

the early 1870s, as Table 40 exhibits. The Scottish banks for the first time since the early 1840s sensed 'a possible, if not probable danger'[53] of losing their note issues.

Confronting this dangerous situation, the Scottish banks took two steps. On the one hand, they argued for their right to issue, citing other examples such as the Irish, Indian and Colonial banks though, at the same time, they brought pressure on the Clydesdale Bank not to show further aggression. Fortunately for the Scottish banks, the Goschen bill was dropped, and the subject was sent to a Select Committee of 1875 which also failed to report. By their joint effort the Scottish banks were again successful in protecting their note issues.

However, on the other hand, efforts to lessen the published amount of the Scottish notes were made in two ways. In the first place, some of the Scottish banks agreed to issue drafts on each other which would take the place of their notes. The Union Bank made arrangements with the Aberdeen Town & County, the British Linen, the Bank of Scotland and the Clydesdale to this effect.[54]

In the second place, the Scottish banks agreed to do a daily exchange of notes, the announcement of which was issued in November 1875,

It has been arranged that in future, and until further notice, in every town in Scotland, where there are two or more Banks represented, there shall be an Exchange of Notes daily, Monday excepted, with a second exchange on Saturday afternoon.... The balance arising on their exchanges will be settled daily by draft on Edinburgh.... The objects of the daily exchange are:

I   To prevent the circulation throughout the week and the figures in the published balance sheets of the Banks, being unduly swelled by the notes in the hands of other Banks, and

II. To economise the working stock of notes required to be kept on hand at the various offices of the Banks.[55]

The result of the two steps is clearly seen in Table 40, which shows decreases of 27% in the growth rates of note issues in both cases of the Scottish total and the Union Bank from 1873 to 1879.

The decline in the growth rate of the Scottish notes indicated that their significance in Scottish banking was changing, or had already changed. In April 1875, when the Select Committee of 1875 was about to start its investigation into note issues, the Scottish bank managers thought that,

The right of issue enjoyed by the Scots Banks ... is a very valuable one both to the Banks and to the country. Its value does not now consist to any great extent in the profit accruing to the Banks from the actual circulation; it rests in the right to issue notes to such an extent as the public may at any time require/subject always to immediate convertibility into coin/whereby the Banks are enabled to carry on business at upwards of 800 Branches without the large extraction of Capital which the use of any other circulating medium would entail.[56]

Indeed, the profitability of note issuing was enjoyed primarily by private banks and provincial banking companies, which had by this time entirely gone. The proportion of notes in circulation in the total Scottish liabilities had already diminished to 6% in 1850 and remained around this figure in the years of 1866/1879. In particular, the Union Bank had £178,000 of its notes in circulation in 1831 — 24% of its total liabilities, and the proportion of notes in its total liabilities reduced to 6.8% on average between 1866 and 1879. The predominance of large-scale joint-stock banking with a tremendous network of branches to gather deposits changed a feature of the structure of Scottish bank liabilities, and cheques were increasingly taking the place of notes. However, it was also true that the Scottish note issues were larger than their Irish counterparts and helped the Scottish banks to economise their use of gold and silver coins as their managers suggested.[57]

Over the years of the conflict between Scottish and English banking, the Clydesdale Bank showed remarkable initiative under the managership of George Readman, even considering amalgamations with at least three banks in the West of England and opening a London office in December 1877.[58] The Clydesdale Bank captured the initiative from the Union, the senior Glasgow bank, which, at last, began preparations for opening a London office in December 1877.

The London office of the Union Bank opened its doors in March 1878 with a staff of twelve whose former occupations are shown in Table 41. Notably, half of the staff was recruited from other banks, particularly from the overseas banks. This must have been due to the character of the London business which required special expertise in international banking business. As a result of the institution of another managership at the London office, the Glasgow manager was first termed 'general manager'.[59]

Simultaneously with the opening of the London office, the Union Bank made three arrangements which were indispensable for the operation of the

TABLE 41

London Office Staff in March 1878

Officer	Former Occupation
1 Manager (J A Fradgley)	Discount Dept of Bank of England
2 Assist. Manager (J E Murray)	Leith Agent of Union Bank
3 Cashier (F Hart)	City Bank, Alliance Bank, London Bank of Mexico, Bank of South America
4 Accountant (W MacMillan)	National Bank of Scotland
5 Senior Clerk (O I Baggally)	London Bank of Mexico
6 Senior Clerk (W I P Robinson)	Unknown
7 Senior Clerk (J Neville)	Glasgow Head Office of Union Bank
8 Senior Clerk (A B Shand)	Merchants Bank of Canada
9 Junior Clerk (unknown)	Edinburgh Head Office of Union Bank
10 Junior Clerk (unknown)	Coatbridge Branch of Union Bank
11 Apprentice (unknown)	
12 Apprentice (unknown)	

Sources: UBM, 19/12/1877 and *passim*

London business. Firstly, the Bank proposed that,

> the Bank of England be requested to open two accounts of the Bank, one for the Head Office at Glasgow to be operated by drafts from Glasgow and Edinburgh, and from such of the Bank Branches, . . . and a separate account for behoof of the London Branch.[60]

Drafts were to be signed by any of two of Gairdner (general manager), A B Henderson (inspector), J A Fradgley (London manager), J E Murray (London assistant manager) and W MacMillan (London accountant).

Secondly, the Bank informed the agents that,

> In the event of your having occasion to draw on London at a currency after date, you will draw on our branch there, instead of on Messrs Glyn & Co as hitherto. In the event of your being asked for a draft on a London bankers, other than ourselves/whether payable on demand or at a currency after date/, you will in that case draw on the Bank of England.[61]

However, there remained certain customers who preferred to 'obtain drafts on a London West-End Bankers'[62] who were doing business with landlords.[63] With regard to this kind of customer, the Union Bank allowed its agents to draw on Coutts & Co.

Thirdly, the Union Bank granted power of attorney regarding 'dividends and transfers of public stocks &c' to Gairdner, Fradgley, Murray, Henderson, J Affleck (Glasgow assistant manager) and A Butter (Edinburgh manager).[64] The grant was executed for the purpose of making transactions of Consols and other securities more conveniently as well as speedily. Consequently, the Union Bank of Scotland became directly connected with the London money market.

3   Consolidation of the Organisation

(a) CHARLES GAIRDNER, THE GENERAL MANAGER

After the death of Sir Adam Hay, the influential Edinburgh director, in 1867, there was only one survivor, D Anderson, of the late partners of Sir William Forbes & Co in the directorate of the Union Bank. The number of directors was reduced from twelve to eleven in May 1869. However, the contract of co-partnery still stipulated that 'the surviving partner of the late firm of Sir William Forbes, James Hunter & Company, shall be re-eligible'[65] and that two directors should go out of office every year by rotation. The last partner of Sir William Forbes & Co disappeared from the board of the Union Bank when D Anderson retired in 1877, one year before the general crisis of 1878.

From 1869, the usual board of directors, excluding C Gairdner, manager, was to consist of five each from Glasgow and Edinburgh, see Table 42. Under the new directorate, the Glasgow directors divided themselves into two sub-committees of 'A' and 'B' in June 1872, each of which the Glasgow manager, of course, attended. Although the minute of June 1872 is missing, the duties of each committee are known from the later minute which explained that,

A; for the purpose of taking cognizance of the advances by way of discounts, cash credits, overdrawn accounts and loans on stocks and other securities at the head office and branches in Glasgow.

B; for the purpose of taking cognizance of the branches generally and the accounts at Glasgow other than those placed under sub-committee A.[66]

The division of duties was mainly regional, that is, Glasgow and the rest, and the A committee was also to be responsible for revision of salaries. Nevertheless, this division was rather ambiguous. The A committee raised a point regarding a branch in Perthshire, whose direct supervision had already been transferred to the Glasgow head office in 1866, and the B committee, too, frequently had discussions on the subject of salaries and accounts at the Glasgow town branches.[67] Furthermore, the minute book of the A committee tended to be brief, recording from time to time no more than attendance. The A committee does not seem to have done much, at least in this period.

TABLE 42

Directorate, 1869

1	D Anderson	of Moredun	Edinburgh
2	J Buchanan	Cadder House	Edinburgh
3	C Campbell	of Colgrain	Glasgow
4	R Dalglish	of Kilmardinny	Glasgow
5	A Galbraith	Manufacturer	Glasgow
6	J Hannan	Merchant	Glasgow
7	D Horne	WS	Edinburgh
8	F Maxwell	Insurance Broker	Glasgow
9	F Pitman	WS	Edinburgh
10	D B Wauchope	Merchant	Leith
11	C Gairdner	Manager	Glasgow

Sources: UB Annual Report, 13/5/1869. R S Rait, 1930, pp. 378–81

One of the main duties of the B committee was inspections of branches all over the country, which will be discussed presently. Another important duty was the supervision of the conduct of business at the Glasgow head office. When the Bank suffered heavily from the Collie fraud in 1875, the B committee recommended a change in the system of how the higher staff conducted the business of the head office, saying that,

Had under consideration the arrangements of the discount department of the head office, and in order to the (*sic*) assistant manager and cashier being relieved as far as possible of transactions of minor importance and to their time being made more available for superintending the discount of bills and the general business of the office, authorise the two chief clerks in the discount department . . . to pass cheques and cash orders presented by the Bank's customers; it being an instruction that they are to consult the assistant manager or cashier in all cases of an exceptional kind of important account.[68]

The organisation of the Union Bank was becoming more modern with senior staff delegating responsibility. The hierarchy within the Union Bank organisation became more powerful.

At the top of the hierarchy came the general manager, Charles Gairdner, who attended not only all committees at the Glasgow head office, but also the Edinburgh committee from 1869 when the contract of copartnery first stipulated a quorum of the meeting of the board to be half of the directors.[69] This stipulation suggests that a small attendance at the board could decide the affairs of the Union Bank, thus effectively controlling its conduct, and it was, of course, the general manager, Gairdner, who was present at all committees.[70] Consequently, it could be argued that Gairdner, the choice of the Edinburgh directors, especially the partners of the late firm of Sir William Forbes & Co, succeeded to the role played by them, effectively presiding over the board of directors. Indeed, Gairdner's caution became more evident in every respect of the business. Gairdner was becoming the most distinguished manager which the Union Bank of Scotland had ever had.

(b) THE FURTHER CONSOLIDATION OF BRANCHES

Intensified inspections of branches in the North, East and Central regions continued in this period. From 1866 to 1870, Gairdner, together with two to three directors, visited the branches in the three regions at least once a year.[71] From 1872 on, the supervision of branches was put under the charge of the B committee at the Glasgow Office, which, selecting some twenty branches on one occasion, had inspectors investigate them closely.[72]

In the course of these inspections, agents were also subjected to scrutiny, and, at least in the North, four of them were dismissed; the Banchory agent replaced by his accountant, the Ballater agent by a member of the Glasgow inspectorate, the Aberdeen West End agent by a clerk of the Whitehaven Joint Stock Bank[73] and someone unknown. Consequently, losses in the North diminished remarkably as Table 43 exhibits.

As Table 43 shows clearly, branches under the charge of the Glasgow head office became a main source of losses particularly from the end of the 1860s. Irregularities were reported especially from the West and South East; Lochgilphead, Paisley, Stewarton, Govan, Glasgow St Vincent Street, Greenock and Peebles. Details of the cause of losses are not known. It might be construed that losses in the West were inevitable because of the large business done by removing resources from the North and East.[74] The case of the Peebles branch, however, seems to be different.

The Peebles branch was one of three in the South East of Scotland where the development of the branch network of the Union Bank was far behind the rest of the mainland, except for the Highlands. All of the three branches were created between 1844 and 1858 when the Union Bank was rapidly growing. In this period, the branches in the South East, especially at Peebles, encountered difficulties which probably resulted from competition with the Edinburgh banks.[75] In 1872, the board resolved that,

> Disappointment was expressed at the want of progress in the business of agency at Peebles; and the manager was instructed to see the agent on the subject.[76]

None the less, the Peebles agent 'was not able to hold out any proposal of improvement in the business of the Branch',[77] which continued to deteriorate. Eventually in 1880, the Peebles branch, together with the other two in the South East, was withdrawn.

The Union Bank increased the number of branches from 99 in 1865 to 125 in 1879.[78] More than four fifths of this creation was due to two circumstances. In 1878 when the City of Glasgow Bank collapsed and the Caledonian Bank temporarily closed its doors, the Union Bank took up four branches of the City Bank and set up a branch at Inverness.[79] More remarkably, fifteen branches were created in the cities of Glasgow, Edinburgh and Aberdeen.[80] The increase of town branches was admittedly due to the concentration of population in the big cities. Thus, the branch establishment of the Union Bank was approaching a turning point in the 1870s under the policy of consolidation pursued by Gairdner.

TABLE 43

Regional Proportions of Losses at Branches, 1866–79*

	Aberdeen†	Perth‡	Edinburgh	Glasgow	Total Amount
1866§	61.2%	0.5%	17.6%	20.7%	£5,367
1867	25.2	0.7	17.9	56.2	6,737
1868	8.6	—	15.0	76.4	6,342
1869	21.1	—	7.7	71.2	8,951
1870	11.1	—	39.1	49.8	2,502
1871	5.3	—	2.2	92.5	2,380
1872	23.5	—	62.8	13.7	14,190
1873	13.9	—	28.4	57.7	1,640
1874	0.8	—	5.0	94.2	15,153
1875	0.6	—	1.9	97.5	27,688
1876	3.0	—	14.4	82.6	4,127
1877	22.3	—	19.0	58.7	5,497
1878	6.3	—	14.5	79.2	5,948
1879	3.9	—	13.2	82.9	18,767

*Division of region as of Table 27
†Accounts consolidated with those of branches under the Glasgow head office in 1880
‡Accounts consolidated with those of branches under the Glasgow head office in 1868
§Date as in April each year

Source: UB (Glasgow), *Abstract Profit and Loss Account Branches*

(c) RECRUITMENT, TRANSFERS AND SALARIES OF THE STAFF

As the Union Bank of Scotland grew older, so did the staff. New blood had to
be infused, but succession from older to younger staff was not always
successful.

The Greenock branch, which was the oldest and one of the most important
in the West, was conducted by A Anderson from 1844. In June 1867 when
Anderson, seventy-seven years of age, tendered his resignation, Gairdner and
the directors were worried about the selection of his successor because the
cashier there was also of too advanced an age to accept the agency.[81]
Eventually, they asked their former inspector, J Norwell, who had resigned
from the service of the Union Bank, to accept the agency. Norwell ran the
Greenock agency for two years before becoming the Edinburgh secretary in
1869.[82]

As a successor to Norwell, Gairdner and the directors appointed F G Bruce,
Officer at Lerwick, who, however, caused a problem. Bruce was a foolhardy
person who was repeatedly engaged in speculative transactions on the stock
exchange, ignoring the warning of the board that,

> any person in the employment of the Bank engaging in speculative business on the
> Stock Exchange or otherwise, shall be liable to be summarily dismissed.[83]

Nevertheless, in May 1874, when Bruce was again found to have engaged
himself in speculative business, the board curiously decided that,

> Directors, while expressing strong disapproval of Mr Bruce being connected with
> such business after the warning given to him by the manager, yet, in the
> circumstances disclosed in the regret, did not think it necessary in this case to carry
> out the Rule that any servant of the Bank so acting should be dismissed.[84]

Though details of 'in this case' are not known and 'Mr Bruce' must have been
a competent person in a sense, the fact that he was not dismissed suggests that
Gairdner and the directors were in a certain difficulty in finding a more
suitable agent for the old and important branch.

When suitable officers were not found among the staff, they did not hesitate
to take over the staff of other banks. In the spring of 1874 when the Aberdeen
cashier, David Wyllie, was retiring, they appointed in his place J Cook, a
member of the staff of the Oriental Bank at Calcutta.[85] As we have already
seen, half of the senior staff of the London office was recruited from other
banks. Moreover, in 1878, the Union Bank, in common with other Scottish
banks, took up the former agents and accountants of the collapsed City of
Glasgow Bank.[86] On the other hand, the Union Bank also lost staff to other
banks. The first Glasgow assistant manager, James Syme, resigned in 1867,
after only two years' service, to become manager of the British Linen Co.[87] In
one case, a young and competent accountant at Tillicoultry, who entered the
Union Bank at Crieff as an apprentice, (aged sixteen), was re-employed in
1876 by an English joint-stock bank.[88] Indeed, the progress of English joint-
stock banking, and probably its overseas counterpart, brought an increasing

demand for qualified clerks, such as those trained by Scottish banking houses. Contemporary bankers had a high regard for bank clerks trained in Scotland, where advanced methods of accountancy and book-keeping were practised.[89] The Scottish bankmen also created with the support of the Scottish banks and under the initiative of A W Kerr, banker and banking historian, the Institute of Bankers, the first example of its kind, in order to improve themselves.[90]

General circulars of the Union Bank provide us with the information about the agents. Of some thirty cases which can be detailed, the Bank selected in twenty cases other agents, accountants at other branches and the staff of the Glasgow head office as successors to the outgoing agents.[91] Secondly came the cases where accountants at the same branches were promoted to agents.[92] Succession from father to son, or between brothers, and appointments of local gentlemen, such as the writer and solicitor, were seen only in three and two cases respectively.[93]

The increasing tendency to transfer agents from one place to another can be exemplified by two persons, that is, J D Sharp, pro-agent at the Glasgow Anderston branch in 1877 and H H Norie, Edinburgh manager in 1881 (see Map 3). Sharp was accountant at Blairgowrie from there he was moved to Rosehearty in 1874. Two years later, he was appointed teller at the Aberdeen office and was promoted to be Aberdeen George Street agent. In only one year or so, he was transferred to be the Auchterarder agent and was eventually promoted to be pro-agent at Anderston in Glasgow.[94] Norie was joint-agent at Kilmarnock where he assisted the senior agents, Gairdners, who were of an advanced age. When the Perth cashier, D Craigie, died in 1866, Norie succeeded him and was later promoted to Edinburgh manager.[95]

The transfers of Bank staff, men who were professional bankers, is a reminder of the eclipse of the 'amateur' agent who dabbled in many affairs including banking. The large scale joint-stock bank of the 1870s and later was similar to the modern corporation requiring highly-trained staff.

The important bank offices also provided more than their share of promoted posts. The Edinburgh manager, H H Norie, was promoted from the Kilmarnock agency; the Glasgow assistant manager, J Affleck, from the Paisley agency, the Glasgow secretary, J Gray, from being Perth secretary, the Edinburgh secretary, J Norwell who was the first full-time inspector, from the Greenock agency and the London assistant manager, J E Murray, from the Leith agency.[96] The five branches at Kilmarnock, Paisley, Perth, Greenock and Leith seem to have been part of the promotion highway, leading to posts at the two head offices, as well as the Aberdeen and London branches. Inside the Glasgow head office, the inspectorate was a useful apprenticeship for the higher posts, as the case of Norwell suggests. In December 1875 when the Glasgow secretary resigned and the accountant was promoted to assistant secretary, the senior sub-inspector succeeded to the office of accountant.[97] Officers of the inspectors' department were also appointed as interim agents while new agents were being selected. Indeed, the large joint-stock bank with the wide network of branches offered both a greater chance of promotion for the clerk, compared to other industry,[98] and a higher status for the inspectorate.[99]

MAP 3

Transfer of Staff

Notes: 1 ———; J D Sharp
Notes: 2 — · —; H H Norie

Sources: UBM, UBGC

As the number of the staff increased, so did the amount of salaries as Table 44 sets out. Salaries at the Glasgow head office increased by more than 150% between 1866 and 1879 which was far more rapidly than in the late 1840s and early 1850s (see Table 18). In addition, in November 1872 when salaries were raised by 3.9%, the board judged it wise to allow bonuses to the staff as a head office circular stated that

> the directors in consideration of the enhanced cost of living, and of other exceptional circumstances affecting this year, have resolved to present the accountants, tellers and clerks of the Bank with a gratuity of 15 per cent on the amount of their salaries, the allowance to be for this year only.[100]

The bonus was probably granted as a result of pressure from the staff who had had the experience of collective bargaining in the early 1850s and who were suffering from the rising cost of living.[101]

TABLE 44

Salaries at Glasgow Head Office, 1866–79

	Amount	Growth Rate: 1866; 100
1866*	£14,681	100
1867	15,861	108
1868	16,481	112
1869	16,842	115
1870	17,883	122
1871	18,618	127
1872	19,318	132
1873	19,914	136
1874	21,153	144
1875	21,660	148
1876	21,991	150
1877	21,592	147
1878	22,300	152
1879	22,881	156

*Date as in April each year

Source: UBPL

The increases in salaries and probable pressure from the staff resulted in Gairdner and the directors considering the establishment of a scale of salaries on the model of Glyn & Co. This was, however, shelved.[102] Consequently, revision of salaries continued to be annual duty of the B committee at the Glasgow head office, or a specially appointed sub-committee.[103]

4   The Union Bank of Scotland in the General Crisis of 1878

At the end of September 1878, the manager of the City of Glasgow Bank confessed at a meeting of the bank managers that the directors of his bank had been deceiving the public by falsifying the balance sheets over the years. He asked for assistance from other banks. On 1 October, the City Bank stopped payment, which precipitated a general crisis. The investigation, held immediately after the stoppage, revealed that the falsification of balance sheets had been made systematically and that the City Bank had committed itself to large scale international financing, doing two kinds of business in which even the Western Bank of Scotland had not been engaged—investment in an American railway company and financing of large scale speculation in New Zealand. Moreover, the City Bank had lent the tremendously large amount of £6,017,000 to four firms; £2,438,000 to J Morton & Co, £1,833,000 to Smith, Fleming & Co, £1,269,000 to J N Fleming and £477,000 to J Innes Wright & Co.[104] In respect of the systematic falsification of balance sheets and large speculative financing, the failure of the City of Glasgow Bank was, indeed, 'the greatest disaster that had ever befallen the commercial community of Great Britain'.[105]

Charles Gairdner and the directors immediately embarked upon emergency measures. They checked the amount of gold held in London, which was brought up to Glasgow on 8 October. At the same time, they were disposing of Consols and US bonds, the proceeds of which would provide for an anticipated run on them. From 2 to 18 October, the Union Bank sold Consols and US bonds for £1,190,000.[106] The large holding of these securities, the growth rate of which was the most remarkable feature of the Union Bank in the 1870s, was, thus, instrumental in strengthening its cash on hand.

In the second place, the Union Bank dispatched two confidential letters to the agents, the first of which read,

> You will please insert in the Weekly Statement of Company's Notes and Coin on hand, the amount of Notes of the City of Glasgow Bank.[107]

It turned out that the Union Bank held £4,000 of City Bank notes in December 1878, the amount of which increased to £82,958 by April 1879.[108] The increase was due to the agreement between the bank managers with regard to retiring the notes on behalf of the City Bank.[109] The second letter was more serious as it read,

> I am instructed to inform you that we are at present very desirous of restricting all advances as much as possible, and this course is also being followed by the other banks. You will please be so kind as keep this in view in respect of the accounts at your Branch. (signed) Secretary.[110]

As a result, from the middle of October to 13 November 1878, no advance of any amount was made at least at the Glasgow head office except to one

customer, the New Zealand and Australia Land Co, whose financial support
fell upon the Union Bank and several other Scottish banks because of the
dropping out of their main bank. The Union Bank allowed an emergency loan
for £83,000.

In the third place, Gairdner and the directors queried as to whether any
shareholder of the Union Bank held stock in the City Bank. If there had been
many double shareholders, it was anticipated that the Union Bank would be
deeply involved in the fraudulent case of the City Bank. A letter of
investigation instructed that,

> I shall thank you to send me a list of the names and addresses of any persons who are
> customers, or under obligations to, this Bank at your Branch, who are holders of
> Stock in the City of Glasgow Bank, either or as Trustees. (signed) Secretary.[111]

Any shareholders, who became bankrupt, were to lose the right of member-
ship and had to dispose of their stock within six months according to the 28th
article of the contract of copartnery. They were removed from the Union
Bank by the middle of December 1878.[112]

Despite every means conceivable, the Union Bank was still not safe and
rumours about a possible danger to the Bank were heard, especially in the East
of Scotland. The Edinburgh office had to cope with them—dispatching a
private letter to agents under its charge that,

> It has been brought under the notice of the Banks that some of their agents have been
> heard, since the failure of the City of Glasgow Bank, to express, either openly or by
> insinuation, some degree of distrust of one or other of the Banks represented in their
> district. Whether the motive for such expressions may have been to attract business
> from rival establishments, or whatever else it may have been, the Banks consider it
> their duty to announce their disappointment in the strongest possible manner.[113]

Although the agents were addressed by 'the Banks', one could venture to say
that the only surviving large scale Glasgow-based Union Bank was exposed to
more critical attention than any other.

Indeed, while the Union Bank was restricting authorisation of advances,
offers of Bank stock started as they did in the 1857 crisis. From 20 November
to 11 December 1878, the stock offered amounted to £18,700, that is, 374
shares of £50 paid, which was already more than one fourth of the total offered
stock in the 1857 difficulties. The situation was critical, and Charles Gairdner
and the directors were eventually forced to issue a special report, an
unprecedented step in the Bank's history, which stated that,

> The Directors deem it right to make a Special Report to the Proprietors on the extent
> to which their interests have been affected by the suspension of the City of Glasgow
> Bank and subsequent failures, and this more particularly as four months must elapse
> before the Annual Meeting is held.
>
> The amount due to the Bank by the City of Glasgow Bank, exclusive of the Notes
> retired in the public interest, is only £4,000. These claims, it is believed, will be paid in
> full; and the Directors have the satisfaction of informing the Proprietors that, on a
> careful estimate of all other bad and doubtful debts, the provision required from the
> profits of the current year is under £3,700.

The Directors believe it will also be satisfactory to the Proprietors to receive at this time an explicit assurance that the Accounts of the Bank are closely and constantly scrutinized by them; that the Advances are safe and well distributed; that losses are invariably provided for as they arise; that the Securities and Investments are of greater value than they stand at in the Books; and that the Bank's Capital of £1,000,000, and Rest of £330,000 are intact. The Proprietors will have observed that an unusual fall has recently taken place in the market price of the Bank's Stock. In connection with this, it is right to mention that a considerable amount of the Stock offered for sale belongs to Proprietors who, unhappily for themselves, are involved as Shareholders in the City of Glasgow Bank. The Bank sustains no loss from this circumstance; and as sales are effected, this depressing influence will, no doubt, pass away.

The Directors have delayed issuing this Report until the effects of the commercial and financial disorder of October have been so far developed as to admit of the Board reporting with confidence on their bearing on the Bank.

Charles Gairdner
General Manager.[114]

As the report suggested, the considerable amount of offered stock between the middle of November and middle of December might be that of the unhappy double shareholders. As also suggested in the report, Gairdner closely and frequently examined the accounts, and, indeed, there remains no evidence of great risk in advances made by the Union Bank.[115] Arrangements regarding advances given to J Morton & Co, which were not particularly for the Union Bank, had already been agreed to among the Scottish banks.[116]

In spite of the guarantee given in the special report, offers of the stock did not cease, even increasing as the annual meeting of 1879 was drawing nearer, as Table 45 clearly shows. This situation was extraordinary and far worse than in the 1857 crisis in which offers of the stock ceased in about three months.[117] The price of the offered stock slipped sharply down from £270 in November 1878 to £160 in December 1878 from which it had not recovered even by April 1879. The falling rate was more than 40% which was also worse than in the 1857 crisis and the largest among those of the Scottish banks.[118] This suggests that the public image of the Union Bank was seriously damaged by the general crisis of 1878 in which many proprietors deserted the Bank. The public and those partners might consider that the large Glasgow-based joint-stock bank, well supplied with branches, was 'jinxed', just like the Western Bank of Scotland, and, therefore, that the next to go would be the Union Bank. Gairdner and the directors sought to weather this terrible storm and by taking an extraordinary step, that is, the adoption of an external audit system, which they believed would be convincing proof that they had nothing to hide.[119]

The general crisis of 1878 had a tremendous effect on Glasgow banking as Diagrams 5 and 6 show. In terms of total liabilities and profits, Glasgow-controlled banking diminished by one third. 1878 marked a turning point in Scottish banking and established a new supremacy of Edinburgh banking. Consequently, it could be argued that the failure of another large joint-stock bank, following the experience of the Western Bank, finally deprived Glasgow of any possibility of becoming another financial centre of Scotland. All Gairdner's instincts for caution were re-inforced and the Union Bank of Scotland shared the fate of Glasgow banking.

TABLE 45

Offers of Union Bank Stock* between November 1878 and April 1879

	Value	Number of Shares	Offered Price
November 1878	£6,700	134	£180–270
1st half of Dec 1878	12,000	240	176–181
2nd half of Dec 1878	10,655	214	160–190
January 1879	8,760	176	—
February 1879	7,500	150	—
March 1879	6,200	124	—
April 1879	31,675	634	165–190
Total	£83,490	1,672	160–270

*20,000 shares (10,000 stock), £50 paid

Source: UBM, 20/11/1878 and *passim*

DIAGRAM 5

Proportions of Total Liabilities: Edinburgh, North and Glasgow Based Banks, 1866–85

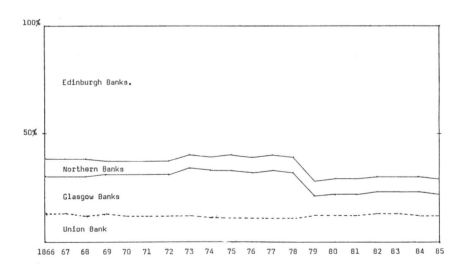

Source: SGC and A B MacDonald, 1973

DIAGRAM 6

Proportions of Profits: Edinburgh, North and Glasgow Based Banks, 1866–85

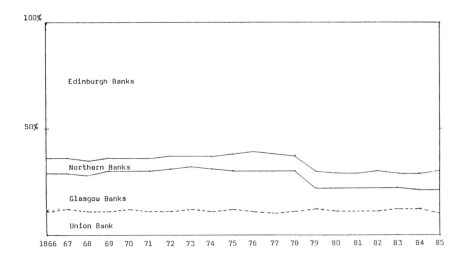

Source: as of Diagram 5

Chapter 5
Stagnation, 1879–1885

The growth rates of total liabilities, deposits and advances of the Union Bank of Scotland in this period were all over the Scottish totals as Diagrams 7 and 8 show. The rapid growth of investments, which was the remarkable performance of the Union Bank in the previous years, became common in Scottish banking during this period. Although the growth of total liabilities, deposits and advances began to lose ground from 1883 on, no extraordinary situation can be found in their movements. The only uncommon feature might be the sharp fall of profits from 1883 to 1885 which was a reflection of the real situation of the Union Bank.

Indeed, the years between 1879 and 1885 witnessed great difficulties. At the commencement of this period, Charles Gairdner and the directors had to cope with increasing offers of the Bank stock. Throughout almost the whole period, they had to support a firm of large shipbuilders, that is, J & G Thomson. These critical circumstances led them to resort to two extraordinary experiments, that is, the adoption of an external audit system and interference in the management of J & G Thomson.

1 The Adoption of an External Audit

Prior to 1879, the Scottish banks in general voluntarily made audits of their accounts.[1] The Union Bank of Scotland in particular stipulated that;

> at the (annual) meeting, it (balance sheet) shall be laid down upon the table for inspection of the Partners, and the substance thereof read or stated by the Chairman; and it shall be in the power of each meeting, if they shall think fit, to appoint a private Committee, consisting of three Partners of the Company . . . for auditing and reporting upon such yearly states, at a future general meeting to be called for the purpose.[2]

Nonetheless, there is no record that even an internal audit was actually undertaken. Even in the aftermath of the 1857 crisis and Collie fraud, Gairdner and the directors had not thought it necessary to undertake an audit. The circumstances confronting them in early 1879 were totally different from any previous experience.

Examinations of all accounts, which were executed between the end of 1878 and the spring of 1879, revealed that there was no particular danger in lending. The special report was also, exceptionally, issued in December 1878, trying to persuade the shareholders to remain with the Bank. Nevertheless, these steps could not stop the tremendous offers of Union Bank stock, the largest of which was made in April when the annual meeting of 1879 was approaching. It was alarming. Gairdner and the directors resolved to take very strong measures to re-assure public opinion. They decided to adopt a compulsory external audit, which had already been suggested by journalists and some of the Scottish MPs in the aftermath of the failure of the City of Glasgow Bank.[3] On 9 April 1879, the board resolved to adopt the system, and Gairdner immediately sent a letter to the deputy chairman, H E Crum Ewing, of Strathleven, who was asked to take emergency action, stating that,

> they are serious that arrangements should be made to have the annual balance sheet now in preparation, submitted to independent auditors, and they hope that you, as the deputy chairman of the Bank, in the absence through ill health of the chairman, and thus the official representative of the proprietors, as distinguished from the board of directors, will kindly take the necessary steps to have suitable auditors appointed. On hearing from you with the names of the gentlemen you propose, I shall at once ask them to attend at the Bank.[4]

DIAGRAM 7

Union Bank; Growth Rates of Total Liabilities, Deposits, Advances, Investments and Profits, 1879–85

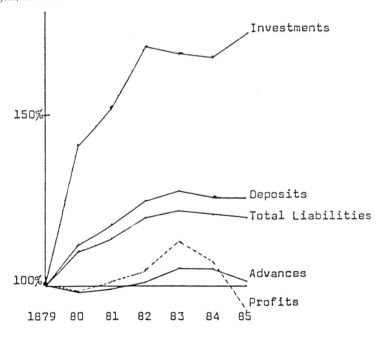

Source: SGC and A B MacDonald, 1973

DIAGRAM 8

Scottish Total; Growth Rates of Total Liabilities, Deposits, Advances, Investments and Profits, 1879–85

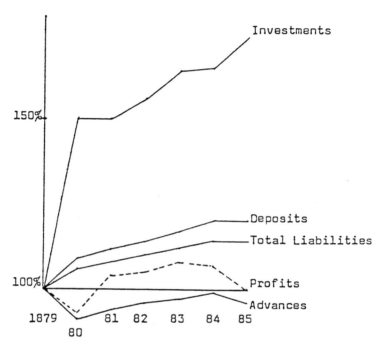

Source: as of Diagram 7

The deputy chairman at once nominated as independent auditors,

> two gentlemen who to the best of my judgment are well fitted to undertake the duties, and these are, Mr William MacKinnon of M'Clelland, MacKinnon & Blyth; and Mr James Haldane of Lindsay, Jamieson & Haldane, Edinburgh.[5]

On receiving the nomination, the board soon carried a resolution in which they confessed their serious anxiety.

> 1. That while the existing system of inspection maintained continuously throughout the year, is satisfactory to the board, there is no reason why an independent audit should not be made, provided it be entrusted to gentlemen qualified by status and experience for so confidential duty.
> 2. That the appointment of auditors of this description would be welcomed by the board as tending to strengthen and confirm the confidence of the proprietors in the management of the Bank.[6]

At the same time, the board obtained the oath of two auditors which read that, we will in no manner of way reveal directly or indirectly of the transactions of the Bank either on its own account or on behalf of its customers.[7]

Consequently, it took only three days for Gairdner and the directors to set the auditors to work. The speed with which the external audit system was established suggests that the whole process was pre-arranged, presumably by Gairdner, who had a surprisingly strong relationship with one of the auditors, W MacKinnon.[8] From this, it must be assumed that the external audit was not necessarily an independent audit. Indeed, MacKinnon, thereafter, deepened his involvement in the daily conduct of the Union Bank, exemplified by Thomson's affairs.[9] Therefore, it could be argued that 'auditing in the modern sense was practically non-existent'.[10]

The appointment of another auditor should also be subjected to scrutiny because J Haldane was one of the liquidators of the City of Glasgow Bank.[11] His appointment is, thus, considered to be quite similar to the experience of Gairdner himself who, being a liquidator of the Western Bank, was asked by the Union Bank to investigate its accounts, successfully confirming to the public the safety of the Bank. The same effect, as in the aftermath of the 1857 crisis, was obviously expected by Gairdner and the directors. It is hard to resist the conclusion that it was 'a put-up job'.

The response of the public to this venture was generally favourable to the Union Bank. *The Times,* for instance, reported that;

> The audit introduced appears to have been of a very thorough character and completely independent, and the Board deserves great credit for having this frankly met one of the most urgent of the popular demands in regard to banks.[12]

The Glasgow Herald, which itself was a shareholder of the Union Bank, also supported it saying,

> The object was to guarantee the shareholders against mismanagement, of which we have had such reckless specimens in the doings of Taylor, of the Western Bank, and of the Stronachs, of the City of Glasgow; as well as to protect the Directors from concealment on the part of the officials. . . . Till some better system of audit for Banks is invented, that adopted by the Union has the first claim to recommendation.[13]

It should be noted that *the Economist* was most sceptical, commenting that,

> a good system of accounts may exist with bad business.[14]

The Economist obviously had in mind the case of the Royal Bank of Liverpool, which earlier in 1860 adopted the external audit system but failed in 1876.[15]

The external audit served its purpose for the public image was improved. One journal commented that,

> The City of Glasgow disaster has had less effect upon the Union Bank of Scotland than was to have been expected.[16]

Indeed, the market price of the Union Bank shares, for the first time since the autumn of 1878, showed a sign of strong recovery going up from £165 to £190 in a few days after the announcement of the adoption of the external audit.[17]

MacKinnon and Haldane inspected the accounts, books and all kinds of documents for nearly ten days giving ten suggestions to the Union Bank. As well as making suggestions such as, 'The Balance Sheet might . . . be rather more detailed,'[18] the auditors surprisingly 'interfered' in the ordinary conduct of banking business as the memorandum read that,

> II. Acceptance by the Bank; acceptances issued in Glasgow and London should be passed through the Books when issued as is done in Edinburgh. The acceptances at the Branches are made 'overdrafts'/has been accepted./
>
> III. Marginal Credits; These ought to be bound up and numbered with progressive numbers in order that no blank forms may be improperly used . . ./has been accepted./
>
> IV. Deposit Receipts; There ought to be special care in issuing the forms to the clerk/The accountant now takes charge of./. . .
>
> VII. System of Audit in Cashier's Department; General Manager has had this matter under consideration and it is now to be dealt with/audit will be conducted by the Inspector of Branches./[19]

All suggestions made by the auditors were readily accepted by the board. It is probable that the general manager, Charles Gairdner, himself instigated the recommendations. He certainly co-operated with the auditors for he was aiming at disciplining the organisation by tightening up book-keeping procedures.

It should also be noted that acceptances at the branches were to be booked as overdrafts. Gairdner probably regarded acceptance business, mainly unsecured, as risky business and, therefore, that a smaller amount of this business was more acceptable to the public. Indeed, *the Glasgow Herald* seems to have felt relieved when it found that,

> The acceptances by the Bank in Scotland and in London amount to £183,007, a very moderate sum, it must be admitted.[20]

The change in the book-keeping probably accelerated the decrease of the amount of acceptances, which was falling considerably from 1879 to 1885 as Table 46 sets out. Although the external audit system was instrumental in recovering the public image of the Union Bank, it, unfortunately, forced the Bank to become ever more timid in pushing its business.

It was also in the aftermath of the 1878 crisis that the seven Scottish joint-stock banks did register as limited companies, although reluctant to do so. They thought that limited liability might encourage more irresponsible banking thus destroying public confidence. In the meantime, the Gladstone government was preparing a bill which would enable joint-stock banks to avail themselves of limited liability. The three Scottish public banks, which had already claimed limited liability by virtue of their charters, raised objections, preparing private bills with intent to protect their privilege. This attitude provoked the Scottish unlimited banks, whether Glasgow or

TABLE 46

Acceptance Business, 1879–85

	Amount	% of Total Liabilities
1879*	£183,007	1.7
1880	189,785	1.6
1881	167,915	1.3
1882	191,914	1.4
1883	111,858	0.8
1884	70,619	0.5
1885	85,166	0.6

*Date as in April each year

Source: UB *Annual Reports*

Edinburgh based, into joint action. They recognised that the government disliked the independence of the Scottish banking system and given an excuse would move to impose conformity, thus threatening the Scottish note issue.[21]

Eventually in July 1881, the seven joint-stock banks jointly agreed to avail themselves of the Companies Act of 1880.[22] The Union Bank called a special meeting in February 1882 carrying a resolution that,

> the Union Bank of Scotland, being a Bank of issue, be registered under the Companies Acts, 1862–1880, as a limited Company, under the name of The Union Bank of Scotland, Limited, ... the nominal amount of the Capital of the bank being One Million Pounds, represented by 100,000 shares of £10 each, fully paid up, be increased to Five Million Pounds by the nominal amount of each of its shares of £10 being increased to £50; provided always that no part of such increased Capital shall be capable of being called up, except in the event of and for the purpose of the Bank being wound up.[23]

This was 'reserve liability' under which no additional call was required unless the bank was being wound up and all the unlimited Scottish banks became limited companies on the basis of having nominal capital five times as large as their existing paid up capital.[24]

2   Business In 'The Great Depression'

(a) MONEY FLOW TO LONDON

Methods of advances and their proportion to deposits and total liabilities on three different levels are set out in Tables 47, 48 and 49, that is, the Union Bank of Scotland as a whole, Glasgow head office and London office. All accounts of branches, except those under the charge of the Edinburgh head office, had already by the spring of 1879 been consolidated at the Glasgow head office, and, therefore, direct comparisons between regions are not available in this period.

TABLE 47

Methods of Advances of the Union Bank as a Whole, 1880–85

	(1) Credit Accounts/ Overdrafts	(2) Loan on Securities	(3) Bills	(4) 1 + 2 + 3	(5) Deposits	(6) 4/5
1880*	£3,011,537	£799,042	£3,352,350	£7,162,929	£9,587,492	74.7%
	42.0%	11.2%	46.8%	59.1%	79.1%	
1881	2,982,628	1,013,634	3,356,166	7,352,428	10,150,931	72.4%
	40.6	13.8	45.6	58.5	80.7	
1882	3,160,618	1,165,633	3,153,786	7,480,037	10,679,642	70.0%
	42.2	15.6	42.2	56.5	80.6	
1883	3,095,592	1,568,074	3,184,599	7,848,265	10,937,157	71.8%
	39.4	20.0	40.6	58.4	81.3	
1884	3,037,734	1,555,978	3,286,874	7,880,586	10,774,189	73.1%
	38.5	19.7	41.7	59.2	80.9	
1885	3,272,620	1,200,255	3,062,132	7,535,007	10,764,218	70.0%
	43.4	16.0	40.6	57.0	81.5	
Average	41.0%	16.1%	42.9%	58.1%	80.7%	72.0%

*Date as in April each year
% of columns 1–3; as of column 4
% of columns 4 and 5; as of total liabilities.

Sources: UB *Annual Reports*

TABLE 48

Methods of Advances at the Glasgow Head Office, 1880–85

	(1) Credit Accounts/ Overdrafts	(2) Loan on Securities	(3) Local Bills	(4) Bills of Exchange	(5) Bills from Branches	(6) 3 + 4 + 5	(7) 1+2 2+6	(8) Deposits	(9) 7/8
1880*	£831,737	£550,768	£715,383	£655,149	£396,730	£1,767,262	£3,149,767	£1,080,320	292%
	26.4%	17.5%	22.7%	20.8%	12.6%	56.1%	26.0%	8.9%	
1881	663,535	743,583	673,858	550,723	762,736	1,987,317	3,394,435	1,216,915	279
	19.5	21.9	19.9	16.2	22.5	58.6	27.0	9.7	
1882	813,618	831,643	714,830	535,443	738,935	1,989,208	3,634,469	1,339,990	271
	22.4	22.9	19.7	14.7	20.3	54.7	27.4	10.1	
1883	761,268	1,100,724	811,898	551,994	717,281	2,081,173	3,943,165	1,381,097	286
	19.3	27.9	20.6	14.0	18.2	52.8	29.3	10.3	
1884	747,348	1,001,182	696,628	630,895	812,540	2,140,063	3,888,593	1,308,974	297
	19.2	25.7	17.9	16.3	20.9	55.1	29.2	9.8	
1885	903,384	717,551	597,048	602,868	572,188	1,772,104	3,393,039	1,133,845	299
	26.6	21.1	17.6	17.8	16.9	52.3	25.7	8.6	
Average	22.2%	22.8%	19.7%	16.6%	18.6%	54.9%	27.4%	9.6%	287%

*Date as in April each year
% of columns 1–6; as of column 7
% of columns 7 and 8; as of total liabilities.

Sources: UB Annual Reports; UBPJ

TABLE 49

Business at the London Office, 1881–84

Sources: UBM, as at dates; UB Annual Reports

	(1) Credit Accounts/ Overdrafts	(2) Bills of Exchange	(3) Inland Bills	(4) Loans to Customers	(5) 1+2+3+4	(6) 5/Total Bank Deposits	(7) Loan to Bill Broker	(8) Loan to Stock Broker
18 Mar 1881	£117,237 20.5%	£266,884 46.6%	£11,941 2.1%	£176,157 30.8%	£572,219 17.9%	5.6%	£1,065,500 33.3%	£772,000 24.1%
21 Mar 1882	198,261 28.6	227,819 32.9	14,006 2.0	253,500 36.5	693,586 27.0	6.5	1,000,000 39.3	70,600 2.7
26/27 Oct 1882	121,567 18.4	199,276 30.1	5,101 0.8	335,351 50.7	661,295 24.8	6.1	595,000 22.3	690,000 25.9
14 Mar 1883	85,222 16.1	157,714 29.7	6,691 1.3	280,537 52.9	530,164 15.8	4.8	800,000 23.9	581,225 17.4
25/26 Oct 1883	196,713 29.4	200,363 29.9	6,387 1.0	265,868 39.7	669,331 20.9	6.2	690,000 21.6	310,575 9.7
17 Oct 1884	40,676 5.1	112,093 14.2	7,839 1.0	630,376 79.7	790,984 25.8	7.3	640,000 20.8	226,326 7.4
Average	19.7%	30.6%	1.4%	48.4%	22.0%	6.1%	26.9%	14.5%

	(9) 7+8	(10) 9/Total Bank Deposits	(11) 5+9	(12) 11/Total Bank Deposits	(13) Consols	(14) Other Balances	(15) 11+13+14	(16) 15/Total Bank Deposits
18 Mar 1881	£1,837,500 57.4%	18.1%	£2,409,719 75.3%	23.7%	£700,000 21.9%	£88,968 2.8%	£3,198,687 25.4%	31.5%
21 Mar 1882	1,070,600 42.0	10.0	1,764,186 69.0	16.5	701,000 27.5	81,526 3.5	2,546,712 19.2	23.8
26/27 Oct 1882	1,285,000 48.2	11.9	1,946,295 73.0	18.0	717,587 27.0	—	2,663,882 20.0	24.6
14 Mar 1883	1,381,225 41.3	12.6	1,911,389 57.1	17.5	1,300,000 38.9	134,753 4.0	3,346,142 24.9	30.6
25/26 Oct 1883	1,000,575 31.3	9.2	1,669,906 52.2	15.4	1,350,000 42.2	178,001 5.6	3,197,907 23.9	29.5
17 Oct 1884	866,326 28.2	8.0	1,657,310 54.0	15.4	1,300,496 42.4	112,354 3.6	3,070,160 23.1	28.5
Average	41.4%	11.6%	63.4%	17.8%	33.3%	3.3%	22.8%	28.1%

% of columns 1–4 as of column 5. % of columns 5, 7, 8, 9, 11, 13 and 14 as of column 15. % of column 15 as of total liabilities. Denominators of columns 6, 10, 12 and 15[(a) the months of March in 1881, '82 and '83; '82 and '83: total bank deposits or liabilities in April each year; (b) Octobers of 1882, '83 and '84; total bank deposits or liabilities on the average between the years.

Figures of advances as percentages of deposits clearly show two features of the performance of the Union Bank. The figures for the Bank as a whole diminished from 75% in 1880 to 70% in 1885 being 72% on average which was considerably below that of the Scottish total (82%).[25] The Union Bank continued to lose initiative in pushing their lending business. The figures of the Glasgow head office, though also substantially declining compared to those of the previous period, were evidence of the dominant position of Glasgow business and the money flow from the rest of Scotland to Glasgow, which is supported by figures in Tables 50 and 51. At the Edinburgh head office and its branches, only 40% of their deposits were lent. At the rest of the branches, a little more than one third of their deposits was advanced. Thus, money flow from the rest of Scotland, especially from the North and East, to the West, especially to Glasgow, was the established pattern of the Union Bank even in the last quarter of the nineteenth century.

TABLE 50

Deposits and Advances at the Edinburgh Office and its Branches,* 1880–85

	(1) *Deposits*	(2) *Advances†*	(3) *2/1*
1880‡	£643,576	£283,555	44.1%
1881	658,464	268,073	40.7
1882	686,613	254,165	37.1
1883	641,084	286,556	44.7
1884	633,388	267,562	42.2
1885	719,057	298,333	41.5
Average	—	—	41.7%

*Lerwick, Kirkcaldy, Leith, Kirkwall and town branches in Edinburgh
†Credit accounts/overdrafts and discounts
‡Date; as in April each year

Source: UBGL

TABLE 51

Deposits and Advances at Other Branches, 1880–85

	(1) *Deposits*	(2) *Advances**	(3) *2/1*
1880†	£7,142,654	£2,717,234	38.0%
1881	7,519,292	2,907,713	38.7
1882	7,910,995	2,703,151	34.2
1883	8,124,896	2,698,476	33.2
1884	8,240,161	2,744,823	33.3
1885	8,183,048	2,566,201	31.4
Average	—	—	34.8%

*Credit accounts/overdrafts and discounts
†Date as in April each year

Source: UBGL

TABLE 52

London Deposits (Estimate),* 1880–85

	Figure in Annual Report	Figure in General Ledger	London Deposits
1880†	£9,587,492	−£9,261,646	= £325,846
1881	10,150,931	− 9,691,031	= 459,900
1882	10,679,642	−10,213,366	= 466,276
1883	10,937,157	−10,414,398	= 522,759
1884	10,774,189	−10,424,533	= 349,656
1885	10,764,218	−10,403,330	= 360,888

*It might be suspected that this estimate has been made arbitrarily, because there remains no evidence which would support the validity of our guess. However, there are two reasons which could be favourable with regard to our guess. Firstly, the gaps between two figures in the annual reports and general ledgers, which constantly amounted to more than £0.3m, are too large to be regarded as a result of the difference in dates in which the two accounts were made up. Secondly, the figures seem to be reasonable for deposits at the London office, compared to those at the Edinburgh office and its branches (see Table 50).

†Date; as in April each year

Sources: UB *Annual Reports.* UBGL

TABLE 53

London Business as Percentages of Estimated London Deposits, 1881–84

	(1) Ordinary Advances*	(2) ⅓+ Loans to Bill & Stock Brokers	(3) Whole London Business
Mar 1881	124.0%	524.0%	695.5%
Mar 1882	148.8	378.4	546.2
Oct 1882	133.7	393.6	538.7
Mar 1883	101.4	365.6	640.1
Oct 1883	153.4	382.8	733.1
Oct 1884	222.6	466.5	864.2
Average	147.3%	418.5%	669.6%

*Credit accounts/overdrafts, discounts and other loans
Denominators; as of note in Table 49

Sources: Tables 49 and 52

On average, any method of advances of the Bank as a whole did not exceed half of the total. Advances on discounts, which were the dominant method of the Bank till the mid nineteenth century, eventually lost ground. Only at the Glasgow head office, they reached 55%. At the London office, where foreign bills must have been centred, their proportion was a little more than 30% of the advances excluding loans to bill and stock brokers. The decrease of discounts was due to the careful lending policy of Gairdner as well as, probably, to the general tendency of a decline in inland bills.[26]

DIAGRAM 9

Proportions of Methods of Advances; Union Bank as a Whole, Glasgow Head Office and London Office, 1880–85

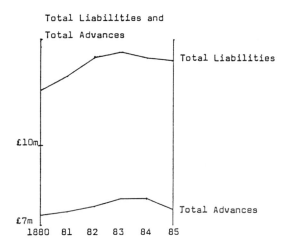

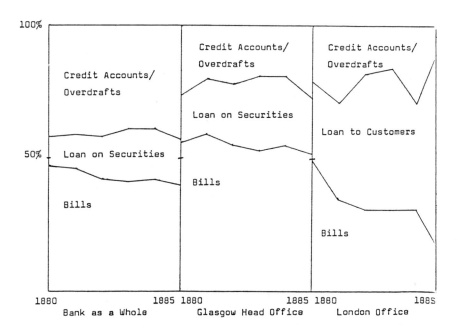

Sources: Tables 47, 48 and 49

Instead of traditional methods, other loans, termed 'loans on securities' and 'loans to customers', were increasing, especially at the offices situated in commercial and financial centres. Details of these kinds of loans are not exactly known, but it is safe to say that they were primarily made on stocks and debentures such as those of railway companies and a growing number of joint-stock corporations in general. Indeed, the Castle Packet Co and the New Zealand & Australia Land Co were usually allowed credits on debentures.[27] Remarkably, the Mexican Railway Co applied for a large loan for £2,000,000, presumably on its debentures, but it was declined.[28] Consequently, these loans, at least a considerable portion of them, are construed to have been quasi-investments. If we added these sums to those of investments, their growth rate would have been more remarkable.

Once the London office was opened in March 1878, another route for substantial money flows made its appearance. Table 49 shows that the advances at the London office, including loans to bill and stock brokers, amounted to 17.8% on the average of the total deposits of the Union Bank. If we include government securities and other balances, more than 28% of the Union Bank deposits proved to be employed in London. There remains no direct evidence regarding the amount of the London deposits, but we can estimate amounts from gaps between figures in the annual reports and general ledgers which are set out in Table 52. If this estimate is assumed to be right, ordinary advances, loans to bill and stock brokers and whole businesses, including government securities and other balances, as percentages of the London deposits, can be obtained, as Table 53 sets out. Even only ordinary advances exceeded the deposits by 50%. Adding loans to bill and stock brokers, the London office lent four times more than its deposits. In all, the London office did business six-and-a-half times larger than its own deposits. From this it must be concluded that the Union Bank of Scotland gathered deposits up in the North and East pouring them into the Glasgow head office and then into the London office which placed them primarily in the hands of bill and stock brokers. This, since the opening of the London office, was a new pattern of money flow for the Union Bank.

The large employment of the Bank resources in London, thus, undoubtedly resulted from the lending policy of Charles Gairdner who, as we already know, preferred safe outlets for money. Indeed, three quarters of the assets at the London office were employed in short term loans to bill and stock brokers (41.1%) and Consols (33.3%). Self-liquidating credits and safe investments, that is, reserve of the banking business, were the purpose of the London business. However, another purpose, more general but minor for the Union Bank, as the small proportion of ordinary advances suggest, should not be ignored. As a young banker argued in his prize winning essay for the Institute of Bankers in 1878 (first published in 1975),

> nowadays it is quite an exception with large mercantile houses in Glasgow and Dundee and other Scotch towns to accept a bill payable in Scotland.[29]

Beyond Edinburgh, the financial centre of Scotland, all payments for commercial transactions were increasingly clustering round the largest international financial centre, London. The Union Bank was not an exception in that the bank follows the customer.

From this point, there emerges a profound question as to whether the money flow from Scotland to London had any substantial effect on the Scottish economy as a whole. A certain effect must have been felt by businessmen in Scotland as the Glasgow Chamber of Commerce complained in 1882 that,

> Your committee feel that the directors of the different Scotch banks should be approached, and strongly urged to modify the unequal rates of discount charged by them in Scotland for certain bills as compared with the discount rates for similar bills in London. In this way, the trading public in Scotland are placed at a great disadvantage in competing with English traders and, several of the members of your chamber have stated that business has actually been driven away from Scotland owing to their competitors being able to finance so much cheaper than can be done in Scotland.[30]

This was probably a result of the money flow to London. However, this subject must be treated from the wider view of the relationship between the Scottish economy and banking, following case studies of other major Scottish banks.

(b) À FULL RANGE OF INVESTMENTS

Following the period of the remarkable growth of investments from 1866 to 1879, the Union Bank greatly diversified its portfolio including the US, Canadian, Australian, New Zealand, Indian Mauritius, Tasmanian, and New Brunswick bonds and American and French railway securities.[31] The largest component of its investments was, of course, British government securities, primarily Consols, to which Treasury bills were added in 1879 when they made their appearance at the suggestion of Sir Walter Bagehot. The amount of Treasury bills soon increased to £400,000 in 1881.[32] Consequently, though the diversification of its portfolio was remarkable, the largest items were the long and short term securities of the British government.

In conducting the business of various investments, the general manager, Gairdner, employed at least nine firms of stock brokers, merchant bankers and an investment company, among which there were definite divisions of business. In London, the firms of Murton & Smallpiece and Pember & Boyle were engaged primarily in transactions with regard to Consols. Rothschild & Son and J Morgan & Co were employed especially for foreign investments, particularly those of foreign governments.[33] In Leeds, R Salmon Backhouse operated for transactions connected with the English railway securities. In Scotland, Bell, Begs & Cowan (Edinburgh), Davidson & Syme (Glasgow), J Watson & Smith (Glasgow) and T F Donald (Glasgow) were engaged in transactions with regard to Scottish securities, mainly those of railway companies.[34] The employment of nine firms suggests that Gairdner was very careful in distributing risks in investments among them.

The purchase of its own stock by the Union Bank almost ceased at the beginning of the 1880s. In March 1881, the Union Bank made a purchase of its stock for £10,322, which was the last large scale one up to 1885.[35] The Union Bank quietly ended this controversial practice in the wake of the adoption of the external audit system.

3 The Union Bank of Scotland and Industries

The number of special advances of £10,000 and over[36] amounted to 120 cases between 1879 and 1885, of which 109 authorisations were made to seven sectors as Table 54 sets out.

TABLE 54

Special Advances, 1879–85

	(1) Number of Authorisations	(2) Average Amount of Authorised Advances	(3) Ranking in terms of 2
1 Trade	31	£27,211	4
2 Shipbuilding & Engineering	21	59,941	1
3 Iron & Steel	18	24,500	6
4 Transport	16	51,781	2
5 Textile	11	25,909	5
6 Public	9	39,778	3
7 Chemical	3	16,000	7
	109		

Source: UBM, *passim*

In terms of the number of authorisations, the transport sector, which we have termed 'the railway sector' because of no special advances being made to shipping companies, dropped behind three industries for the first time since the sectoral preference of the Union Bank appeared in the early 1860s. Instead, the sectors of trade, shipbuilding and iron and steel occupied the first three rankings, which might reflect the coming of the age of steel ship navigation. In terms of the average amount of authorisations, a different ranking can be obtained as column 3 in Table 54 sets out. Surprisingly, the sector for shipbuilding and engineering jumped up to the top of the table, followed by the sectors of transport and public utilities. The appearance of the public sector in the higher ranking was entirely due to one overwhelmingly large credit made to the City of London Commissioners of Sewers for £200,000.[37] Excluding this large advance, its average sum was reduced to £19,750. Consequently, it is reasonable to say that the favourite sectors of the

Union Bank were still trade, transport and shipbuilding and engineering, as they were in previous years, though iron and steel was not negligible. Coincidentally, the Union Bank had three notable borrowers in these three sectors, that is, the Haputale Coffee Co, the Castle Packet Co and J & G Thomson, whose cases would be worth detailing.

(a) THE HAPUTALE COFFEE CO AND THE CASTLE PACKET CO; DIRECTORS' CONCERNS

The Haputale Coffee Co, situated in London, was trading with Ceylon, borrowing exclusively from the Union Bank at its London office (Table 55). As far as the amounts, lengths and rates of interest of advances were concerned, there was neither any remarkable feature nor any foreseeable risk. The average sum of authorised credit (£12,955) was far below that of the trade sector. Lending rates were carefully arranged so that they did not fall below 4%. However, there arose a problem which was a result of the exclusive business of the Union Bank with the Haputale Co.

TABLE 55

Advances to the Haputale Coffee Co

	(1) Amount	(2) Method of Advance	(3) Length, m	(4) Lending Rate
28 Apr, 1880	£20,000	Credit account †	12	BER*(3%) + 1%, not under 4%
8 June, 1881	20,000	Credit account	12	BER($2\frac{1}{2}$%) + 1%, not under 4%
13 July, 1881	25,000	Open credit	—	
24 May, 1882	20,000	Credit account	12	BER (3%) + 1%, not under 4%
30 May, 1883	10,000	Credit account	12	BER(4%) +, not under 4%
18 July, 1883	9,000	Open credit	—	
19 Dec, 1883	10,000	Credit account	12	BER(3%) +1%, not under 4%
19 Dec, 1883	8,000	Open credit	—	
4 June, 1884	2,500	Credit account	—	—
4 Feb, 1885	10,000	Credit account	12	BER(48) +1%, not under 4%
4 Feb, 1885	8,000	Open credit	—	—
Average‡	£12,955			

*BER; Bank of England rate
†Credit account; probably sometimes overdrafts
‡Average; including open credits

Sources: UBM, as at date except 18/7/1883. UB (Glasgow) *Accountant's Minute,* 18/7/1883.
         B R Mitchell and P Deane, 1976, p. 457

Among the directors of the Union Bank, Frederick Pitman (WS, Edinburgh) was very keen to expand the business of the Haputale Co intending to purchase an estate in Ceylon by issuing preference shares of the Company.[38]

To this scheme, some of the shareholders of the Haputale Co raised objections. H M Lang, one objector, who was a relative of Alexander Dennistoun and Seton Thomson, director of the Union Bank, wrote to Gairdner expressing his anxiety over the future of the Haputale Co saying that,

> I am annoyed about these Haputale and Madulsa (another coffee co.) . . . the unsatisfactory grant is that the directors don't seem to indicate what they intend to do in the future. If they cannot see their way to make the estates pay something much better, put them in liquidation as I must say I would decidedly object to any calls being made.[39]

The business of the Haputale Coffee Co was obviously in certain difficulties in which the Union Bank had to involve itself on account of its being the sole lender. The answer of Gairdner is not known, but it is likely that he did not object to the scheme to purchase an estate in Ceylon because he stepped in to arbitrate between the directors and shareholders of the Haputale Co. Gairdner's arbitration was successful, and the scheme was launched in November 1884.[40] Gairdner and Pitman might have seen a bright future in the Ceylon business, as did Thomas Lipton![41]

The Castle Packet Co was created in the late 1870s by Sir Donald Currie of the firm of Donald Currie & Co (Liverpool), which commenced a line of sailing ships between Liverpool and Calcutta in 1862.[42] From the outset of the venture, the Castle Co borrowed money mainly on debentures and this constantly amounted to £200,000 as Table 56 sets out. Although the constant authorisation of credits for £200,000 was very favourable for the Company, advances on debentures were the usual method of financing the transport

TABLE 56

Advances to the Castle Packet Co

	(1) *Amount*	(2) *Method of Advance*	(3) *Length, m*	(4) *Lending Rate, %*
19 Nov, 1879[1]	£50,000	Debentures	12	4.5
26 Nov, 1879[1]	50,000	Debentures	12	4.5
29 Dec, 1879[1]	100,000	Debentures	12	4.5
2 Apr, 1880[2]	70,000	Debentures	—	—
29 Dec, 1880[3]	100,000	Debentures	12	4.5
20 Jan, 1881[3]	100,000	Debentures	12	4.5
20 July, 1881[3]	30,000	Credit account/ overdraft	—	—
2 Apr, 1882[2]	100,000	Debentures	12	4.5
8 Feb, 1883[1]	150,000	Promissory notes	12	4.5
26 Sept, 1883[3]	50,000	Promissory notes	12	4.5
1 Oct, 1883[3]	50,000	Promissory notes	12	4.5
27 Aug, 1884[1]	100,000	Bills	12	4.5
20 May, 1885[1]	50,000	Bills	12	4
Average	£76,923			

Sources: [1] UB (Glasgow) *Accountant's Minute,* as at dates   [2] UBPL, as at dates   [3] UBM, as at dates

sector. In August 1883, the Castle Co, encountering an emergency need for cash in addition to the credit of £150,000 granted in February, asked Gairdner to give another large advance for £100,000.[43] Gairdner did not confine the authorisation despite a plea by James Currie, director of the Union Bank and the brother of Donald Currie. Negotiations took nearly two months, and the credits were sanctioned in the autumn of that year to the extent that the Curries demanded.[44]

The two cases of Haputale and Castle financing had no common feature in terms of method and condition of advances. The only common aspect was that both companies were the Bank directors' concerns. The Ceylon scheme of the Haputale Co, was successfully initiated thanks to the assistance of the Union Bank, and especially to Gairdner. Also in the case of the Castle Co, Gairdner complied with the request of a director of the Bank though negotiations were rather prolonged. From these two examples, it may be concluded that the directors' concerns had priority over the other customers. Indeed, the large additional advances to the Castle Co were sanctioned in the middle of the difficulties over the Thomson affairs. The Castle Packet financing also suggests another point—that the bank found difficulty in separating itself from the large borrower, as the Union Bank did in the case of the Dennistouns in the 1850s and early 1860s. Unfortunately, the Union Bank was trapped by another case in this period, that is, the Thomson affairs.

(b) J & G THOMSON FINANCING

The firm of J & G Thomson was set up in 1847 by James R and George P Thomson, both of whom were trained at the famous shipyard of Robert Napier. The first record of the Union Bank authorising a credit to the Thomsons appeared in the minute of the board in May 1855.[45] Thereafter, the volume of Thomson financing accumulated, standing at £110,000 in the summer of 1879,[46] when the Thomsons asked the Union Bank to allow an additional credit for £25,453 on the ground that,

> We have here with approximate statements of our affairs, and we would beg to accompany same with one or two remarks in explanation. We beg to say, as regards the results of last year's working, that it has been quite apparent to us for some months back, that to push forward the work so as to earn instalments enhanced very heavy extra outlay. Added to this, however, were drawbacks of a much more serious character, which are now removed by the additional alterations recently made, viz: (1) the want of dock accommodation at our yard and the heavy expense for the work in Harbour consequent thereon: (2) the want of adequate Engine shop, thereby entailing very large and costly amounts of over time, to keep pace with the building yard.[47]

As is suggested in the letter, a part of the shipbuilding works had lately in 1874 been transferred from Finnieston to Dalmuir on account of a scheme of the Clyde Trust.[48] The expense of transfer for £50,000 was supplied by the Union Bank.[49] Through the 1870s, the Thomsons were making remarkable progress, building a steel paddle steamer and so competing with other big shipbuilders such as William Denny & Bros of Dumbarton and John Elder & Co.[50] The Thomsons were borrowers with a bright future and the Union Bank must have anticipated good returns from their business.

The partial transfer of their works resulted in heavier fixed capital on account of the want of dock accommodation and an inadequate engine shop, as they complained. Moreover, they had to face the more fundamental problem of a shortage of workers 'owing to the want of travelling accommodation between Clydebank and Partick'.[51] The separation of their works was, thus, apparently a great mistake even though they were forced into it. These circumstances were serious for the Thomsons whose financial burden fell entirely upon the Union Bank, and the result was heavier involvement in the Thomson affairs.

The debts of the Thomsons totalled £123,977 in the spring of 1881 when a tragedy happened as the report, afterwards made by William MacKinnon, external auditor of the Union Bank, revealed that,

> the result of a fire which occurred in the shipyard at Dalmuir in April 1881, destroying totally the joiners' shop, and the greater part of internal fitting of the *Servia* and other ships then in course of construction. The shop was insured but the delay occasioned was great and work had to be given out, which entailed loss.[52]

The *Servia* was the third ocean-going steel ship in Britain, built for the Cunard line, following the two launched by Denny & Bros, and was the largest—with the exception of the *Great Eastern,*—of 515 feet length and 7,392 gross tons.[53] This accident resulted in an unusual relationship between the Union Bank and the Thomsons, not in the way that 'the device of the short-term loan became an instrument of long-term investment'[54] as Professor P Mathias has suggested and, indeed, the Bank hitherto did, but in the way that the bank directly intervened in the management of Thomsons'.

Firstly, the Union Bank considered a conversion of the firm of Thomson into a public company which must have been considered by Gairdner and the directors in order to have a wider choice in raising funds, thus relieving the Union Bank of further involvement in the Thomsons' and also enhancing its capacity. For this purpose, the Bank asked two firms of chartered accountants, Anderson, Muir & Main and M'Clelland, MacKinnon & Blyth, to make a report on '(1) the amount of capital necessary for the new Company, (2) the capability at the works . . . to compete economically with other shipbuilding yards',[55] which was submitted in the summer of 1882 recommending that,

> (1) Capital; £300,000 of which £200,000 might be subscribed in shares and £100,000 borrowed on mortgage or debenture would be sufficient.
> (2) Capability; This being a question which appeared most capable of being determined by a person having large practical experience as a shipbuilder and engineer.
> (3) The advantages which may be expected to result from the concentration of works at Dalmuir; Mr James Thomson estimated . . . £15,000 per annum.[56]

The scheme of conversion into a limited company was met with downright rejection by the Thomsons, and, as a result, only the third recommendation survived.[57] For the purpose of transferring further parts of the works from Finnieston to Dalmuir, the Union Bank immediately allowed a credit for £30,000.[58]

More importantly, Gairdner and the directors ignored, or hesitated, to adopt promptly, the second recommendation in spite of a remarkable letter, written by P Denny of Denny & Bros of Dumbarton and attached to the report, saying that,

> Messrs Thomson, I have looked into your last sheets of *Thames* in comparison with our *Clyde*. In the carpenters' timber in your sheet there must be a considerable error. . . . In the total wages there is a considerable difference in excess of ours. We had several advantages over you. . . . I don't know as to the effect of your disastrous fire on cost of the *Thames*. That may have had the effect of increasing probably.[59]

Denny's letter suggests that 'the Thomson affairs' resulted not only from the disastrous fire, but also from a probable 'mismanagement', especially of a technical kind. It was debatable whether the bank should take any action, say, intervention, when it was acknowledged that its borrower had defects in management. However, in the case of the Thomsons, the hesitation of Gairdner and the directors certainly aggravated their affairs.

The Thomsons were again hit by an accident in December 1882 when a new steam ship, *Aurania,* broke down on her maiden voyage to New York, apparently on account of mechanical faults. Finally, the reluctance of Gairdner and the directors to intervene in the management of Thomsons' disappeared. The real situation of the Thomsons had deteriorated to such a degree that,

> any other course would probably involve the suspension of the business and an enforced winding up in the results.[60]

Thus, in February 1883, Gairdner asked William MacKinnon to investigate closely the financial situation of Thomsons'. MacKinnon made a report upon which Gairdner drew up a reconstruction plan for Thomsons'.

According to the plan, the Thomsons were to be allowed large advances. Firstly, £100,000 was to be lent directly to the firm which should apply this to reducing its arrears of debts. Ironically, the Union Bank had to supply funds to the Thomsons in order to lessen the amount it had lent. This must be an example of a bad loan and certainly a strange one. Secondly, the Bank promised, in order to transfer the entire Thomson works to Dalmuir, to supply to the extent of £100,000, including £30,000 already supplied in August 1882, funds which were to be secured by 'the demand drafts for work done and bond over the works or otherwise'.[61] Thus far was the ordinary business of banking.

Besides the large advances to the extent of £200,000, another loan was stipulated in the reconstruction plan, as the minute recorded that,

> The loan of £40,000, not to claim against the firm in competition with business debts,

contracted after the date of the loan, but to take precedence of the sum of £100,000 referred to . . . which is to be a debt of the partners as individuals.[62]

At the same time, the Bank arranged with MacKinnon to the effect that,

> Mr MacKinnon shall enter into an agreement with the firm in which he will undertake that on the capital at the credit of partners being made up to £60,000 he will lend the firm £40,000 which shall not be repayable until all business debts contracted after the date of the loan shall have been paid, but in a condition, (1) that the loan shall be repayable on 1st January 1888. . . . Mr MacKinnon shall grant a receipt to each contributor to the fund. . . .[63]

According to the agreement, the fund of £40,000 was to be placed in the hands of MacKinnon who was in charge of collecting contributions from the third party to the fund and, thus, making up the capital of Thomsons' to £100,000. This arrangement was, it might be construed, a step towards converting the firm of Thomsons' into an incorporated company because the total amount of loans for £240,000, which the Bank promised, and the expected amount of contributions for £60,000, made up £300,000, which was exactly the same sum as the report of chartered accountants recommended in 1882. If this guess is right, a receipt, which was to be issued by MacKinnon, could be regarded as a kind of debenture. From this, we may deduce that Gairdner and the directors envisaged the financing of the Thomsons in the light of converting the private firm into 'J & G Thomson, Ltd.' Indeed, Thomson Ltd, was formed in 1889, when the loan of £40,000 was to be extinguished. The fund of £40,000 was termed a 'guarantee fund' by the directors who themselves contributed to it.[64]

Compensation for the tremendous amount of advances, naturally, had to be paid by the Thomsons who accepted the following conditions that,

> (1) The management at the works, and the causes which led to the unsatisfactory results of recent years to be examined into by Mr MacKinnon with a view to the introduction of such reforms as may, in his opinion, be necessary for the efficient conduct of business. Every facility shall be afforded to Mr MacKinnon to enable him to carry the purpose into execution.
> (2) As regards the future conduct of business, Mr MacKinnon to be consulted as to the loans and conditions of new contracts, and generally as to all questions of importance which may arise. A manager of first class experience to be got for the work.
> (3) Drawings of future and all outlays, at the work, to be placed on a most economical footing under Mr MacKinnon's supervision.[65]

MacKinnon also recommended that,

> 1st, that an able and thoroughly capable man is secured and put in charge as general manager of the shipbuilding yard.
> 2nd, that engineering department of the business be removed from Finnieston to Dalmuir. It is estimated this will cost something like £30,000.
> 3rd, that a more active and direct superintendence and control of the general conduct of the business be taken and the proposed arrangement points to this being put into operation now.[66]

Regarding the replacement of the general manager, the Thomsons first showed disapproval, preferring the present manager. Their resistance could be understandable if we think of their being proud of 'a thorough practical training and nearly twenty years' experience as engineer and shipbuilder.'[67] The Thomsons could not resist for long, and advertisements to recruit 'A thoroughly qualified manager for a large shipbuilding yard'[68] appeared in newspapers in the middle of March 1883. As a result, J G Wilson, who was formerly superintendent of shipbuilding yards at Leith and Barrow, was to be appointed general manager in July 1883.[69]

MacKinnon's investigation started in the spring of 1883 revealing another two problems. Firstly, there was 'trouble with the iron workers and consequent rise in wages,'[70] although transport facilities had already been provided by the opening of the North British railway line. Details of the rises in wages are not known, but a rise in wages for nearly 5,000 workers must have been another problem for the Thomsons. Secondly, it turned out that 'a further sum of £30,000 is required for the purpose of moving the engine shop and foundry from Finnieston Street to Clydebank.'[71] Though advances to the extent of £100,000 were promised for this purpose, the Union Bank did not immediately allow the credit. Instead they waited until November 1884 when works at Clydebank were nearly completed.[72] Consequently, the management of Thomsons' was put entirely under the control of the Union Bank for at least a year and a half from the spring of 1883 to the autumn of 1884.

The two successive accidents and the consequent financial difficulties gave rise to rumour about the Thomsons and the Union Bank, especially after the institution of the guarantee fund from which people learned about the critical situation of Thomsons'. In July 1883 when subscriptions to the fund were almost completed, James Currie, director of the Bank, expressed his anxiety that,

> Within the last two or three days I have heard that Thomsons are under trust deed and that an allusion in the Glasgow News to the pecuniary difficulties of a firm employing nearly 5,000 men referred to them. My general reply was that some of Mr James Thomson's friends and trustees are interested in the company and that some vague language must have misled the gossips and that I had every reason to believe they were going on as usual.[73]

Despite the confidence of Currie, the Bank could not avoid troubles caused by these rumours which spread even up to Perth. The Perth cashier sent a report to Gairdner that,

> There is a good deal of talk going on in Perth about the report in the paper that several Scotch banks are largely interested in some shipping venture, the Union and Clydesdale being chiefly spoken about . . . it occurred to me that it might be of advantage if you (unreadable) to clear the good name of the Union.[74]

Rumours about the Thomsons and the Union Bank did not cease until February 1884 when the trial of the 'Aurania' was successfully held. Thus, the most crucial stage of Thomson financing had passed. The three years between

1881 and 1884 had really witnessed tremendous difficulties with regard to the Union Bank, as Sir Charles Tennant, deputy chairman, wrote in retrospect that,

> I am inclined to think that we have seen the worst of the business and think we shall see an improvement towards the close of year.[75]

Indeed, as Sir Charles predicted, Thomson financing at last reached the stage at the end of 1884 that 'The work now in progress . . . would yield a fair profit.'[76]

The intervention of the Union Bank in the management of the Thomsons was the result of its heavy involvement in their business which had already developed prior to the two accidents. This was the vicious circle in which the Western Bank of Scotland and the City of Glasgow Bank collapsed. Fortunately for the Union Bank, the general climate of shipbuilding on the Clydeside was so favourable that the Bank had time to convert the firm of Thomsons into an incorporated company thus being able to minimise further involvement.

The Thomsons, though they were suffering from their own technical troubles, were undoubtedly one of the largest shipbuilders on the Clyde, launching many fine ocean-going Cunarders. Gairdner and the directors must have seen that the business of Thomsons would be profitable if it were put on a sounder basis. A bright future was also seen because of 'the increase of Royal Navy'[77] whose business was tremendously profitable as Table 57 clearly shows. Surprisingly, the estimated profit of building the 'Scout' was £13,600 which was 70% of the total profits of Thomsons'. The profit rate was at least twice as large as those of civil ships. This was why the capability and capacity of Thomsons' had to be enhanced by the concentration of their works at Clydebank, and this was also why Gairdner was so generous in supplying large funds and the directors of the Bank were very anxious to obtain orders from the Admiralty.[78] Indeed, the newly-built Clydebank shipyard of Thomsons' was apparently one of the most modernised works with powerful overhead travelling cranes, a complete system of hydraulic machinery in lieu of the usual steam appliance and a locomotive tractor and steam travellers over a railway system. The capacity of their shipyard was, thus, raised from

TABLE 57

Estimated Profits of Thomsons'

	(1) *Estimated Cost*	(2) *Contract Price*	(3) *Estimated Profit*	(4) *Profit Rate*
Lake Superior (Cunard)	£78,000	£82,000	£4,000	5%
Scout (Admiralty)	53,000	66,600	13,600	26
Brayne's Boat	14,000	16,000	2,000	14
Hardie's Boat	17,000	17,000	0	0
Total	£162,000	£181,600	£19,600	12%

Source: TP, 2/12/1884

3,000 tons to 8,000 tons, and the number of workers also increased from 1,500 at Finnieston to 5,000 at Clydebank. Clydebank emerged as a new industrial town with railway stations, a post office, churches and schools.[79] Ironically, the rather unusual example in British banking of the bank intervening in the management of the customer not only relieved the customer of financial difficulties but also contributed to the establishment of Clydebank, from which a large and fine fleet of steel ships was launched.

4   The Structure of the Union Bank of Scotland

(a) DIRECTORS *v.* SHAREHOLDERS

Between 1865 and 1878, the Union Bank of Scotland was not challenged by the rest of the Glasgow-based banks, the Clydesdale and the City of Glasgow Banks, in terms of profits. In 1867 and 1875, the Union Bank was even able to challenge the Edinburgh banks, ranking third. But after the 1878 crisis, it began to face the rivalry of the Clydesdale Bank which, indeed, first caught up on the Union Bank in the two successive years of 1881 and 1882 as is exhibited in Diagram 10. As a result, the Union Bank sank into seventh place in terms of profits among the Scottish banks, which was the worst since 1865 when the balance sheets of the Scottish banks began to be published. Gairdner and the directors of the Union Bank were shocked to find their Bank lagging behind the younger and smaller Clydesdale. It was against this circumstance that 'quasi window-dressing' of the Bank's balance sheet was undertaken, to show an increase in profits.

There was a problem which was undoubtedly shared by other banks as well as joint-stock companies in general, and that was that the larger profits caused claims by the shareholders to enlarge the dividend. In this dilemma, Gairdner and the directors did not hesitate to show larger profits despite possible objections by their shareholders. The concern of Gairdner and the directors is well exemplified in the task of drawing up the annual report, in the spring of 1884 when an influential director, Colin Campbell, wrote to Gairdner that,

> I regret to see that our losses total up to such a large sum and so many . . . I can only hope that the profits may come out as you say £162^m [£162,000] and while I would have liked to have slipped an extra 10^m into a corner, I fear we cannot show less than 137 and if all stories are true I fancy our neighbour cannot do better this year. I only wish that we could think that the worst was over and good times approaching.[80]

From the expectation that 'our losses total up to such a large sum', Gairdner, looking over balance sheets of other banks, started the task of increasing artificially their profits, which is further suggested by letters from Campbell saying that,

> 4^m will certainly . . . enable us to put out of the 5 . . . and make a good show. It is I think a good plan to carry fair and a large sum as when this is added to the profit . . .

The B of S statement looks well but there may be Skeleton somewhere. I fear our deposits will show decrease,[81]

and that,

Some of which (profit and loss accounts of branches) are good and we can only hope the latter tend to go to the good at Head Office . . . shall be well pleased if you turn the 140^m for the public, but anyhow I think we can have 5^m for guarantee.[82]

It was absolutely apparent that the target of Gairdner and Campbell was to 'turn the 140^m for the public'. Indeed, the profits of 1883/1884 turned out to be £140,162, which was a little more than the anticipated sum and a little smaller than those of the Commercial Bank of Scotland, and the Union Bank regained its status of the senior Glasgow bank, though its deposits decreased, as Campbell feared.[83] '5^m for guarantee' might be slipped into the balance sheet. Upon Gairdner's successful task, congratulations were offered by two directors. Seton Thomson wrote that,

My congratulation to you for such a good account. I must say that I like Mr Campbell should like to see us show £140,000. I feel that we can do so and I am confident that the public who have heard how we have got out of recent mercantile troubles, would be disappointed if we showed less.[84]

Frederick Pitman wrote that,

Taking everything into consideration the result is more satisfactory than I expected. The only hope I felt inclined to express was 'Show more than £140,000' and I would have telegraphed this but did not like receiving the risk of publicity of telegram. I am glad to hear . . . that you have so arranged.[85]

It is not clear how and where Gairdner found the sum of £5,000 suggested in Campbell's letter. There is, unfortunately, no record to provide us with a clue. It could be construed that Gairdner transferred a part of the losses or some of the charges for the business year of 1883/84 to the next annual balance account. No matter how it was done, in the case of the Union Bank, 'window-dressing' was made by way of an artificial increase in profits. It was said theoretically that,

Periodically, the banks resort to a device known to the City editors of the newspaper as 'Window-dressing'. That is to say, at times it is considered to be available for the banks to show in their balance sheets large amounts of cash in hand and at the Bank of England. It is sometimes done just before the publication of the monthly statements, and almost always at the half-yearly balancing and publication of accounts. To accomplish the desired result, the banks either let their loans run off, or else call in money from the short loan fund of the market.[86]

On account of a slight deviation from the theory, the case of the Union Bank could be termed 'quasi window-dressing'.

As the profits came out just as Gairdner and the directors had eagerly

DIAGRAM 10

Profits of the Union Bank of Scotland in Comparison with the Clydesdale Bank and the Bank of Scotland, 1879–85

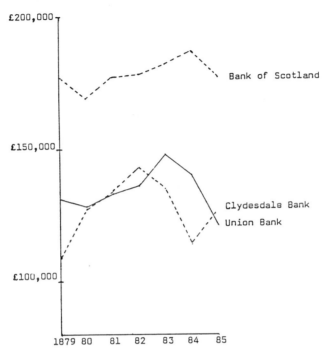

Sources: UB *Annual Reports*
        A W Kerr, 1898, pp. 46–66

hoped, the first barrier to surmount was the external audit. However, that was no problem at all because it is very difficult to believe that William MacKinnon, external auditor, who had already deeply committed himself to the most crucial business of the Union Bank, that is, Thomson financing, could be disapproving of the manipulation of his friend, Gairdner. In fact, the annual balance sheet of 1884 easily 'satisfied the auditors'.[87] Therefore, it should again be claimed that the external audit was quite different from the independent audit.[88]

The last barrier was the annual meeting of the shareholders, whose holdings of the Bank shares are set out in Table 58.

Remarkably, as little as 1.3% of the total proprietors held almost one-third of the Bank capital, and a little more than one-tenth of them owned nearly 60% of the capital stock. The largest shareholders are set out in Table 59; the Dennistouns were the relatives of Seton Thomson, director, C Campbell himself director, C Tennant deputy chairman, J Y Buchanan director, P Stirling extraordinary director and J Buchanan, T R Buchanan and

W D Gairdner relatives of the director and general manager. In the aggregate, holdings of the deputy chairman, ordinary and extraordinary directors, general manager (see also Table 68) and their relatives amounted to 19% of the Bank shares, which certainly made it easier for Gairdner and the directors to get their policy through the annual meeting. Indeed, 'the annual meeting (of April 1884) of the Bank . . . passed off so quietly and so satisfactory. The report . . . pleased the shareholders and all concerned.'[89]

TABLE 58

Ownership of the Union Bank, 1885

	(1) Number of Shareholders	%	(2) Cumulative Number	%	(3) Number of Shares	%	(4) Cumulative Number of Shares	%
Over 1,000	7	0.4	7	0.4	16,550	16.6	16,550	16.6
1,000–501	15	0.9	22	1.3	10,820	10.8	27,370	27.4
500–101	144	9.1	166	10.4	30,627	30.6	57,997	58.0
Under 100	1,422	89.6	1,588	100.0	42,003	42.0	100,000	100.0

Source: UB *List of Shareholders 1885*

TABLE 59

Large Shareholders, 1885

1	A Dennistoun (Golfhill, in trust of Miss Mary Dennistoun)	5,500
2	C Campbell (director of the Bank)	3,100
3	Baron Roissard de Bellet (Paris)	2,250
4	R Dennistoun (in trust of the late)	2,010
5	G C White (Ayr)	1,585
6	C Tennant (deputy chairman of the Bank, MP, of St Rollox)	1,100
7	G Barbour (Edinburgh)	1,005
8	T R Buchanan (MP, Edinburgh)	1,000
9	J F Monteith (of Carstairs)	865
10	J Y Buchanan (director of the Bank)	850
11	F C Buchanan (Helensburgh)	840
12	J A Jamieson & G Dalziel (WS, Edinburgh, in trust)	771
13	J Buchanan (Edinburgh, executors of the late)	737
14	A Russell (Glasgow)	700
14	J Wilson (Killearn Station)	700
14	W D Gairdner (Ayr)	700
17	A R Forbes (University Club, Edinburgh)	657
18	Miss Barbara Anderson (Edinburgh)	650
18	Miss Christina Anderson (Edinburgh)	650
20	A Rutherfurd (Glasgow)	645
21	P Stirling (of Kippendavie, Perthshire)	550
22	R Blair (Confectioner, Edinburgh)	505

27,370

Source: as of Table 58

Whether larger profits provoked claims by the shareholders to increase the dividend is not exactly known, but it can be suspected that there might be certain demands, as C Campbell expressed that,

> I am glad to think we can meet the objection that our profits are always large!!! So that if the shareholders suffer we shall please the public.[90]

In the circumstances of the Bank being confronted with the Thomson affairs and suffering from rumours about even its own financial situation and also being almost overtaken by the Clydesdale Bank, profits, at least larger than those of the fellow Glasgow bank, were of vital importance for Gairdner and the directors to maintain their status. Their policy towards the shareholders was seemingly successful, though the Union Bank was again overtaken by the Clydesdale Bank in 1885. The dividend was not raised during this whole period, remaining at 12%.

(b) THE CHANGE OF THE PATTERN OF BRANCH NETWORK

Between 1879 and 1885, the Union Bank, probably together with other banks, rarely opened a new country branch. Indeed, the Scottish banks were often in negotiation with each other to withdraw their branches. First in February 1880, the board of the Union Bank resolved that,

> This Bank was to withdraw from Neilston in favour of the Clydesdale Bank; and the Clydesdale Bank to withdraw from Bathgate in favour of this Bank. . . . It was further agreed that a donation of £150 should be paid, after the lapse of one year, to the present agent of the Clydesdale Bank in Bathgate, provided their deposits business shall then have been in main transferred to this Bank.[91]

Arrangements to the same effect were made with the Commercial, National Banks and Bank of Scotland which withdrew their business at Kincardine in 1880, Bridge of Allan in 1882 and Johnstone in 1882 respectively. In exchange for these withdrawals, the Union Bank retreated from Peebles, Selkirk and Montrose, and Innerleithen in favour of the Commercial Bank, the National Bank and the Bank of Scotland respectively.[92] In addition, the Union Bank independently discontinued four branches at Hatton, Kincraigie, Lumsden and Bothwell and also reduced branches at Stonehouse and Blairgowrie to sub-branches.[93] Apparently, the Union Bank was following the policy of tightening the branch network.

Maps 4, 5 and 6 suggest that a fundamental change in branch distribution during the whole period from the outset of the Union Bank to 1885 happened between 1844, a year after the Bank adopted the national title, and 1858, when it accomplished rapid growth. From Map 4, we can see how moderate the branch network of the Union Bank was despite its claim of being a national bank. More than two-thirds of the branches were located in the West and South and there were no branches in the Grampian area and Tayside, as Table 60 shows. At first, the branch network of the Bank covered the whole nation in the late 1850s as Map 5 exhibits, numbering 99. By comparison with this

MAP 4

Regional Distribution of Branches of the Union Bank of Scotland, 1844

TABLE 60

Number of Branches, 1844, 1858 and 1885

		1844	1858	1885
1	Strathclyde	15	29	45
2	Grampian	0	22	24
3	Tayside	0	16	17
4	Lothian	1	3	9
5	Dumfries & Galloway	3	9	9
6	Central	4	8	8
7	Fife	3	5	6
8	Shetland & Orkney	1	2	5
9	Highlands	0	2	2
10	Borders	0	3	0
	Total	27	99	125

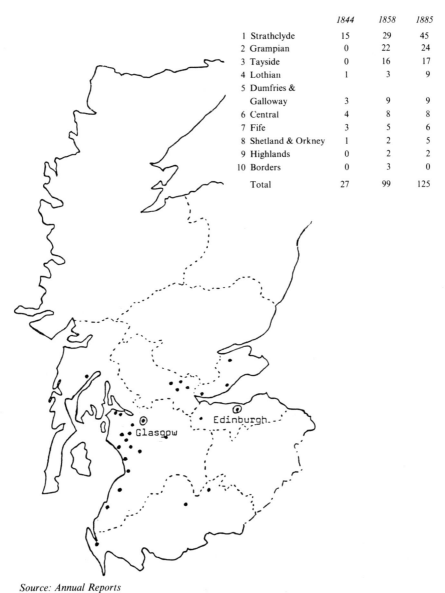

Source: Annual Reports

MAP 5

Regional Distribution of Branches of the Union Bank of Scotland, 1858

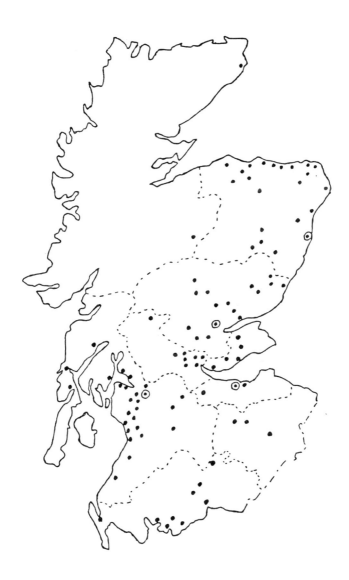

Note: ⊙; Glasgow, Edinburgh, Perth and Aberdeen

Source: UB *List of Branches 1858*

MAP 6

Regional Distribution of Branches of the Union Bank of Scotland, 1885

Note   ⊙ ; Glasgow, Edinburgh, Perth and Aberdeen
          ✗ ; Branches withdrawn since 1858

Source: UB *List of Branches 1885*

tremendous development, any fundamental or remarkable change cannot be seen from 1858 to 1885. It could be, therefore, argued that the pattern of the Union Bank branch establishment was basically settled by the late 1850s.

However, it was also true that the number of branches had increased. In terms of regional distribution, thirteen were created in the North and East, among which five were in Edinburgh and two in Aberdeen, and sixteen were created in the West, among which five were in Glasgow.[94] This pattern of establishing branches suggests that the money of the Union Bank was flowing increasingly from the North and East to the West and was also due to the further concentration of population in big cities where large deposits were expected to be gathered, as we have seen in the 1870s.

What factors did slow down the further development of branch establishment? One thing is obvious, that the retardation resulted from the agreed withdrawals of branches negotiated among the Scottish banks. The number of Scottish bank branches might be approaching a limit. Indeed, the average increase of the Scottish branches per year was seven from 1879 to 1885, in contrast to fifteen in the period between 1865 and 1879.[95]

The Union Bank in particular was led by Charles Gairdner who from the earlier years of his office hesitated before creating branches[96] and still, or increasingly, held to this attitude as the Edinburgh manager, H H Norie reveals that;

> The BLCo. are to open in Fraserburgh in a few days, and No. of Scotland opened in Lerwick. I am afraid I can no longer prevent our board from entertaining the offers of agencies which every now and then crop up. You know my opinion on this subject is the same as your own, you can easily understand that it is difficult for me to persuade our directors that we ought not to endeavour to enlarge our business.[97]

It is not known where the directors wished to create branches and what the results were, but it is quite clear that Gairdner and his fellow Edinburgh manager objected to any further creation of branches. Norie's letter also suggests that Gairdner, together with the Edinburgh manager, was reluctant 'to enlarge our business' in general. It could be argued that the development of branch network was a 'highly important expansive factor'[98] as S E Thomas suggested and, therefore, that the Union Bank of Scotland lost the initiative to develop its overall business when its leader, Charles Gairdner, preferred a policy of maintaining the *status quo*.

Intensive inspection of branches continued. In one case, a branch with a small deficiency of £20 had to undergo a special investigation by the head office inspector.[99] Otherwise, reports of irregularities in the conduct of agencies almost disappeared from the minute book. Dismissal of an agent was reported in only one case, at the Doune branch, whose agent ignored instructions from the head office, causing a large decrease in deposits.[100] In addition to regular inspections, Gairdner, together with some of the directors, undertook holiday trips making surprise inspections especially in the North.[101] Regular and thorough branch inspections were a rooted policy of Gairdner.

The largest and most important branch of the Union Bank was, of course, the London office which increasingly placed funds in short-term lending and government securities as has been discussed already. In order to supervise this office, the Union Bank instituted a London committee which was composed of Gairdner, three to four directors and the head inspector, A B Henderson. The committee usually visited London twice yearly, in March and October.[102] In inspecting the London office, Gairdner attached the most importance to portfolios of investments and securities of short-term loans to bill and stock brokers. Usually one of the directors, accompanied by the London manager, proceeded to the Bank of England verifying its books in which the government securities purchased by the Union Bank were actually kept. It was also on these occasions that sales and purchases of government securities, on a large scale, were planned and executed. Inspections of the London office did not reveal any irregularities, at least until 1890.[103]

(c) THE STRUCTURE, 1885

Various records regarding the staff and salaries in this period provide us with more details than at any previous period—from which we can re-build the structure of the Union Bank of Scotland in 1885.

Important changes in the posts of the higher staff in this period occurred exclusively in the London and Edinburgh offices. In January 1880 when the London assistant accountant, A B Shand, was re-employed by the Bank of Africa, a clerk at London succeeded to the office.[104] In April 1883 when the London assistant manager, J R Murray, successfully applied for the vacancy as Kirkcaldy agent, another clerk at London succeeded to the office.[105] Furthermore in November 1884 when the new assistant manager resigned to go to an unknown bank, the Aberdeen secretary, A Gordon, was transferred to the office. The vacancy for the Aberdeen secretaryship was filled by the sub-inspector of the Glasgow head office, W Mitchell.[106] In Edinburgh, two changes were made. In May 1881 when the manager, A Butter, requested a transfer to Perth on account of an unknown conflict between him and his staff, the directors accepted it, appointing the Perth cashier, H H Norie, to be Edinburgh manager.[107] In October 1882 when the Edinburgh secretary, J Norwell, died, the confidential clerk to the manager and secretary at Edinburgh succeeded to the office.[108]

These examples of staff movement suggest some features of branch character. In the first place, London was the place where Scottish young bankers were recruited by other banks, especially by overseas banks. This case is exemplified by A B Shand, who was obviously a native of Scotland and who probably started his banking career there, possibly in the Union Bank. He was recruited by the Union Bank from the Merchants' Bank of Canada at the opening of the London office[109] and, in a brief tenure of less than two years, resigned to take office in another overseas bank. London must have been regarded by young Scottish bankers as a gateway to success. Indeed, some of the Union Bank staff were very anxious to go to London even without an increase in their salaries.[110]

In the second place, three vacancies for higher posts, that is, London assistant manager, Edinburgh manager and secretary, were filled by the staff at the London, Edinburgh, Aberdeen and Perth offices. None of the Glasgow head office staff was appointed to these offices. The fact that notable transfers of the higher staff happened entirely between London and cities on the east coast of Scotland suggests that there might be a certain similarity in the character of business in these cities, especially between London and Edinburgh both of which were financial centres.

In the third place, there emerged another higher ranked branch to which staff wished to be promoted, that is, the Kirkcaldy office. The case is illustrated by J E Murray who was promoted from the Leith agency to be assistant manager at London office in 1878. When the vacancy at the Kirkcaldy agency occurred, Murray, successfully applied, although competition with a solicitor at Kirkcaldy and three of the Kirkcaldy staff was severe.[111] Consequently, we may add the Kirkcaldy office to the group of important branches of Kilmarnock, Greenock, Paisley, Perth and Leith.[112]

Regarding recruitment for the junior staff, only the case of the Edinburgh office is known, and this is set out in Table 61. Remarkably, nearly 85% of the Edinburgh staff, who were in the service of the Union Bank between 1879 and 1885 were recruited from the offices under the charge of the Edinburgh directors. The Stranraer branch, which was under the Glasgow head office, used to be the branch of the banking firm of Sir William Forbes & Co. The Perth branch also had a close relationship with the Edinburgh office as the case of the Perth cashier being promoted to be Edinburgh manager indicates. It is quite understandable that the Edinburgh directors selected their staff from branches with which they were well acquainted. It should also be noted that nearly two-thirds of the Edinburgh staff were recruited inside the city of Edinburgh, that is, from the head office and town branches. D R Kemp entered the Union Bank at the Edinburgh head office in April 1862, being

TABLE 61

Years and Places of Entrance to the Union Bank of Edinburgh Staff

	Prior to 1858	1858/ 1865	1866/ 1878	1879/ 1885	Total
1 Edinburgh Head Office	6	5	6	1	18
2 Edinburgh Town Branches*	0	0	9	0	9
3 Other Edinburgh Branches†	1	3	5	1	10
4 Other Branches & Bank					
(a) Elgin	0	0	1	0	1
(b) Kilmarnock	0	1	0	0	1
(c) Perth	0	0	0	3	3
(d) Stranraer	0	1	0	0	1
(e) Ship Bank	1	0	0	0	1
Total	8	10	21	5	44

*Downie Place, Forrest Road, Haymarket, Hunter Square, Morningside, Newington and Norton Park in 1885
† Lerwick, Kirkwall, Leith and Kirkcaldy

Source: UB (Edinburgh), *Staff and Salary Records*

TABLE 62

Salaries of the Union Bank Staff, 1880–85*

	(1) Glasgow Head Office	(2) Edinburgh Head Office	(3) London Office	(4) Glasgow Branches	(5) Edinburgh Branches	(6) Total
1880	£23,444	£7,057	£4,456	£43,510	£5,460	£83,927
	28%	8%	5%	52%	7%	100.0%
1881	23,920	6,947	4,761	43,471	5,480	84,579
	28	8	6	52	6	100.8
1882	24,000	6,862	5,251	42,624	5,505	84,242
	28	8	6	51	7	100.4
1883	23,990	5,952	5,338	42,515	5,770	83,565
	29	7	6	51	7	99.6
1884	23,305	6,272	5,498	42,537	6,060	83,672
	28	7	7	51	7	99.7
1885	23,320	6,422	5,358	42,674	6,345	84,119
	28	8	6	51	7	100.2

*% of columns 1–5; as of total. % of column 6; growth rate; 1880; 100. Date as in April each year

Sources: UB (Glasgow), MSS. UB (Edinburgh), Staff and Salary Records

transferred to the George Street branch as receipt clerk. Next, he was promoted to clerk at that branch and returned to the head office in 1864 as receipt clerk, continuing until 1870 when he was given the higher duty of ledger clerk. In four years, he was again transferred, this time to the Canongate branch (discontinued before 1885) as agent and returned to the head office in 1876 as confidential clerk, which was the highest post among clerks. Eventually in 1883, when the secretary died, he succeeded to that office.[113]

TABLE 63

Salaries of Major Officials of the Union Bank, 1885

1	General Manager (C Gairdner)	£3,500
2	Glasgow Assistant Manager (J Affleck)	2,000
3	London Manager (J A Fradgley)	1,750
4	Glasgow Cashier (G N Hill)	1,500
5	Edinburgh Manager (H H Norie)	1,000
5	Glasgow Secretary (J Gray)	1,000
5	Edinburgh Secretary (J Norwell)	1,000*
5	Glasgow Inspector (A B Henderson)	1,000
9	Aberdeen Cashier (J Cook)	850
10	Edinburgh Secretary (D R Kemp)	700
11	Glasgow Accountant (G Willock)	600
11	London Assistant Manager (J E Murray)	600†
11	Perth Cashier (A Butter)	600

*Died in 1883 and succeeded by D R Kemp
†1880

Sources: UB (Glasgow), MSS. UB (Edinburgh), *Staff and Salary Records.* UBSB

Comprehensive material on the salaries of the Union Bank staff are for the first time available in this period. The total amount of their salaries did not visibly increase as Table 62 shows, in contrast to the sharp increase in the years of 1866/79, and even decreased from 1881 to 1883 when the Bank was suffering severely from the Thomson affairs. Gairdner and the directors must have been keeping increases in the staff salaries, which were a major item of the Bank charges in the profit and loss account, in check. The decline in the cost of living was also a factor, enabling the Bank to keep salaries down.[114]

Salaries of the major officials of the Union Bank are set out in Table 63. Eight of the thirteen officials enjoyed salaries of more than £1,000 which 'represented considerable worldly success ... and placed a man, economically speaking, well towards the top of the middle classes'.[115] Above all, £3,500 for the general manager, which was double the initial salary of £1,750 in 1862, was far more than most incomes of the upper middle classes and thirty times larger than the average salary of the staff at the secretary's department of the Edinburgh office in 1885 (see Table 65). Indeed, the Scottish general manager was a grandee 'of a somewhat remote kind'[116] as Professor Checkland argued. The list of salaries of major officials also suggests that there was

TABLE 64

Edinburgh Staff of the Union Bank, 1881–85   Source: as of Table 61

		(1) Office Duty	(2) Place & Year of Entrance		(3) Salary 81/82	82/83	83/84	84/85
A	**Officials**							
1	H H Norie	Manager	Kilmarnock	1859	£1,000	£1,000	£1,000	£1,000
2	J Norwell	Secretary	Ship Bank	1835	1,000	1,000	(r)	
3	J Smith	Accountant	HO	1846	400	400	400	400
4	D R Kemp	Secretary	HO	1862			500	700
	sub total				2,400	2,400	1,900	2,100
B	**Cashier's Department**							
5	C W Cowans	Teller	HO	1857	300	300	(r)	
6	J R MacGibbon	Teller	HO	1862	200	200	(t)	
7	R Glegg	Teller	HO	1863	180	180	200	200
8	J R Jones	Teller	HO	1869	160	160	170	170
9	P Peace	Teller	Kirkwall	1858			220	220
10	J Shand	Teller	Lerwick	1868			150	150
	sub total				840	840	740	740
C	**Secretary's Department**							
	(a) Securities, dividend, transfer and enter special correspondence							
11	D R Kemp	Confidential clerk	HO	1862	350	350	(to A4)	
12	J Shand		Lerwick	1868	120	120	(to B10)	
13	A Sinclair		George Street	1878	45	55	65	75
14	W Graham		HO	1871			160	160
	(b) Correspondence							
15	W Graham		HO	1871	120	120	(to C14)	
16	C Keene		Downie Place	1876	60	70		
17	G J Deas		HO	1857			160	170
18	P S Irvine		Perth	1879			60	70
	sub total				695	715	445	475
D	**Accountant's Department**							
19	P Peace	Check clerk	Kirkwall	1858	210	210	(to B9)	
20	R S H Ponnie	Check clerk	Lerwick	1858	190	190	200	200
21	H G Laurie	Clearing house clerk	HO	1852	200	200	200	200
22	A R Forbes		HO	1856	140	140	150	150
23	J MacPherson	Cash sheets	HO	1856	190	190	190	200
24	G S Deas	Cash sheets	HO	1857	150	160	(to C17)	
25	A Thomson		Leith	1855	170	170	180	190
26	W Jones	Bill clerk special a/c	HO	1861	210	210	250	250
27	J Mason		HO	1868	110	120	(t)	
28	G Martine		HO	1873	100	110	(r)	
29	J D Lawson	Check clerk	Stranraer	1864	150	150	165	165
30	J Crichton	Bill collecting	HO	1873	100	100	100	110
31	Clerk a		HO	1866	110	120	(t)	
32	b		Leith	1871	100	120	120	130
33	c		Kirkwall	1862	130	150	150	160
34	d		Elgin	1868	100	100	115	115
35	e		Leith	1868	160	(r)		
36	f		George Street	1866	115	(r)		
37	g		George Street	1878	45	55	(t)	
38	h		Downie Place	1871		80	(t)	
39	i		HO	1862			120	130
40	j		Canongate	1877			60	70
41	k		Perth	1879			60	(to C18)
42	l		Downie Place	1876			90	100
43	m		Leith	1878			65	75
44	n		Newington	1878			50	60
45	o		HO	1883			40	50
46	p		Newington	1873			180	180
47	q		Leith	1872				90
48	r		Perth	1879				70
49	s		Perth	1881				50
	sub total				£2,680	£2,575	£2,485	£2,745
E	**Porters**							
50								
51	}				242	242	242	242
52								
	Total				£6,857	£6,772	£5,812	£6,302

(r) retire;   (t) transfer to other office

emerging a certain ranking among them. Next to the general manager came the Glasgow assistant manager who was effectively the head of the Glasgow head office. The third official was the London manager whose ranking overtook that of the Edinburgh manager. The Edinburgh manager, despite the fact that the Edinburgh office was termed head office, came next to the Glasgow cashier, ranking with the Glasgow secretary and head inspector. This ranking apparently resulted from two features of the policy of the Union Bank, that is, money flow from the North and East to Glasgow, from thence to London, and strict inspections of branches. The Edinburgh head office might simply be regarded as a large branch, by Gairdner and the directors.

TABLE 65

Average Salaries of Lower Staff at the Glasgow and Edinburgh Head Offices of the Union Bank, 1882–85

Glasgow Head Office

		Cashier's Dept	Secretary's Dept	Accountant's Dept	Inspector's Dept
1882*	a†	£281	£197	£—	£154
	b‡	8	10	—	12
1883	a	281	204	—	162
	b	8	9	—	12
1884	a	232	187	155	170
	b	8	10	47	11
1885	a	243	192	152	156
	b	8	10	47	12

Edinburgh Head Office

1882*	a†	£210	£139	£141
	b‡	4	5	19
1883	a	210	143	143
	b	4	5	18
1884	a	185	111	133
	b	4	4	19
1885	a	185	119	125
	b	4	4	21

*date as in April each year
†a, average salary
‡b, number of staff

Sources: UB (Glasgow), MSS. UB (Edinburgh), *Staff and Salary Records*

A complete list of salaries of the Edinburgh staff (Table 64) and the average amount of salaries of the staff in seven departments and the two head offices (Table 65) give us some more details of the staff organisation. From the list of the salaries of the Edinburgh office, it is fair to say that a rise in salary was allowed approximately every two years and to the extent of £10. Increases larger than £40 were sanctioned only for the officials and for clerks who were to be promoted from the lower staff to the officials as the case of Kemp illustrates. In terms of salary, the clerks of the cashier's department, that is, tellers, were most favourably treated. But it seems to have been the secretariat and inspectorate who had more chances of being promoted, as exemplified by Kemp and the Glasgow inspectors.

There was a wide difference in the salaries of the agents as Table 66 shows. The salary of the Kilmarnock agent was eight and a half times larger than that of the Banchory agent. Salaries at the Kilmarnock, Paisley, Glasgow St Vincent Street and Kirkcaldy offices could well rank with those of the officials at the chief offices. From this, the Glasgow St Vincent Street branch must be added to the group of highly ranked branches. On the other hand, the salaries of the agents of minor importance such as at Cupar Angus etc. were well below those of the accountant's staff at the Glasgow head office. Consequently, it could be argued that the Union Bank had four levels of discrimination in salaries, that is, between the officials and the clerks, between the departments at the head offices, between the head offices and chief offices and the agents, and between the agents themselves.

TABLE 66

Salaries of Some Agents of the Union Bank, 1879–85

1 Kilmarnock	£850	15 Fraserburgh	£200
2 Paisley	750	15 Leslie	200
2 Glasgow St Vincent Street	750	18 Aberdeen West End	180
		19 Buckie	170
4 Kirkcaldy	400	19 Edzell	170
5 Ayr	350	21 Tarbert	160
6 Stirling	300	22 Cupar Angus	150
6 Stranraer	300	22 Doune	150
8 Glasgow Anderston	275	22 Dunkeld	150
9 Peterhead	260	22 Helensburgh	150
10 Blairgowrie	250	22 Keith	150
10 Glasgow Partick	250	22 Kirriemuir	150
10 Troon	250	22 Tillicoultry	150
13 Moffat	230	29 Turriff	130
14 Govan	225	30 Aberlour	120
15 Aberfeldy	200	31 Banchory	100

Sources: UBSB, *passim.* UB (Glasgow), MSS

The Union Bank for the first time established a scale of salaries, though it was only at the Glasgow head office, presumably on the model of Glyn & Co.[117] The scale had seven grades as Table 67 sets out. The duty of the clerk in the first grade was to make entries in books and write drafts and vouchers. The clerk in the second grade was also termed the second or supplementary clerk and he was engaged in giving notice of bills due, posting daily lists of bills and dealing with the London accounts. The clerk in the third grade was entrusted with more sophisticated duties, being termed the first clerk. Because of his specialised duties, he was also called the assistant cheque clerk or protested bill clerk or sub-inspector. The clerk in the fourth grade was simply more senior than the third-graded clerk, being termed the second or senior discount clerk, or senior or first senior ledger clerk, or assistant accountant, or sub-inspector. The clerk in the fifth grade was authorised to sign 'pro manager',[118] assisting the head of the department.

DIAGRAM 11

Structure of the Union Bank of Scotland, 1885

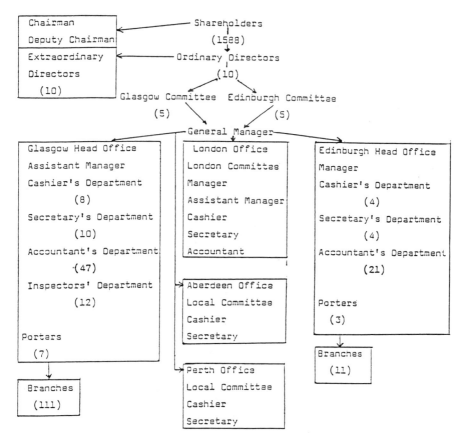

Key: ( ); number of shareholders/directors/staff/branches
———➤ direction of control/selection

Sources: UBC, UBSB, UBGC, UB (Glasgow), MSS, UB (Edinburgh), *Staff and Salary Records*

From the variety of data we have used, we can re-build the structure of the Union Bank of Scotland in 1885 and this is shown in Daigram 11. Inside the Glasgow head office, the inspectors' department ought to be distinguished from the rest because the duty of the department was to investigate all accounts and the conduct of business of the Union Bank, Glasgow head office included. Outside the two head offices, the London, Aberdeen, and Perth branches ought to be distinguished from the rest because of their importance. The most important staff member was undoubtedly the general manager, Charles Gairdner, whose career and personality should be worth detailing.

TABLE 67

Scale of Salaries at the Glasgow Head Office in the early 1880s

Grade	Salary
Apprentice	£20, 25, 35
Clerk 1st grade	£60–100
Clerk 2nd grade	100–160
Clerk 3rd grade	160–240
Clerk 4th grade	240 and over
Clerk 5th grade	average 280
Clerk 6th grade	average 282

Source: UB (Glasgow), MSS (no date, but undoubtedly in the early 1880s)

5 Charles Gairdner: Accountant, Stock-broker, Economist and Banker

The general managership was certainly the most important post of any bank, and the Union Bank of Scotland was no exception. By 1885, Charles Gairdner had already been the general manager for twenty-three years. Even George Readman, who took the initiative in publishing balance sheets, making an experiment in taking time deposits and leading the Clydesdale Bank in its invasion of England, held the office of general manager only for twenty-eight years between 1852 and 1880.[119] After the retirement of Readman, Gairdner was undoubtedly the most senior general manager in Scottish banking as his letter to J A Wenley, treasurer of the Bank of Scotland suggests,

> I have your letter of yesterday and am sorry that another meeting (of the Scottish bank managers) would be thought necessary. If it be so it would require to be tomorrow at 3.45 p.m. I send you minute amended in a way which would, I think, be a considerable improvement and I hope the other gentlemen may be able to adopt it and so avoid the meeting of our having to have (*sic*) tomorrow.[120]

Although the treasurer of the Bank of Scotland was traditionally in the chair at the general managers' meetings, it was Gairdner who presided over the meetings, behind the scenes.

Charles Gairdner, born in January 1824 at Ayr, was the son of Charles Dalrymple Gairdner who had just entered the services of Hunters & Co in 1821. Charles Gairdner was educated at Kilmarnock Academy and Edinburgh. He was then apprenticed to James M'Clelland, accountant and stock broker at Glasgow and later a senior partner of M'Clelland, MacKinnon & Blyth, chartered accountants. In 1843, at nineteen years of age, he entered the firm of Peter White, stock broker and accountant at Glasgow, becoming a partner in 1845. Later, Gairdner joined two institutions; the Institute of Accountants and Actuaries in Glasgow, established in May 1855, in which he was one of the original forty-nine members, and the Glasgow Stock Exchange Association, in which he became a member of the committee of 1855/56. Consequently, Gairdner was accountant and stock broker till the age of thirty-two in 1856. This earlier experience would certainly have predisposed the directors in his favour when they were looking for a general manager of the Union Bank. Indeed, his energy was poured into investigations of the accounts and branches of the Bank, in which his qualification as chartered accountant must have been tremendously useful, and the portfolio of the Bank's investments during his managership grew extraordinarily as has been already mentioned.[121]

The years between 1857 and 1862 were crucial for Gairdner. In January 1858 when a group of liquidators of the failed Western Bank of Scotland was to be formed, Gairdner became a liquidator and continued his duty until 1865 when Western Bank affairs were handed over to the firm of M'Clelland & MacKinnon, chartered accountants and intimate friends of Gairdner, and which Gairdner's eldest son afterwards joined as a partner.[122] It was during this duty that Gairdner was also asked by the directors of the Union Bank to investigate its accounts. He came up to their expectation, finding out many doubtful accounts. His connection with Scottish banking, thus, commenced from being the liquidator of a failed bank and the investigator of the surviving bank, which led to him becoming a bank manager in 1862.

It should be noted that Gairdner volunteered to become a liquidator of the Western Bank, as a contemporary writer revealed.[123] The liquidation of the large joint-stock bank was undoubtedly a tremendous task through which an ambitious youth could enhance his reputation and train to become a banker. There might have also been the influence of his father, a partner of the late firm of Hunters & Co and the acting agent of the Union Bank at Kilmarnock. Indeed, he had already become a shareholder of the Union Bank earlier in April 1858[124] and was well known by 1857 at the latest, by the directors of the Union Bank, especially by the Edinburgh directors, who had begun to doubt their manager, J Robertson.[125]

The first three years of Gairdner's joint-managership were very successful as the late manager, J A Anderson, had predicted,

I think Mr Gairdner will prove a great acquisition in the Glasgow office.[126]

Indeed, owing to Gairdner, the Bank could discipline the branches and develop its business, reaching a place second only to the Royal Bank of Scotland in the Scottish banking league table in 1865. Nevertheless it is another matter to judge whether the success of the Union Bank in the 1860s is due to Gairdner's intervention or to general trading conditions.

During the whole period of his office, Gairdner was very careful about his public appearance. He did not directly raise his opinion on any public affairs. *The Glasgow Herald* wrote down in his obituary that,

> The controversy of any kind he had a rooted aversion, and his voice was rarely if ever raised in the discussion of political or municipal questions.[127]

As *the Glasgow Herald* also suggested, he took a leading part in social and academic activities, joining social clubs, supporting charitable and benevolent institutions and writing essays on economics. His attitude of standing neutral in political affairs was one of the most important qualifications of the good banker, as J W Gilbart argued.[128]

Was Gairdner really uninterested in the wider questions? The reverse is more likely. Ironically, his ambition was disclosed in the prospectus of a social club, 'the Adam Smith Club', established in 1868, which read that,

> The idea . . . had been suggested to him (Gairdner) from having been present, shortly before, at a dinner of the Political Economy Club of London, when the discussion of the evening was conducted in a manner which was highly interesting and instructive .
> . . that during the period of its existence the leading Parliamentary and other authorities on economical questions had been members of the Club, and that it had thus become the arena in which the views and opinions of the statesmen who during the last generation had taken the chief part in reforming our commercial and social laws had been matured.[129]

Though the Adam Smith Club itself was merely a social club, it is obvious that Gairdner was very anxious to have a certain influence in politics, despite the claim of *the Glasgow Herald*.

Indeed, Gairdner gathered many notable gentlemen around him in the Club—Edward Caird, Professor of Moral Philosophy, George C Ramsay, Professor of Humanity, W T Gairdner, Professor of Medicine, John Veitch, Professor of Logic, James Robertson, Professor of Conveyancing, John Young, Professor of Natural History, A B M'Grigor, Writer in Glasgow, James A Campbell, afterwards MP for the Universities of Glasgow and Aberdeen, James S Fleming, Writer in Glasgow and afterwards Cashier of the Royal Bank, R H Leadbetter, Merchant in Glasgow, Francis W Clark, Advocate, Sheriff Substitute and afterwards Sheriff of Lanarkshire. There were twelve[130] original members. Through these people, Gairdner would hear stimulating discussion on 'political or municipal questions'. In a sense, he might be a real 'politician'.

In the presence of such distinguished people, Gairdner enjoyed giving papers, the themes of which, surprisingly, ranged from business subjects such as,

What are the advantages and disadvantages of joint-stock companies as compared
with private companies, and to what kinds of enterprise ought they in prudence to be
confined?[131]

which was given in the middle of 1869, to politics such as 'The Caucus',[132]
which was given in November 1882 when the Union Bank was suffering from
the Thomson affairs. Indeed, Gairdner both maintained a close relationship
with a prominent Liberal MP, Henry Campbell-Bannerman, who was a late
partner of J & W Campbell (warehousemen, Glasgow) and afterwards prime
minister, and, personally contributed to Conservative party funds.[133]

Gairdner was also a writer of economic and banking theory. This started in
1866 when he was asked by the Glasgow Chamber of Commerce to reply to
questions addressed by the Conseil Supérieur du Commerce de France
regarding the Scottish note issues.[134] By 1885, his writing produced three
pamphlets.[135] One of the three, *The Rate of Discount and Bank Acts* (1872)
discloses a part of his theory that;

> 1st.   That the main consideration that influences Bankers in fixing the rate of
> discount is the necessity of maintaining a due proportion between their specie
> reserves and other forms of assets.
> 2nd.   That this due proportion is not a fixed arithmetical proportion, but may, with
> propriety, vary under varying circumstances.
> 3rd.   That the question what is the due proportion that ought at any particular time
> to be maintained, must be referred for determination to the judgment of experienced
> men.[136]

Having formulated this theory, he advocated the repeal of the Bank Acts of
1844/45 and in lieu of them that,

> it were required that all new Banks desiring to issue notes should give proof of their
> responsibility and bona fides, by possessing a paid up capital of large amount—say
> one million sterling; by unlimited liability, as regards the partners, or if 'limited',
> then by liability on the shares for a substantial amount beyond the sum paid up; and
> by publishing their balance sheets periodically, in a form to be prescribed. Let us
> suppose that this system were extended to England, with the exception only of
> London and its immediate neighbourhood, and to Ireland.[137]

On the surface, his arguments resembled those of the Banking School in that
no rule could be laid down on the proportion of specie.[138] The idea that
'liability on the shares for a substantial amount beyond the sum paid up' was
the same as that of reserve liability, under which the Scottish joint-stock banks
became limited companies,[139] though it is not certain whether he was the first
to suggest the idea. These were the most notable aspects of his argument. His
suggestion of new banks of issue being extended to England and Ireland
sounds an anachronism in the 1870s, even though many non-issuing joint-
stock banks were promoted in England and Wales between the 1860s and
early 1870s and the anti-Bank Acts mood still dominated a considerable part
of Glasgow businessmen in the early 1870s.[140]

Without regard to its quality, his writing undoubtedly made him famous as an economist. Indeed, it was for this reason that the University of Glasgow made him an honorary LLD in 1889, and Professor Robertson said at the graduation that,

> As is well known to his fellow citizens, Mr Gairdner has won for himself a position in the very front rank of bankers by his profound and philosophical knowledge of the subject of banking and by the enlarged and liberal views which he entertains and has expounded regarding it.
>
> These considerations, however important though they be, are not the ground on which I am to ask you, Mr Vice Chancellor, to confer the degree of Doctor of Laws on Mr Gairdner, What the Senate are desirous of recognising is the great merit of the various contributions which from time to time Mr Gairdner has made, and still continues to make, in the department of political economy,—a department in which we of this University may well be supposed to take a deep and abiding interest, recollecting, as we do, that its principles were first expounded within our walls—this, too, by one of our own professors. On this subject Mr Gairdner has written—I shall not say has written much—but assuredly what he has written clearly shows that few have studied the subject more successfully, and fewer still have expressed their views upon it with greater consciousness and eloquence.[141]

It may have been too great an exaggeration when Professor Robertson compared Gairdner with 'one of our own professors', Adam Smith, though his words may have been ceremonial and diplomatic ones. The honorary degree must have further enhanced his fame as a scholar.

TABLE 68

Directorate, 1879–85

		Term of Office	Share Holding
1	Sir Thomas J Boyd (Edinburgh)	1876/1901	100
2	J Y Buchanan (Edinburgh)	1879/83, 1884/1900	850
3	C Campbell (of Colgrain)	1857/62, 64/69, 71/85	3,100
4	A Crum (of Thornliebank, Merchant, MP)	1874/92	100
5	J Currie (Leith, Merchant)	1877/99	100
6	C D Donald (Glasgow, Writer)	1871/86	200
7	A Galbraith (Glasgow, Manufacturer)	1863/86	360
8	F Pitman (Edinburgh, WS Lord Provost)	1868/84, 85/89	360
9	D Ritchie (Dowanhill)	1873/82, 1883/1914	220
10	S Thomson (Glasgow, Insurance Broker)	1879/1917	185
11	D B Wauchope (Leith, Merchant)	1869/85	340
12	C Gairdner (General Manager)	1869/95	300
			6,215

Sources: UB *Annual Reports.* UB *List of Shareholders 1885.* R S Rait, 1930, pp. 378–81

The crucial question remains, was Gairdner a success as general manager of the Union Bank? This subject can be dealt with by examining relationships between Gairdner and the directors, and these are illuminated by two affairs, that is, selection of the directorate and authorisation of credits to the directors' companies.

During the period between 1879 and 1885, the Union Bank had twelve directors, as Table 68 sets out. The most senior and influential director was undoubtedly Colin Campbell, who was the second largest shareholder (see Table 59) and who had continued in office from 1857. He was the only person in the directorate of this period who had witnessed the 1857 crisis from the boardroom. None of the other directors could rank with Campbell, who wrote to Gairdner in January, when S Thomson expressed his willingness to retire, saying that,

> I called on Seton Thomson . . . I called again yesterday in the hope of having some talk with him, but found Mr T had passed a very bad night and he had gone to his (unreadable) and ordered that he should not be disturbed. . . . She is very weak/cannot stand/. So I fear the end is approaching. I note (*sic*) all yesterday as to him as a director. What I wanted to find out was whether in the event of her death he has made up his mind to leave Glasgow altogether. . . . We must have old P (Pitman) in place of W (Wauchope).[142]

On the following day, Campbell wrote again that,

> We (Campbell and Thomson) talked over some matters connected with this Bank and then I spoke to him as to the acting directors . . . he also quite agrees we should get back Pitman, and strengthen the Glasgow end as much as possible, his idea would be Bolton's partner, he has not known of the retirement of the old partner in that corner, but is he coming to Glasgow? . . . I do hope Galbraith and Ritchie may not fail you.[143]

Indeed, the serious talk between Campbell and Gairdner resulted in Thomson making up his mind to stay in the directorate and Pitman being elected a director in place of Wauchope.[144]

Clearly, the selection of the directorate was carefully prepared by a couple of the directors and Gairdner. Both directors, that is, C Campbell and S Thomson, had tremendously large shareholdings behind them; Campbell himself was the second largest proprietor and Thomson was a relative of the largest, Dennistoun (see Table 59).

In the second place, a kind of faction was emerging in the boardroom, which was probably composed of Campbell, Thomson, Galbraith, Ritchie (all Glasgow directors), Pitman (Edinburgh director) and Gairdner. The existence of this group is also suggested by a telegraph sent by Gairdner that,

> If Mr Campbell in City ask him if he would approve purchase of one or two hundred and half at about yesterdays price Ritchie and Galbraith approve.[145]

It is clear that an inner caucus of six men was the real power in the Union Bank.

In the third place, it should be noted that Campbell expressed his desire to 'strengthen the Glasgow end'. A supposition that there might have been a conflict between the Glasgow directors and Edinburgh counterparts could be possible, but there remains no trace of any disagreement between them. The existence of Pitman, an Edinburgh director, in the inner caucus of the directorate, might on the contrary, suggest the opposite. Therefore, the words of Campbell might have been uttered simply because he felt weak on account of his ill health and because he was hoping for a competent person to succeed him. He died in 1886.[146] These three features further confirm that Gairdner was 'a king-pin' of the Union Bank.

Gairdner's power may be more strongly illustrated by authorisations of advances, a remarkable example of which is given in the case of the Castle Packet Co.[147] In August 1883 when the Castle Packet Co applied urgently for a large additional credit for £100,000, Gairdner first did not confirm its authorisation. Encountering the set face of Gairdner, J Currie, director of the Bank, had to write on behalf of the Castle Co that,

> My brother Donald tells me tonight that although you seemed to see no objection, when he met you in London, to giving the Castle Co £100,000 more on loan yet on reconsideration and consultation you do not like to go so far to our company. With this decision in general principles, I don't quarrel and situated as I am I feel precluded from saying all I might otherwise do. But I may say generally that the position of the Castle Co as expounded to you, is thoroughly sound and under the circumstances I think such a loan would be quite safe. But if you don't see your way to such an advance then the next question is whether you consider it expedient to advance any lesser sums, say £50,000 to the Castle Co and £50,000 to Donald Currie & Co, who would in turn advance on their own responsibility to the Castle Co. It comes to this that the Co and DC & Co are undoubtedly good for a very much greater amount, and the Castle Co alone are (*sic*) quite safe, and having thought all was arranged must now at once arrange either with you or elsewhere for meeting the requirements of the position. They are building new vessels, which they would prefer not to pay in bills, but in cash, and as Donald goes to Garth tomorrow morning, I suggest that you write to him there on receipt saying what you can see your way to do or what you would suggest so that he may take measures accordingly.[148]

Despite the detailed explanation and revised proposal, Gairdner did not still proceed to authorise the credit, and more than two weeks later Donald Currie himself had to reiterate his plea to Gairdner's stating that,

> The Co is in a sufficient strong position to finance; but at the same time I can understand you thinking after consideration that perhaps £250,000 (that is, £100,000 in addition to £150,000. See Table 56) was too much for one Co. Your suggestion that DC & Co shall give the Bank their promissory note or draw on the Company for £100,000. . . . Please arrange them to give the £100,000 which may be wanted about a fortnight.[149]

The credit was eventually given a month later at the end of September.

The negotiations between the Castle Co and Gairdner reveal two important characteristics of this general manager. In the first place, Gairdner was very, or excessively, careful in lending, though it is understandable that the Union Bank should have restrained large advances in the middle of the Thomson affair. In the second place, surprisingly, negotiations for advances were taking place entirely outside the boardroom of which the correspondence itself was indisputable evidence. The minute of the board of directors in 1883 has not recorded any trace of this kind of negotiation at all.

There was a further element which strengthened Gairdner's power, that is, 'inside-trading' of Union Bank stock, the existence of which is suggested by some affairs of 1884. A Galbraith, director, wrote an undated letter to Gairdner ordering a purchase of the Bank stock and stating that,

> I saw the Clydesdale quoted $21\frac{1}{2}$, no Union quote but if still to be had at 21, would you (unreadable) £1,000 value for me. I do not like the Union to be down lower than the Clydesdale, so at 21 I would have 50 shares.[150]

The letter reads as though Galbraith was purchasing the Union Bank shares in order to support its market price. This was merely one of two reasons for the purchase as Galbraith confessed that,

> I have taken £1,500 of the Bank stock which yields $5\frac{1}{2}$ int.[151]

A query about purchase of the Bank stock also came from outside the boardroom and read,

> Would you recommend the present time as a favourable time for the purchase of the Union Bank shares. If so could you supply Ten or Fifteen shares and at what price? I see that the present price is £21. Your answer in course will oblige.[152]

Furthermore, Gairdner himself bought the Bank shares, recommending purchases to his relatives. William Gairdner replied that,

> I received your letter this afternoon and have no objection to your registering the shares you have purchased in my name. I am only sorry I can't see my way to invest some money of my own in the same way as you describe the investment. The only money that I shall have . . . are some Australian and New Zealand debentures which fall in, in December. It might be worth while to find out what price I can get for the £8,500 of that stock.[153]
>
> I have just written to David and asked him to communicate with you without loss of time, for I think from all you say that I should not miss this chance of making a safe investment which will give such a good return. The New Zealand bonds are constantly falling in and can only be received at 4%. So if you will take them over in the part of the Bank and allow me the difference it will be better, as it will give me the use of the money in one sum, and an opportunity of buying 400 shares in the Union Bank stock now.[154]
>
> I . . . am obliged to you for looking after the purchase of the Union Bank stock. It is very good of you to let me have 300 you have.[155]

The letters imply that Gairdner supplied to his relative the Bank money by way of buying up the New Zealand bonds which were, indeed, to be held by the Union Bank under 'investments' in May 1884.[156] The same facilities were given to at least another two persons, that is, a trustee of the late C D Gairdner and the Edinburgh manager, H H Norie.[157]

We have other evidence on inside-trading. In April 1883, Sir Charles Tennant, deputy chairman of the Union Bank, daringly circulated inform-ation that the Bank business would show a poor result, and then sold his shares repurchasing them and gaining a margin. These were typical actions with regard to inside-trading which, naturally, offended his fellow direc-tors.[158] In comparison with this typical example, Gairdner, of course, did not proceed any further than giving his relative and friends advice and facilities for buying the Union Bank stock. However, both actions should be regarded alike, because Tennant and Gairdner must have made use of inside information available only to them. Although inside-trading was not illegal, it was very offensive to other shareholders[159] and, therefore, had to be kept secret. Naturally, Gairdner was extremely careful, specially employing a firm of stock brokers, Penny & MacGeorge, 24 George Square, Glasgow, whose names never appeared in relation to the ordinary business of investments.[160]

Charles Gairdner was a formidable man both inside and outside the Union Bank of Scotland. By the public, he was regarded as devoting himself to writing and giving papers on economic and banking subjects, besides his banking job. Inside the Bank, he was the general manager who selected the directors, decided on authorisations of important advances and supervised 'inside-trading'. He was, therefore, accountable for the overall policy decisions of the Union Bank. Under his managership, the Union Bank fell from second in 1865 to sixth place in 1885.[161] In these twenty years, he put forward clearly two features of his banking policy—increase in investments and discipline of overall business conduct, especially that of branches—which suggests that he was the banker of prudence and discipline. None the less, it was Charles Gairdner who gave large advances to Alexander Collie, who had been involved in fraud, during the early 1870s without taking any written documents, and involving the Union Bank in the heavy loss of £150,000. This was a fundamental mistake which the careful banker should not make. The Thomson affair might eventually have deprived him of any initiative, which once lost is hard to regain, as a modern banker has argued.[162] Indeed, the advances of the Union Bank were the smallest among major Scottish banks at a time when the West of Scotland was one of the world's leading centres of industry.[163] Consequently, if lending was the most vital business for the bank, in order to develop itself and the economy, it could be argued that Charles Gairdner fell far short of the ideal.

Conclusion

Development and Stagnation of the Union Bank of Scotland

In conclusion, it is intended to examine the performance of the Union Bank of Scotland at three levels. In the first place, the Union Bank will be reviewed in terms of its role and relative position in Scottish banking. There are three themes here; the Glasgow challenge, the amalgamation movement and competitiveness. In the second place, four particular features of the Union Bank will be examined, namely, assets management, sectoral lending, money flow and leadership. Finally, the life cycle of the Union Bank of Scotland will be reviewed.

1 The Glasgow Challenge

Our first concern then is with the Union Bank of Scotland as a component of the Scottish system.

The Union Bank led the Glasgow challenge to Edinburgh banking in two respects. The establishment of the Union Bank reflected the eagerness of Glasgow businessmen to set themselves up as bankers. The Union Bank was, thus, the pioneer of Glasgow joint-stock banking and it had a direct impact on the creation of at least three joint-stock banks in Glasgow; the Western Bank of Scotland, the Clydesdale Bank and the Glasgow Joint Stock Bank. Eventually, the successful establishment of the Union Bank was followed by seven Glasgow joint-stock banks. The Union Bank also started its notable take-overs in 1836, initiating the early age of amalgamation in Scottish banking up to 1844.

Through the 1840s and indeed until the late 1850s, the Union Bank, together with the Western Bank, did indeed make a successful banking challenge. If the number of shareholders and number of branches are considered adequate criteria, then Glasgow could claim to have established another financial centre in Scotland. But it was a Pyrrhic victory, and much was lost in 1857 in terms of Glasgow leadership with the collapse of the Western Bank.

In the aftermath of the 1857 crisis, the Union Bank, whose financial situation in the crisis was somewhat similar to that of the Western Bank, was forced to change its management and began to divorce itself from an expansionist policy. The disappearance of the Western Bank and the change of the policy of the Union Bank marked the beginning of the eclipse of the Glasgow challenge.

Between 1865 and 1878, the Union Bank became increasingly conservative.

There were few attempts either to push advances or to set up new branches. The poor performance was accelerated especially after the Collie fraud in 1875. The Glasgow challenge lost ground. Indeed, the City of Glasgow Bank had begun to falsify its balance sheets as early as the Gurney crisis of 1866. The Clydesdale Bank remained fairly passive although it did set about invading northern England by opening branches there.

The crisis of 1878 was in effect the fatal blow to the Glasgow banking challenge. The collapse of the fraudulent City of Glasgow Bank rocked the city and had wide repercussions. The Union Bank had to struggle for six months with the loss of value of its stock, eventually resorting to the adoption of an external audit system to reassure the market. Consequently, the Glasgow challenge, born with and led by the Union Bank of Scotland, ceased to exist by the late 1870s, when Glasgow was deprived absolutely of any opportunity of becoming another financial centre of Scotland.

Professor C P Kindleberger has argued that in certain industrialized countries 'money and capital markets were centered at the capital'.[1] Regarding British banking, Professor Kindleberger has argued that,

> it is hardly necessary to explain how London became the metropolitan apex of the financial network. Whether the correspondent system, the Bank of England branches in the provinces, or the nationally spread joint stock banks with their head offices also in the provinces, the system had no choice but to center in London. London had an ancient tradition and it was a major port, the capital seat, and hub of the railroad network; all forces were brought to bear on this locality, which was itself somewhat divided between the City and the West End. The different banking systems in Ireland and Scotland reached across boundaries and linked up with London.[2]

How far is this argument applicable to Scottish banking? Edinburgh had the oldest banking tradition, which created the Bank of Scotland, established only a year later than the Bank of England, and was the political and cultural centre of Scotland. Though she was rivalled by Glasgow during the 1840s and 1850s, Edinburgh firmly re-established her supremacy over Glasgow after the mid 1870s, especially after the 1878 general crisis, and continued to be the sole financial centre. No joint-stock bank based on Edinburgh ever failed, and, in this respect, Edinburgh was a more solid financial centre than London. Thus far, Professor Kindleberger's argument can be acceptable with regard to the Scottish case.

One important difference between the two financial centres could be found in the fact that one of the three remaining Scottish banks, the Clydesdale Bank, still continues to base itself on the city other than the Scottish financial centre, that is, Glasgow. The continuance of the Clydesdale Bank's head-quarters in Glasgow is partly due certainly to the fact that it was affiliated with the Midland Bank, based on London, earlier in 1919, and thereafter the London headquarters of its parent bank was, in effect, the head office of the Clydesdale Bank. This fact probably made it unnessary for the Clydesdale Bank to move to Edinburgh. Indeed, as Professor Kindleberger has suggested, the existence of the largest financial centre in the world, London, directly connected by railway only 400 miles away, was certainly a factor to weaken the status of Edinburgh. Especially after the mid 1860s, when London eventually became the international financial centre, Scottish banking increasingly deepened its involvement in London business as the openings of London offices of the Scottish banks and the money flow of the Union Bank of Scotland suggested.

Moreover, it must be noted that differences between the two biggest cities in Scotland, Edinburgh and Glasgow, were not so noticeable in all respects as those between London and other English towns. Glasgow was the largest Scottish city in terms of size and population. It was situated at the very centre of the industrial West and was equipped with two large ports, Greenock and Port Glasgow. Half of the railway lines running across the border from England reached Glasgow. These factors must have joined forces to deprive Edinburgh of some qualifications as the Scottish financial centre.

In terms of British banking as a whole, it is indisputable that London was always the ultimate source of liquidity and, thus, the sole financial centre. Scottish banking was not an exception and had to place a not insubstantial amount of funds in London. However, inside Scotland, 'the concentration theory' could not have been valid. Indeed, Scotland had two financial centres in the mid nineteenth century, Edinburgh and Glasgow. In terms of branch banking and number of shareholders, Glasgow dominated the Scottish banking scene, a status which neither Liverpool nor Birmingham could claim in England. Furthermore, though it was from time to time accused of 'speculative banking', Glasgow banking was enthusiastic in supplying funds to the expanding economy, thus developing energetically during the 1840s and 1850s. Therefore, it could be argued that Glasgow would have had an opportunity to continue to be another financial centre of Scotland if the Western Bank of Scotland and/or the City of Glasgow Bank could have survived, or had not been eliminated in, the crises. The two successive failures of these large banks in Glasgow had a tremendous effect on the Glasgow challenge and the structure of Scottish banking.

2 The Amalgamation Movement

The Union Bank of Scotland amalgamated with seven banks; three in the North and East and four in the West. This trend started in 1836 and ended in 1857. It was the most remarkable performance in Scottish banking as Tables 69 and 70 set out. Nearly one-third of the major amalgamations in Scottish banking between 1830 and 1858 were undertaken by the Union Bank. The process of assimilation, giving the Union Bank offices all over Scotland, did much to enhance its reputation as a national bank.

The amalgamation movement of the Union Bank produced three further noteworthy results. Firstly, the acquisition of the firm of Sir William Forbes & Co gave the Bank invaluable access to Edinburgh banking, that is, banking in the financial centre, and raised the status of the Bank, whose manager was regarded by his Edinburgh counterparts as their peer. Secondly, the amalgamations resulted in the tremendous development of a branch network which greatly increased the resources of the Bank. The take-overs of the Aberdeen and Perth Banks were particularly important in that money flow from the North and East to the West developed inside the Union Bank. Finally, the amalgamations widened outlets for increased resources, though at the same time there emerged borrowers such as the Dennistouns, where there was more than an element of risk. The amalgamation movement was undoubtedly the main factor of the development of the Union Bank by the late 1850s.

TABLE 69

Major Amalgamations, 1830–79; Location of Absorbed Banks

(1) *Absorber*	(2) *Number of* *Absorbed Banks*	(3) *Location* (a) *North and East*	(b) *West and South*
Edinburgh Banks*	10	6	4
Glasgow Banks†	16	6	10
Union Bank	7	3	4

*BS, RBS, BLC, CBS, NBS, and Edinburgh & Glasgow Bank
†UB, Western Bank and Clydesdale Bank

Source: SG, 1975, Tables 11 and 16

Even after the last amalgamation in 1857, the Union Bank had opportunities to take over the Dundee Bank in the late 1850s and the Caledonian Bank in the early 1860s, which were indeed anxious to make their business over to the Union Bank. The Union Bank, however, did not proceed to take them over, preferring consolidation of business to further development—especially that of branch network, which would naturally result from amalgamations. This policy was deliberately pursued by the general manager, Charles Gairdner. However, it was also true that opportunities for bank amalgamations became increasingly less in Scottish banking, because of the reduction of number of banks as well as of the enlargement of dimension of each bank. Further amalgamations would thus have involved a change from large banks mopping up small ones to unions between almost equally large concerns. In these circumstances, the Union Bank began to lose relative importance in

TABLE 70

Major Amalgamations, 1830–79; Periodical Distribution

(1) *Absorber*	(2) *Period* (a) *1830/1844*	(b) *1845/1858*	(c) *1859/1865*	(d) *1866/1879*
Edinburgh Banks*	8	0	1	1
Glasgow Bank†	11	4	1	0
Union Bank	5	2	0	0

Notes and Source: as of Table 69

Scottish banking. It could be argued that the Union Bank was literally a union of banks and could continue to develop as long as it could unite with other banks smaller than itself.

3   Competitiveness

Competitiveness should first be assessed by performance in price competition. In this sense, the Union Bank stood in the middle, between the Edinburgh banks, which tended to offer lower deposit rates and charge higher lending rates, and the other Glasgow banks, which accepted lower margins. The Union Bank was, thus, moderate in price competition. Such competition, however, disappeared from Scottish banking in the early 1860s when the general managers adopted a co-ordinated policy.

In the assessment of performance in non-price competition, two criteria could be put forward. Firstly, branch banking was considered to represent the overall method of offering services to customers and of gathering deposits. The Union Bank was one of the most energetic creators of branches over the years between the late 1840s and the late 1850s, expanding to a network of one hundred branches in 1858, which was primarily due to its remarkable amalgamation movement. Therefore, when it ceased to take over other banks, the rate of its development of branch banking diminished, and consolidation of the existing branches became the policy of the Union Bank. Thus, in terms of spatial competition, the Union Bank became less energetic from the early 1860s.

Another criterion of competitiveness was the readiness to respond to the needs of the customer, that is, lending. Again in this respect, the Union Bank seemingly began to lose ground from the mid 1860s with the sole managership of Charles Gairdner. As his managership advanced, this tendency grew and this was well illustrated in the case of the Castle Packet Co. Consequently, in all respects, except the Thomson financing (which, however, should be regarded as an unusual case), the Union Bank became less competitive from the mid 1860s. This attitude of the Union Bank and its general manager was also perceived in some particular features of the Union Bank, especially, in its assets management.

4   The Management of Assets

We turn now to our second set of themes, namely the particular features of the Union Bank. The first of these concerns asset management. The two main assets of the bank were, of course, advances and investments. The Union Bank preferred two methods of advances, that is, discounts and credit accounts/overdrafts, presumably in common with other Scottish banks. Between the two methods, advances on discount were a major element in developing the overall business of the Union Bank till the late 1870s. During this period the business of the Bank increased when advances on discount did so. Advances on discount, however, ceased to be the primary method, presumably in the mid 1870s, owing to the experience of the Collie fraud. From it, the Union Bank learned its lesson that bills of exchange, especially those originating from foreign trade, were risky. This attitude resulted in the remarkable reduction of advances as a percentage of deposits, as Table 71 sets out, as well as in the stagnation of the overall business. The decrease in the proportion of discounts was not supplemented by an increase in that of credit accounts/overdrafts.

TABLE 71

Advances and Investments as Percentages of Deposits, 1866–85

	Advances		Investments	
	Union Bank	*Scottish Total*	*Union Bank*	*Scottish Total*
1866	98.30	95.24	11.99	17.85
1867	95.74	93.89	12.63	17.75
1868	94.48	91.93	14.35	18.84
1869	95.96	94.38	14.37	18.40
1870	94.74	95.64	13.90	18.08
1871	91.11	97.32	15.93	18.16
1872	94.01	95.41	15.56	19.22
1873	94.24	96.77	15.65	19.36
1874	94.60	97.87	14.60	18.10
1875	89.24	98.07	16.76	17.31
1876	93.91	99.08	15.02	16.89
1877	84.13	97.44	19.30	18.40
1878	90.90	103.61	17.06	16.42
1879	88.25	99.64	16.91	16.01
1880	76.96	83.21	21.41	22.09
1881	74.08	83.42	21.74	21.38
1882	71.84	83.63	23.10	21.83
1883	72.78	82.55	22.33	22.42
1884	73.80	82.17	22.29	22.09
1885	70.79	80.05	23.45	23.19

Source: SGC and A B MacDonald, 1973

The third method, ambiguously termed 'other loan', made its appearance in the mid 1870s. These loans were mainly given against the medium and long term securities of a growing number of joint-stock companies. These were quasi-investments, and were chiefly granted at large offices such as the Glasgow head office and the London office. They represented a departure from the Scottish tradition of short term self liquidating lending.

Another asset, i.e., investments, increased remarkably in the 1870s, during which the growth rate was far larger than that of the Scottish total. Previously, however, as Table 71 shows, investments as a percentage of deposits had been far below the Scottish total from 1866 to 1874, barely reaching the Scottish level in the mid 1870s. It could be argued that the Union Bank exerted itself to maintain the Scottish pattern, presumably that of Edinburgh banking, by rapidly increasing the investment share of its assets. It is, therefore, suspected that 'Edinburgh banking' might be planted in the conduct of the Glasgow-based Union Bank, as will be discussed later. The trend in investment policy could thus be interpreted as a move to less venturesome banking, less intimately concerned with Scottish commercial and industrial needs.

In sum, then, the Union Bank changed its assets management in the mid 1870s and thereafter preferred safer assets, that is, loans on stocks to advances on discount, and investments to advances in general. The Union Bank was certainly aiming at the safer management of its assets from the third quarter of the nineteenth century.

5   Sectoral Lending

The Union Bank preferred borrowers in three sectors, transport, trade, and shipbuilding and engineering.

The transport sector, especially railways, was the favourite throughout the whole period, right up to 1885. Prior to 1845, railway companies in the West and Lowlands, especially the Glasgow, Paisley, Kilmarnock & Ayrshire and the Edinburgh & Glasgow Companies, were large borrowers. More importantly, the financing of the Ayrshire Railway was one of the causes which led the Union Bank to amalgamate with Hunters & Co and the Glasgow & Ship Bank. The financing of the Edinburgh & Glasgow Railway resulted in a lending cartel arranged between the Union Bank and the Edinburgh banks. From the late 1840s to the early 1850s, the Union Bank, together with other Scottish banks, was involved in heavy railway investments, which were inspired by the operations of exchange companies. Though the Bank did not continue its large scale investments, railway companies remained the biggest borrowers.

The trade sector was favoured throughout almost the whole period. Particularly between 1845 and 1857, the Union Bank supplied large funds to enterprising merchants—engaged in American, Australian and Indian trade—such as the Dennistouns (whose financing, however, involved the Bank in great danger during the 1857 crisis). Thereafter, the policy of the Union Bank towards this sector gradually changed and, though this sector remained a favoured one, the Union Bank increasingly preferred incorporated companies to private firms of merchants. This policy was accentuated by the Collie fraud in 1875.

Shipbuilding and engineering became another preferred customer from the 1850s in accordance with the development of the Clydeside shipyards, overtaking the railways as borrowers by the 1880s. The Union Bank supplied funds to at least ten firms of shipbuilders and engineers. Among them, one of the largest shipbuilding firms, J & G Thomson, emerged as the largest borrower of the Bank during the 1870s. Although the Thomson financing resulted in difficulties for the Bank, and there was an unusual relationship between them, the Union Bank survived this difficulty, and continued to contribute to the fame of Clydeside as the shipbuilding centre of the world.

It could be argued that the Union Bank supplied funds to the Scottish economy primarily through the sectors of transport and shipbuilding and engineering, as well as assisting Scottish merchants to trade abroad. But it was also true that the Union Bank was placing substantial resources in London.

TABLE 72

Liquid Assets as a Percentage of Deposits, 1866–85

	Union Bank	Scottish Total
1866	15.80	19.72
1867	16.46	19.66
1868	18.53	21.18
1869	18.33	21.07
1870	17.53	20.31
1871	19.87	19.95
1872	19.21	20.98
1873	19.12	20.64
1874	17.62	19.43
1875	20.02	18.63
1876	17.76	18.38
1877	22.56	20.03
1878	19.71	17.51
1879	19.35	18.43
1880	24.23	24.86
1881	24.33	23.29
1882	25.58	23.34
1883	24.45	23.49
1884	24.14	22.96
1885	25.13	23.90

Source: as of Table 71

6   Money Flow

Two directions of money flow appeared in two different stages of the development of the Union Bank.

After the last two take-overs of the banks in the North and East, the first substantial money flow emerged, that is, the movement of resources from the agricultural North and East to the industrial West. The same kind of money flow was also perceived in England in the early nineteenth century, where bills in industrial Lancashire were discounted through bill brokers in London using money from agricultural Norfolk, Suffolk etc., and this was still going on in the 1870s as Sir Walter Bagehot stated. However, the money flows of the Union Bank and English banking were significantly different. The money flow of the Union Bank happened inside its own structure, that is, through the wide network of the branch system, which was peculiar to the Union Bank and other large scale Scottish banks. Therefore, it could be assumed that the money flow, taking place in the Union Bank, was common in Scottish banking as a whole, with most banks having something approaching national branch coverage.

Another money flow in the Union Bank made its appearance immediately after the opening of the London office in 1878, namely that to London. It was the result of commercial and banking needs. All payments of both domestic and international trade increasingly clustered around the world's largest financial centre, London, during the 1860s. The widest range of opportunities for various types of investment and short term lending, which were the main components of the Bank's reserve, was available in London.

Just as in the case of the Union Bank money flow in Scotland, there is a presumption that other Scottish banks were in similar situation. There has been no case study of other banks, and, therefore, we must rely on rough data, i.e., investments and liquid assets as percentages of deposits, which are construed to reflect the London business of the Scottish banks to some extent. As Tables 71 and 72 set out, investments and liquid assets as percentages of deposits constantly exceeded 20% from 1880 when the six major Scottish banks, excluding the Commercial Bank, had opened their London branches.[3] Consequently, it is not unreasonable to conclude that the two kinds of money flow, though evidenced only by the case study of the Union Bank, were more or less common to Scottish banking.

7 Leadership

This theme may be examined by dividing the period into four sub-periods; 1830/1844, 1845/1857, 1858/1865 and post 1865.

It is rather difficult to find anyone who really headed the Union Bank throughout the formative years of 1830/1844. Robert Stewart, director, was certainly a leading figure in establishing the Bank in 1830, but thereafter his voice was rarely heard on the board. John Leadbetter, director, was very active and competent in obtaining railway business and thus competing with other banks, but it is hard to say that he was the sole leader. He seems to have been more interested in railway companies in which he, indeed, took office as chairman and as director. Four partners of the firm of Sir William Forbes & Co joined the directorate of the Union Bank in 1838 and must have had prestige on the board, but there remains no strong evidence which suggests their leadership over the Bank as a whole. Indeed, their responsibility was to a considerable degree confined to Edinburgh business till the mid 1840s, when the firm of Sir William Forbes & Co was finally assimilated with the Union Bank. The manager, J A Anderson, though competent, cannot be regarded as a leader in any respect. Consequently, it is safe to say that collective responsibility, rather than individual direction, determined the policies of the Union Bank in its formative years.

The rapid growth of 1845/1857 witnessed the emergence of leading figures in the Union Bank, who appeared on both the Glasgow and Edinburgh boards of directors. Immediately after the amalgamation with the Glasgow & Ship Bank, some of the original directors of the Bank, including J Leadbetter, retired from the directorate, which was then filled by the late partners of the Glasgow & Ship Bank. Thereafter, the Glasgow board was seemingly taken over by them. On the other hand, the Edinburgh board was firmly constituted by the late partners of Sir William Forbes & Co though they were joined by one member of the Glasgow & Ship Bank. This dual-board system, instituted in 1844, was represented by two directors, that is, Alexander Dennistoun on the Glasgow board and Sir Adam Hay on the Edinburgh board. As an enterprising merchant, Dennistoun pursued an expansionist policy which undoubtedly led the Bank to develop greatly. Hay, as a leader of the late firm of Sir William Forbes & Co, followed the policy of playing safe and from time to time raised objections to Dennistoun's policy. Together they represented the classic Glasgow versus Edinburgh dichotomy of speculativeness versus caution. The manager, Anderson, had to remain neutral between his two masters. He retired in 1852. His successor, James Robertson, stood nearer to the Glasgow board, recommending the expansion of branch network, though it is untrue to say that he led the Bank in any sense. Thus, the leadership of the Union Bank was based on a balance of power between the two boards, represented by Dennistoun and Hay. This was lost in the mid 1850s and led to difficulties in the 1857 crisis.

In the 1857 crisis, A Dennistoun, whose business involved the Union Bank in great danger, dropped out of the directorate and the expansionists on the board lost ground. Moreover, two successive failures of large borrowers in the early 1860s caused a great change in the management and in this the Edinburgh directors, especially A Hay, took the initiative. Indeed, the Glasgow manager, J Robertson, together with his secretary, was forced to resign. The Union Bank appointed Charles Gairdner, the choice of the Edinburgh directors, as joint-manager. He immediately instituted an energetic investigation into the whole conduct of business of the Bank, successfully responding to the expectation of the Edinburgh directors. The years of 1858/1865 witnessed the transition of the leadership of the Union Bank.

Charles Gairdner commenced his sole managership in 1865. A year after, the most influential director, A Hay died. Gairdner became a formal member of the board of directors according to the change of the contract of copartnery in 1869. He attended both Glasgow and Edinburgh boards from the early 1870s, supervising the whole conduct of business in the Bank. Though his office was not termed general manager until 1878 (when another managership was instituted at the London office), he became the most powerful man in the Union Bank. His career was not challenged by any director, except Colin Campbell, who was the most senior, and the only director in the early 1880s who had witnessed the difficulties of 1857 from the boardroom. In effect the leadership of the Union Bank was assumed by Gairdner from 1865.

Charles Gairdner occupied a position of great power and influence from

1862 to 1895, unsurpassed by any other general manager. He must therefore be considered accountable for the overall policy decisions made by the Union Bank. During this period, the Union Bank lost ground and fell to sixth in order of importance of Scottish banks. After his initial enthusiasm, he showed a lack of initiative in challenging effectively Edinburgh banking and developing the Union Bank. Although he came from the West of Scotland, ill-famed for speculation, he was a man of more than average caution, and of Edinburgh temperament. Indeed, his father's concern, the banking firm of Hunters & Co, had strong connection with the firm of Sir William Forbes & Co and the directorate of the British Linen Co. He was also educated in Edinburgh. He was certainly brought up with Edinburgh caution, and as such he was an Edinburgh nominee. Therefore, it could be argued that the Glasgow challenge to Edinburgh banking, led by the Union Bank, was ended partly because the Edinburgh mentality was planted in the seat of power, namely the general managership of the most senior Glasgow-based joint-stock bank. The Gairdner regime was, thus, the outcome of the Edinburgh-dominated selection process in filling the office of general manager and also of the choice of a man of too much caution. Being subject to the reinforcing effect of the experience of the Western Bank and the City of Glasgow Bank and his own errors— the Collie fraud and the Thomson financing—of ageing, and perhaps of an element of intellectual dilettantism, Charles Gairdner, concerning banking, failed to give leadership from the only direction from which it could come, namely the general manager's office.

8   The Phasing

Our third facet of the behaviour of the Union Bank of Scotland is concerned with its general performance over time. Here the same phasing as used in the text is appropriate.

(a) FORMATIVE YEARS, 1830–44

The first Glasgow-based joint-stock, Union Bank, created in 1830, embarked upon an extraordinary amalgamation movement earlier in the mid 1830s, growing by leaps and bounds, taking over two private and three provincial banks and displaying all the attributes of large scale joint-stock banking in the industrial West. Through the acquisition of the fine firm of Sir William Forbes & Co, the Union Bank also became firmly based in Edinburgh. The success and development of the Union Bank was followed by a great spate of Glasgow enterprise.

(b) RAPID GROWTH, 1844–58

The Union Bank entered upon a stage of vigorous competition during the hectic years of British economic growth and developed its business by financing foreign trade and railways. Another two take-overs accelerated the development of the Union Bank. The expansionist policy was prevalent in every feature of the performance of the Union Bank during the 1850s. As a result, there were difficulties in the 1857 crisis. The storm was weathered by its well-balanced branch network and reserve policy which the collapsed Western Bank of Scotland had not established.

(c) ZENITH, 1858–65

The experience of the 1857 crisis and its aftermath resulted in a great change in the conduct of the Union Bank, which was heralded by the appointment of the cautious Charles Gairdner. However, the reserve of energy, which accumulated in the years of rapid growth, elevated the Union Bank in 1865 to second to the Royal Bank of Scotland in order of importance, so the zenith of the Union Bank of Scotland was attained in the mid Victorian age.

(d) YEARS OF DIFFICULTY, 1865–79

These fourteen years, commencing from 1865, witnessed incessant hazards. The failure of Overend, Gurney & Co in 1866 and the Collie fraud in 1875 resulted in the shrinkage of the Union Bank, which, from then on, became less go-ahead in pushing advances, thus reducing its overall business. The general crisis of 1878 greatly damaged the last surviving large Glasgow-based, Union Bank. In these circumstances, carefulness dominated aggressiveness in every facet of its business. The Union Bank lost initiative and the Glasgow spirit of enterprise was eclipsed.

(e) STAGNATION, 1879–85

In addition to the task of recovering the public image damaged in the 1878 crisis, the Union Bank was confronted with another problem which was caused by the Thomson financing. Although the Union Bank weathered the Thomson affair, its prestige in Scottish banking continued to diminish; it sank into sixth place in 1885, its lowest ebb since the disclosure of the Scottish bank balance sheets in 1865. Initiative lost was hard to regain, and the Union Bank of Scotland stagnated.

(f) SCOTTISH BANKING AND THE UNION BANK OF SCOTLAND

The Scottish banking system in 1830 comprised thirty-six banks; this figure included the public banks, the private banks, the provincial banking companies and the joint-stock banks. The number of the banks was reduced to ten by 1885—seven nation-wide Edinburgh- and Glasgow-based banks, and three local North-based banks. By this time, the major amalgamations among the Scottish banks had for a time ceased. There were few chances for any new bank to enter the system. In England, on the other hand, there was still room for many promotions and amalgamations. A change in the feature of Scottish banking, the main spring of banking initiative and invention in the world, brought drama to banking history as Professor Checkland has argued, the Scottish banking system, from being the most open and competitive in the world before 1830, had become by 1880 one of the most tightly controlled.[4]

Scottish banking matured earlier than its English counterpart.

The life cycle of the Union Bank of Scotland exemplified the aggregate trend of Scottish banking. The Union Bank of Scotland was born in the enthusiasm of Scottish joint-stock banking and developed by leaps and bounds, reaching its zenith in the mid 1860s, when Scottish banking was also at its highest ebb. Thereafter, when Scottish banking was consolidating its system, the Union Bank of Scotland lost its initiative and sank remarkably from second in 1865 to sixth in 1885 in the system. Glasgow, too, succumbed to the supremacy of Edinburgh. Certainly, the Union Bank of Scotland became more conservative than its fellow Scottish banks. In this sense, the Union Bank of Scotland was, perhaps, a symbol of the fate of Glasgow banking, rather than of Scottish banking as a whole.

Postscript

The Union Bank of Scotland in 1885 still had another sixty-seven years to live before it was to merge with the Bank of Scotland, during the years of 1952–54. Sixty-seven years, though a long period for a short postscript, are worth a survey. Although archive materials are not available for most of the period,[1] this study will produce an overview of the Union Bank of Scotland in the latter half of its whole history.

Towards the end of the nineteenth century, the minute books of the boards of directors of the Scottish banks, which had by that time recorded a large number of banking inventions and initiatives, were becoming less exciting,[2] and those held at the Glasgow Chief Office of the Bank of Scotland, namely the former Head Office of the Union Bank, were not an exception. In this tendency, however, the minute books of the Union Bank recorded three features of its banking policy.

Firstly, the London business of the Union Bank was becoming increasingly important during a quarter of a century prior to 1914. The most remarkable record on the London business was attached to the minute of 26 October 1899 which reads that,

There was submitted to the Committee a Certificate dated 21st October by the Bank of England certifying the sum of £189,403 3s. 3d.

To have stood at credit of the Account of the Union Bank on the evening of the 14th October as compared with £182,832 11s. –d.

in the book of the latter.
The Discrepancy was explained by Mr Downie.
There was also submitted the Bank of England's Certificate that the under-mentioned amounts of Stock were standing in the names against which they are placed.
In the name of the Union Bank of Scotland Ltd.

Consols	£450,083	12s.	1d.
Annuities $2\frac{3}{4}\%$ 1905	135,000	0	0
Annuities $2\frac{1}{2}\%$ 1905	45,000	0	0
India $2\frac{1}{2}\%$	104,000	0	0
London County Consolidated $2\frac{1}{2}\%$	100,000	0	0
Birmingham Corporation 3%	10,000	0	0

In the name of Union Bank and Chairman for Commissioners of Inland Revenue.

Consols	105,412	13	4

In the name of Union Bank and Chairman for Board of Customs.

Consols	40,000	0	0

In the name of Hadgley and Andrew Gordon.

Consols	4,800	0	0
Metropolitan $3\frac{1}{2}\%$ Consols	1,229	9	9
India $3\frac{1}{2}\%$	2,346	16	4

The Meeting examined the detailed list of securities held against loans to Stockbrokers and called for at random, and have produced a large number of these securities, which were examined, counted, and found in order.

The Meeting also examined the Bills held on account of Head Office and also held in security of advance to Billbrokers, and considered them in conference with Mr Hadgley.[3]

The business done at the London Office was very similar to that carried out prior to 1885. What surprises us is the fact that this was the only type of business constantly and minutely recorded in the minute books between 1885 and 1919.[4] Through the London Office, the Union Bank also started to allow large credit accounts to foreign customers operating in London.[5] The London business was probably the most profitable as well as indispensable for the Union Bank and perhaps for other Scottish banks when London was enjoying the status of sole international financial centre at least up to 1914.

Secondly, the rapid growth of investments was a characteristic of the Union Bank's policy from the late 1870s, and this tendency continued during the last two decades of the nineteenth century. The growth was this time led by increases in foreign, especially colonial, investments as the minute of 3 November 1888 reveals.

The following investments held by the Bank in London Office, on account of Glasgow Head Office, had been examined and found in order;

Egyptian Government 3% Loan	£150,000
Great India Peninsula Railway $3\frac{1}{2}\%$ Bonds	50,000
Ond and Rohilkund Railway $3\frac{1}{2}\%$ Bond	45,000
Cape of Good Hope Government 6% Bonds	7,100
New Zealand Government 5% Bonds	32,000
Australian Land and Finance Company 4% Bonds	23,000
Victoria Railway 4% Bonds	60,000
Victoria Government $4\frac{1}{2}\%$ Bonds	75,000
New South Wales Government 5% Bonds	88,000
New South Wales Government 4% Bonds	5,000
India Midland Railway $3\frac{1}{2}\%$ Bonds	85,000
India 3% Loan	200,000[6]

These foreign investments continued to be one of the Bank's vigorous activities till the outbreak of the First World War.[7] The increasing foreign investments were a factor which enhanced further the importance of the London business.

Thirdly, a remarkable change was seen in the increasing volume of each advance. The largest lump sum of credit before the War, namely £322,000, was given to the Lanarkshire and Ayrshire Railway Co.[8] Shortly after the War, the Union Bank sanctioned an extraordinary amount of credit of £3,000,000 to Lloyd Royal Belge (Great Britain) Ltd against their steam ships.[9] This advance was authorised at the London Office and was certainly the largest loan the Bank ever allowed. The extraordinary figure of this loan was probably due partly to the inflated general prices during the post-World War period,[10] but it was also true that the amount of each advance was becoming larger in the twentieth century.

Prior to 1919, there were three notable incidents worth mentioning. In the first place, the firm of J & G Thomson, which had by the early 1890s fully recovered from its difficulties, proposed in January 1890 to convert itself into an incorporated company. The Bank, supported the scheme, resolved that,

It was of great importance to the Bank that the Limited Company should be constituted, and there being no prospect of this being accomplished without the Bank's aid, it further resolved to authorise the advances recommended by the General Manager and approved by the Sub-Committee 'A' namely

1.   An advance on the joint and several responsibilities of Messrs James R and George P Thomson of £150,000 to enable them to take up the Ordinary Shares of the Limited Company, which will then be held in manner approved by the Bank's Law Agent as security for this and any other indebtedness of Messrs Thomson to the Bank.

2.   An advance in same manner to Messrs Thomson on £25,000 to be placed by them to the credit of the Preference Dividend Reserve Fund in the Books of the Limited Company.[11]

This arrangement was soon carried out, and, as a result, both the Bank and J & G Thomson were put on more solid footing as the lender and the borrower respectively, though Thomson was later in 1899 taken over by an English company based in Sheffield, Brown & Co.

In the second place, the Union Bank joined the fellow Scottish banks in helping a firm of merchant bankers, Baring Brothers & Co in London, during the so-called Baring Crisis. The firm of Baring Brothers which for a long time was involved in Argentinian business, encountered difficulties in November 1890, which frightened the Chancellor of the Exchequer, G J Goschen who thought that the '1866 (crisis in which Overend, Gurney & Co collapsed) would be a trifle in comparison'.[12] Goschen suggested that the bankers should establish a guarantee fund to which the great City houses, the Bank of England and large joint-stock banks both based in London and Scotland should contribute. The Scottish banks contributed £2,100,000 to this guarantee fund and the Union Bank £300,000.[13]

In the third place, the Union Bank embarked energetically upon foreign banking towards the end of the First World War. In January 1917, anticipating a recovery of the world trade in the post-war period, the Union

Bank discussed with the Royal Bank and the British Linen Bank a matter of setting up con-jointly an overseas bank based in Scotland.[14] The negotiations did not make good progress perhaps because of unwillingness of the Royal Bank and the British Linen Bank. The Union Bank could not resist losing good opportunities of establishing a new business and launched its own foreign exchange department in October 1918. The Union Bank re-employed a member of the staff of a firm of merchant bankers in London as manager of the department.[15] Meanwhile, the Union Bank continued to search for institutions which would join the Bank in forming the proposed overseas bank. The Bank's effort came to fruition in April 1919 when the British Overseas Bank Ltd was founded.[16] Seven banks participated in the scheme, namely the Anglo–South American Bank, the Dominion Bank, Glyn, Mills, Currie & Co, Charles Hoare & Co, the Imperial Ottoman Bank, the Northern Banking Co (Belfast) and William Deacons Bank.[17] The authorised capital, £5m, was divided into 300,000 shares of which the Union Bank took 50,000.[18] The general manager of the Union Bank, Arthur C D Gairdner, transferred his office to the new Bank where he became the chairman of the board of directors. The chairmanship of Gairdner, who continued to sit on the board of the Union Bank, indicates that the British Overseas Bank was effectively the project of the Union Bank. The British Overseas Bank, responding to the expectation of the Union Bank, developed its business especially into the Baltic coast such as Poland, Latvia and Estonia. Unfortunately for the British Overseas Bank, the political and financial situations of Europe during the inter-war period did not favour its business, and the Overseas Bank encountered difficulties in the mid 1930s, eventually making the business over to Glyn & Co in 1944.[19]

Save the three topics mentioned, the content of the minute books of the Union Bank was becoming increasingly monotonous and less interesting, particularly from the turn of the century. The directors do not seem to have participated in the daily conduct of business. Yet in the late 1880s the minute of the board of directors showed that the directors themselves were very active in superintending their business. This was exemplified by the record that,

> The Committee appointed for the current year, Messers Clapperton, Galbraith, Ritchie and Thomson as Sub-Committee for the purposes of superintending the advances by way of Discounts, Cash Credits, Overdrawn Accounts and Loans on Stock and other Securities at the Head Office and Branches. The General Manager to be ex-officio a member of Committee, and three to be a quorum.[20]

This was effectively the last record of the directors involving themselves directly in the daily conduct and of the Bank minuting banking policy. From then on (more accurately speaking, up to 1919 when our free access to the minute books in the Bank Archives expires), there was never the slightest whisper of any policy statement. The minute books, especially in the twentieth century, became formal, following a regular pattern of recording. Invariably there was the list of transfers of shares at the beginning of each meeting of the board. This was followed by another list of advances, and then came the report of the inspector about which no information was given in the minute book. As far as the minute books between 1885 and 1919 are concerned, it is impossible for us to know from them what policy the Union Bank was following and what decision the board of directors was making. This fact, however, suggests one point, that is, the management of the Union Bank, and perhaps of the bank in general, was entirely dependent upon the general manager and the hierarchy which he governed.

Between 1895, when Charles Gairdner retired from his office, and 1952, when the amalgamation of the Union Bank and the Bank of Scotland was negotiated, the Union Bank had five general managers;[21] Robert Blyth (1895–1910), Arthur C D Gairdner (1910–19), George J Scott (1919–20), Norman L Hird (1920–45) and John A Morrison (1946–54). Among them, some features of three general managers can be outlined.

Robert Blyth had been a partner of the firm of M'Clelland, MacKinnon and Blyth, chartered accountants in Glasgow, and then became the manager of the Scottish Amicable Life Assurance Society.[22] As a partner of the well known firm of chartered accountants, from which the first external auditor of the Union Bank came, Blyth must have been an intimate friend of his predecessor, Charles Gairdner, formerly chartered accountant. As such he was probably a nominee of Charles Gairdner. As a result, the Union Bank had two general managers who were chartered accountants and who controlled the Bank for nearly half a century. The accountants regime was interrupted by the appointment of Arthur C D Gairdner. Younger Gairdner was born in 1872 and was a son of D C Gairdner, brother of Charles Gairdner. Arthur Gairdner had already been some time the London manager of the Union Bank by 1910 when he was promoted to the general manager's office. His tenure was only nine years, the shortest compared with those of his predecessors, but he contributed to the Union Bank in two respects. Firstly, he introduced the first and only superannuation scheme in 1913.[23] Secondly, he was enthusiastic in embarking upon foreign banking business as we discussed above.

Norman Hird was born in 1886 and a son of a captain of the Mercantile Marine. He enrolled as a student at London University and was presumably one of the first bank general managers who had a university education. He entered the Union Bank at the London Office in 1903. In 1911 he was transferred to Glasgow where he was put in the Inspector's Department. Then he was promoted to Assistant Accountant in the London Office in 1914, later to Accountant, to Assistant Manager and to Manager in London in 1919. In 1920 when G J Scott, who had succeeded Arthur Gairdner, deserted the Union Bank to be Treasurer of the Bank of Scotland, Hird became his successor. He was the youngest general manager the Union Bank ever had.[24] He took a vigorous initiative in building an American style new Head Office in St Vincent Street, Glasgow, creating the first independent trustee department and the first bank nominee company and further developing a modern foreign exchange service following Arthur Gairdner. He was also enthusiastic in developing Scottish industries during difficult years of the inter-war period. These accomplishments were, however, somewhat counteracted by his formidable temperament displayed against his bank clerks and fellow general managers.[25]

TABLE 73

Comparisons of Growth Rates of Some Items of Balance Sheets of the Union Bank of Scotland under Three General Managerships: 1895 = 100, 1910 = 100, 1920 = 100

	(1) Total Liabilities/Assets		(2) Deposits		(3) Advances		(4) Investments		(5) Liquid Assets		(6) Profits	
	(a)*	(b)†	(a)	(b)	(a)	(b)	(a)	(b)	(a)	(b)	(a)	(b)
Blyth (1895–1910)	114%	113%	118%	113%	119%	112%	100%	100%	108%	124%	150%	139%
Gairdner (1910–19)	250	231	253	245	247	159	309	458	210	239	177	174
Hird (1920–45)	177	210	179	211	45	73	462	381	213	224	113	139

*Union Bank   †Scottish total

Source: SGC and MacDonald, 1973

TABLE 74

*Comparisons of Assets Managements under Three General Managerships:
Advances, Investments and Liquid Assets as Percentages of Deposits*

	(1) *Advances*		‡(2) *Investments*		(3) *Liquid Assets*	
	(a)*	(b)†	(a)	(b)	(a)	(b)
Blyth (1895–1910)	63%	72%	23%	25%	36%	29%
Gairdner (1910–19)	62	57	29	35	31	31
Hird (1920–45)	40	42	56	53	24	26

*Union Bank   † Scottish total
‡ Figures are average of each tenure

Source: as of Table 73

Table 73 sets out growth rates of main items in balance sheets of the Union Bank and the Scottish total during three periods, namely under general managerships of Blyth, Gairdner and Hird. Under the management of Blyth, the growth rates of total liabilities, deposits and advances were slightly above those of the Scottish total. No remarkable characteristic was perceived in the trend of these items. It could be said that Blyth's management of assets laid a little stress on liquid assets, as Table 74 shows. During Gairdner's leadership, the Union Bank grew in terms of total liabilities by nineteen points more than the Scottish standard. This growth apparently resulted from increases in advances as Table 73 and 74 set out. The rapid growth of advances was due certainly to the expansion of heavy industries responding to war demands, for which the West of Scotland was far more responsible than any other place in Britain,[26] and to which the Union Bank must have supplied much resources.

Under the headship of Hird, the growth rate of total liabilities was considerably below the Scottish total. The same situation was seen in the trend of deposits, which were, of course, the largest component of liabilities. On the assets side, advances decreased substantially between 1920 and 1945. Advances as a percentage of deposits slipped down to 16.6% in 1945 and was 40% on average during these twenty-five years. On the contrary, investments grew nearly five times larger than those in 1920. Investments as a percentage of deposits reached the highest point of 74.4% in 1944 and were 56% on average. From the figures in Tables 73 and 74, it is not unreasonable to say that two factors were responsible for the relatively weak growth of the Union Bank. First on the liabilities side, deposits failed to increase enough to sustain the development of the business rivalling those of other banks. This probably resulted from the lack of competitiveness in expanding branch banking. Second on the assets side, advances lost ground. The low proportion of advances and the subsequent high proportion of investments in asset management were common in Scottish banking from 1920 as Table 74 shows. This tendency appeared more strongly in the case of the Union Bank. This suggests that the Union Bank was losing lending opportunities faster than its fellow Scottish banks. Unfortunately for Norman Hird, who was perhaps the last of the classic type of Scottish bank manager, the Union Bank could not show any remarkable performance between 1920 and 1945 and, indeed, it could not advance beyond sixth place in Scottish banking.

From 1950, five years after the death of Norman Hird, a surge of Scottish bank amalgamations, which had some time ceased from 1907/1908 commenced reducing the number of Scottish banks from eight to five; the Clydesdale Bank and the North of Scotland Bank amalgamated in 1950, the Union Bank and the Bank of Scotland in 1952–54 and the Commercial Bank and the National Bank in 1958. There was one distinct difference between the first and third cases and the case of the Union Bank. In the former cases, two English banks, the Midland and Lloyds, were essential in promoting the mergers.[27] On the contrary, no English initiative was involved in the case of the Union Bank and the Bank of Scotland. Independence from English control was the established policy of the Union Bank led by Norman Hird and of the Bank of Scotland, the most senior Scottish bank.

In other respects, the amalgamation of the Union Bank and the Bank of Scotland reflected a common problem of the Scottish banks. In the post-Second World War period, there emerged giant corporations which demanded tremendously large amounts of advances.[28] For instance, A P Anderson, the general manager of the British Linen Bank, told the Radcliffe Committee that,

Individual advances may be anything up to £1m.[29]

Only the giant bank could respond to demands of gigantic customers. In addition there were situations challenging the Scottish banks. To the south of the border, the English banks, which had already by this time consolidated into the Big 5, were further strengthening their positions and were prepared to deprive their Scottish counterparts of their customers as this really happened in the 1960s.[30] There was another formidable competitor. Hire purchase companies, which had recently been freed from any official restrictions, started to invade banking business, especially short term lending. Anderson complained that,

There has been very much more competition from the hire purchase concerns,[31]

though it was a Scottish bank which first took an interest in a hire purchase company.[32] In these circumstances, the smallish Scottish banks, such as the Union Bank and the Bank of Scotland, compared with their English counterparts, had no choice but to amalgamate with each other in order to become larger units.

There was a particular factor, too, for the case of the Union Bank and the Bank of Scotland. As *The Economist* argued,

A significant feature of this merger, by contrast with the earlier one (the Clydesdale/North of Scotland merger in 1950) is that the business of the two banks are competitive rather than complementary, and that both embrace extensive networks of branches throughout Scotland. The potentialities for the concentration of branch business should therefore be a good deal wider than those presented by the Clydesdale–North merger.[33]

The concentration of branch networks, of course, involved both Banks in reducing the number of offices and the staff. Simultaneously, there were prospects for the amalgamated Bank of strengthening more specialized and up-to-date departments such as foreign exchange, trustee business, hire purchase etc, and these perhaps mitigated the staff problem. Eventually, some fifty branches were closed in ten years.[34] The amalgamation of the sixth and fourth Banks elevated the new Bank to the top of the Scottish ranking in terms of total liabilities in 1955. The Union Bank of Scotland, being proud of the longest Glasgow banking tradition, was at last assimilated with the oldest Edinburgh based Bank.

The Union Bank of Scotland was created in 1830 by enthusiastic Glasgow men who were energetically developing industries in the West of Scotland. In the 1860s when the high prosperity of industries was about to arrive in Glasgow, the Clydeside and the West, the Union Bank reached its zenith. During the latter half of the Victorian age, the Bank continuously fell in importance in Scottish banking, but was a financier of vital importance in sustaining the prosperity of heavy industries, trade and transport in the West. In the post-First World War period when the industries in the West could not reshape themselves, failing to challenge difficulties and thus losing ground, the Union Bank did not show a remarkable performance which could once again attract the public and enhance its fame. Indeed, the Union Bank of Scotland shared the fate of decay with the industries, whose financing was the *raison d'être* of the bank, and was absorbed by the wave of the amalgamation movement which the Bank had pioneered in Scotland some 120 years earlier.

Notes

Introduction

1 SGC, 1975, Chapter 6. CWM, 1981, Introduction.
2 SGC, 1975, Tables 3 and 9. CWM, 1981, Chapters 4 and 5.
3 SGC, 1975, Chapter 10.
4 E Nevin and E W Davis, 1970, p. 58.
5 T Joplin, 1827, p. 10.
6 *Ibid.* p. 54.
7 T C Smout, 1969, pp. 196–7, 233. A Slaven, 1975, pp. 97–102.
8 T C Smout, 1969, p. 243.
9 SGC, 1975, pp. 417–18. A Slaven, 1975, pp. 52–3.
10 T Devine, 1975, p. 93.
11 SGC, 1975, Chapters 5 and 6.
12 *Ibid.* p. 125.
13 *Ibid.* pp. 124–34.
14 Anon, 1966, 'Glasgow Financial Scene', *TBR,* pp. 37, 42–3.
15 'of Ulbster, statesman, agriculturalist, philanthropist and prolific writer' (J Irving, 1880, p. 476) and the compiler of the first *Statistical Account of Scotland* (1791). *See also* R Mitchison, 1962.
16 SGC, 1975, p. 168.
17 *Ibid.* Tables 5 and 6.
18 R S Rait, 1930, p. 204.
19 R H Campbell, 1965, p. 148.
20 CWM, 1981, Table 49.

Chapter One   *Formative Years, 1830–1844*

1 The title of the Bank will be termed Union Bank, even in discussion of the period before 1844, when the Bank actually changed its title to this.
2 UBM, 15/1/1830.
3 *Ibid.* 15/1/1830.
4 R Renwick, 1916, vol. XI, p. 326.
5 UBM, 15/1/1830.
6 *GH,* 28/12/1829.
7 UB *Prospectus* 1830.
8 UBM, 15/1/1830.
9 *Ibid.* 21/1/1830.
10 *Ibid.* 20/1/1830.
11 UBC.
12 Anon, 1886, *One Hundred Glasgow Men,* p. 175.
13 *Ibid.* p. 97. See also J S Jeans, 1872, pp. 36–7, 41. Anon, 1896, *Old Glasgow,* p. 147.
14 Anon, 1886, *One Hundred Glasgow Men,* p. 9.
15 UBM, 19/2/1830.

16 CWM, 1981, p. 164.
17 *See* Chapter 1.2.
18 CWM, 1981, p. 164.
19 UBM, 23/3/1830.
20 *Ibid.*
21 UB, *Manager's Circular,* 10/4/1830.
22 UBM, 6/5/1830.
23 UB, *Annual Report,* 12/5/1831.
24 UBM, 30/12/1830.
25 *Ibid. passim.*
26 A Slaven, 1975, pp. 26–7.
27 UB *Annual Report,* 12/5/1831.
28 UBM, 18/10/1830, 13/12/1830, 30/12/1830.
29 S E Thomas, 1934, p. 257.
30 UBM, 28/2/1831, 13/3/1831.
31 *Ibid.* 4/3/1830, 27/5/1830, 18/6/1830, 20/1/1831.
32 Appendix A.
33 SGC, 1975, Table 13.
34 UB, *Annual Report,* 10/5/1832.
35 *Ibid.* 8/5/1834.
36 UBM, 4/2/1834.
37 *Ibid.* 20/12/1831.
38 SGC, 1975, Table 13.
39 CWM, 1981, p. 120.
40 R Cameron, 1967, p. 75.
41 UBM, 27/9/1831.
42 *Ibid.* 3/12/1833 and *passim.*
43 *Ibid.* 18/10/1831.
44 *Ibid.* 9/7/1833.
45 *Ibid.* 11/10/1831, 6/12/1831.
46 *Ibid.* 24/12/1833.
47 *See* Chapter 3.2.
48 UBM, 13/5/1834, 19/5/1835.
49 UB, *Annual Report,* 8/5/1834.
50 UBM, 7/10/1830.
51 *Ibid.* 21/8/1832.
52 *Ibid.* 2/4/1833, 9/4/1833.
53 *See* Chapter 1.2.
54 UB, *Annual Report,* 8/5/1834.
55 *Ibid.* 14/5/1835.
56 *See* Chapter 2.3.
57 UBM, 31/1/1832.
58 UB *Prospectus* 1830. *See also* UBM, 8/1/1833.
59 UB, *Annual Report,* 9/5/1833, *see also* Map 1.2.
60 UB, *Petition for a charter,* —/12/1835. For the purpose of obtaining a charter, *see* Chapter 2.1.
61 UB, *Annual Report,* 9/5/1839.
62 *Ibid.* 9/5/1839.
63 RBS *Minute of the Board of Directors,* 28/7/1842.
64 UBM, 21/1/1840.
65 *See also* Table 10.
66 UBM 14, 23/8/1838, 5/2/1839.

67 *Ibid.* 18/1/1842.
68 T R Gourvish, 1969, p. 294.
69 UBM, 17/10/1838, *passim.*
70 CWM, 1981, p. 127.
71 SGC, 1975, p. 386.
72 UBM *Scroll Book,* 28/11/1841.
73 UBC.
74 CWM, 1981, p. 127.
75 UBM, 15/4/1845.
76 *Ibid.* 14/5/1844 *passim.*
77 *Ibid.* 8/11/1845 *passim.*
78 *Ibid.* 8/2/1842.
79 *See* Chapter 2.2.
80 UBM, 27/7/1841, 19/7/1842, 7/3/1843.
81 *Ibid.* 1/11/1836, 7/9/1837.
82 *Ibid.* 21/8/1838.
83 *Ibid.* 26/10/1841.
84 *Ibid.* 25/6/1839, 2/7/1839, 8/10/1839, 22/10/1839, 12/11/1839.
85 *Ibid.* 1/8/1843.
86 *See* Chapter 1.3.
87 J Thomas, 1971, p. 63.
88 Anon, 1886, *One Hundred Glasgow Men,* p. 175.
89 UBM, 1/5/1840.
90 *Ibid.* 19/10/1841.
91 *Ibid. Scroll Book,* 10/5/1842.
92 T B Gourvish and M C Reed, 1971, p. 216.
93 UBM, 16/8/1836.
94 UBCUBM, 28/6/1836, 1/8/1837, 22/8/1837.
95 *Ibid.* 29/5/1838.
96 *Ibid.* 8/8/1837. *See also* 15/8/1837.
97 UBME, 15/6/1843.
98 D S MacMillan, 1967, p. 323.
99 UBM, 21/6/1836, 7/2/1843, 28/3/1843.
100 R S Rait, 1930, p. 128.
101 UBM, 21/6/1836.
102 *Ibid.* 21/6/1836.
103 *Ibid.* 21/6/1836.
104 R Richardson, 1900, p. 33.
105 SGC, 1975, p. 157.
106 C D Gairdner, 1902, p. 19.
107 R S Rait, 1930, p. 251.
108 UBM, 17/4/1838.
109 *Ibid.* 17/4/1838.
110 UB, Edinburgh, *Private Letter Book,* 18/9/1839 and *passim,* R S Rait, 1930, p. 117.
111 UB, *Annual Report,* 10/5/1838.
112 C F Freebairn, 1924, p. 115, SGC, 1975, p. 171.
113 C F Freebairn, 1924, p. 117. R S Rait, 1930, pp. 200–1.
114 *See* Chapter 1.3.
115 R S Rait, 1930, pp. 173–4, 180–1.
116 *Ibid.* p. 184.
117 C D Gairdner, 1902, p. 19.

118 Glasgow & Ship Bank, *Minute of the Board of Directors*, 8/11/1843.
119 *Ibid.* 9/3/1843, 23/3/1843, 30/3/1843.
120 *Ibid.* 8/11/1843.
121 UBM, 10/10/1843.
122 UBMGB, 13/10/1843, Glasgow & Ship Bank, *Minute of the Board of Directors*, 9/11/1843.
123 *See* Chapter 2.1.
124 UBM, 17/3/1842. Regarding advantages of obtaining a charter, *see* Chapter 2.1.
125 UBC amendments.
126 UB, *Special Report*, 8/11/1843.
127 UBC amendments.
128 UBM, 4/4/1843.
129 *Ibid.* 28/12/1841.
130 Anon, 1886, *One Hundred Glasgow Men*, pp. 175–6. Anon, 1896, *Old Glasgow*, p. 106.
131 UBM, 12/12/1843.
132 *Ibid.* 13/5/1841.
133 *Ibid.* 19/9/1843, 2/11/1843.
134 *Ibid.* 8/1/1833, 23/8/1838, Glasgow & Ship Bank, *Minute of the Board of Directors*, 9/11/1843. *See also* C F Freebairn, 1924(a), p. 240.
135 *See* SGC, 1975, Diagram 2.
136 *Ibid.* Table 42, C W Boase, 1867, pp. 422–3.

Chapter Two   *Rapid Growth, 1844–1858*

1 F W Fetter, 1965, *passim.*
2 Select Committee, 1841, Q.1727.
3 *Ibid.* QQ.1683, 1685, 1790, 1794, 1797.
4 8 & 9 Vict. c.38.
5 C W Boase, 1867, p. 432. S E Thomas, 1934, pp. 526–8. SGC, 1975, p. 458.
6 UB, *Annual Report*, 14/5/1846.
7 *Ibid.* 14/5/1846.
8 UBM, 20/2/1850.
9 UB *Annual Report*, 8/5/1856. *See also* S E Thomas, 1934, pp. 590–1.
10 UBM, 31/1/1851, 8/1/1854 and *passim.*
11 T R Gourvish, 1969, p. 301.
12 *See* Chapter 2.2.
13 Select Committee, 1841, Q.1924.
14 *See* Chapter 1.3.
15 UBM, 10/9/1844, 17/9/1844, UBMGB, 12/9/1844.
16 UBM, 12/11/1844.
17 *Ibid.* 29/1/1847, 3/2/1847.
18 *Ibid.* 8/11/1845, 10/11/1847, UBMGB, 25/1/1847. NBS *Minute of the Board of Directors*, 10/11/1845, 17/11/1847.
19 UBM, 3/2/1847.
20 *Ibid.* 10/7/1850.
21 *Ibid.* 12/5/1854.
22 SGC, 1975, p. 486.
23 UB *Annual Report*, 13/5/1847.
24 *See* Chapter 2.5.

25 UB *Annual Report,* 8/5/1856.
26 *See* Chapter 2.4.
27 R Cameron, 1967, p. 77.
28 UBM, 28/10/1853.
29 H D MacLeod, 1889, pp. 327–8.
30 W T C King, 1936, p. 94.
31 R W Hidy, 1949, p. 133. Gillet Brothers' Discount Co, 1952, part II. Metropolitan College, n.d., pp. 13, 182.
32 UBM, 23/3/1853.
33 *Ibid.* 23/9/1847.
34 *See* Chapter 2.5.
35 UBM, 28/10/1853.
36 *Ibid.* 25/9/1851.
37 *Ibid.* 13/9/1848.
38 R H Campbell, 1955(a).
39 UBM, 29/9/1852.
40 *See* Chapter 5.3(2).
41 UBM, 13/1/1847.
42 UBMGB, 4/2/1850, 9/1/1851.
43 UBM, 14/2/1849.
44 P Deane and W A Cole, 1969, p. 231.
45 UBPL, 5/10/1838 and *passim.*
46 G Kinnear, 1848, p. 11.
47 *Ibid.* p. 19.
48 UBM, 14/6/1848.
49 SGC, 1975, p. 342.
50 UBM, 5/3/1847.
51 G Kinnear, 1847, pp. 3–4, 5.
52 UBMGB, 19/3/1847.
53 UBM, 31/3/1847.
54 *Ibid. Scroll Book,* 13/1/1847.
55 UBM, 14/6/1848, 21/6/1848.
56 'A proposal' was made known in the annual meeting held on 13 May 1852.
57 B R Mitchell and P Deane, 1976, p. 456.
58 UB *Annual Report,* 13/5/1852.
59 UBMGB, 12/8/1852.
60 B R Mitchell and P Deane, 1976, p. 455.
61 UBMGB, 13/1/1853.
62 UBME, 28/2/1853, 8/8/1853.
63 UB *Private Journal* (Edinburgh), 19/4/1856, 20/4/1857, 20/4/1858.
64 UBC.
65 UBMGB, 13/5/1846.
66 *Edinburgh Almanac,* 1849, quoted by J W Gilbart, 1849, p. 544.
67 Select Committee, 1841, QQ. 2411, 2443.
68 UBMGB, 9/7/1846, UBM, 22/7/1846, 5/7/1848.
69 *Ibid.* 19/1/1851.
70 UBME, 7/11/1844 and *passim.* UBMGB, 8/1/1852 and *passim.*
71 UBM, 22/7/1846, UBMGB, 8/1/1852.
72 UBME, 21/3/1840. *See also* UBMGB, 13/4/1848.
73 *See* Chapter 2.5.
74 UBMGB, 14/11/1844.
75 UBM, *Scroll Book,* 14/1/1845.

76 UBME, 30/5/1846.

77 UBM, 7/7/1852.

78 J W Gilbart, 1849, pp. 240–1.

79 SGC, 1975, pp. 340–1, 466.

80 UB *Annual Report,* 14/5/1846.

81 UBMGB, 29/10/1845.

82 *Ibid.* 11/3/1847, 3/6/1847.

83 The number of Dennistoun's shares in this period is not clear. However, the list of shareholders later in 1885 reveals that the Dennistoun family held 7,570, a tremendous sum, of which 5,500 were the holding of A Dennistoun (UB *List of Shareholders 1885*).

84 UBM, 18/9/1845, 2/10/1845.

85 *See* Chapter 2.2.

86 *See* Chapter 2.5 and Chapter 3.1.

87 UBMGB, 9/12/1847.

88 *Ibid.* 9/12/1847.

89 *Ibid.* 12/10/1848.

90 *The Glasgow Stock Exchange Daily List, passim.*

91 UBMGB, 12/8/1847 and *passim.*

92 UBM *Scroll Book,* 16/5/1845.

93 UBM, 9/12/1857, 10/3/1858, 24/3/1858.

94 *Ibid.* 30/5/1835.

95 UBME, 5/5/1856.

96 UBM, 24/6/1845, 2/9/1846, 9/9/1846.

97 *Ibid.* 24/6/1845, 27/8/1845, 26/8/1846, 2/9/1846.

98 *Ibid.* 22/1/1851.

99 Select Committee, 1857/58, reproduced in: Anon, 1858, *The Western Bank Failure and the Scottish Banking System,* p. 50.

100 UBM, 23/2/1853. *See also ibid.* 19/1/1853.

101 *Ibid.* 22/4/1857.

102 UBMGB, 13/1/1848.

103 *Ibid.* 21/5/1850.

104 UBM, —/5/1861.

105 *Ibid.* 28/8/1850. *See also* UB *Annual Report,* 9/5/1850, UBMGB, 6/6/1850.

106 Select Committee, 1858, reproduced in: Anon, 1858, *The Western Bank Failure and the Scottish Banking System,* p. 37.

107 *Ibid.* p. 42.

108 UBM, 15/5/1850.

109 *Ibid.* 26/6/1850 and *passim.*

110 CWM, 1981, p. 90.

111 H MacKenzie, 1953, pp. 250, 263.

112 UBM, 1/6/1849.

113 *Ibid.* 1/8/1849.

114 CWM, 1981, p. 97.

115 Perth Bank, *Minute of the Board of Directors,* 13/7/1857.

116 *See* Chapter 1.3.

117 CWM, 1981, p. 97.

118 UBME, 25/2/1851, 18/2/1856.

119 R S Rait, 1930, p. 263.

120 CWM, 1981, p. 97.

121 *See* Chapter 3.3.

122 R S Rait, 1930, p. 292.

123 UBM *Scroll Book,* 22/9/1847.

124 *Ibid.* 29/9/1847, 17/11/1847, 5/1/1848.
125 UBME, 28/8/1847. *See* Chapter 1.3(2).
126 *See* Chapter 2.5.
127 R H Campbell, 1955.
128 BS (Edinburgh) *Private & Confidential Letter Book,* 20/10/1857, which was read by Blair before the court of directors.
129 UB (Edinburgh) *Letter Book,* Samuel Hay to Sir Adam Hay, 14/11/1857.
130 A Blair's *Memorandum,* 22/10/1857, in: Anon, 1858, *The Western Bank Failure and the Scottish Banking System,* p. 78.
131 Western Bank *Minute of the Board of Directors,* 23/10/1857, in: *ibid.* p. 79.
132 *Minute of the Edinburgh banks,* 26/10/1857, in: *ibid.* p. 79.
133 J Stirling, 1865, p. 32.
134 C W Boase, 1867, pp. 481–3.
135 Anon (R H Patterson), 1864, The Economy of Capital, *Blackwood's Edinburgh Magazine,* p. 316, R H Patterson, 1865, p. 110.
136 UB (Edinburgh) *Letter Book,* J Robertson to S Hay, 9/11/1857.
137 UBM, 10/11/1857.
138 UBME, 2/11/1857.
139 UBM, 10/11/1857.
140 R Fulford, 1953, p. 162.
141 A Alison, 1883, vol. 2, p. 192.
142 UB (Edinburgh), *Letter Book,* S Hay to Sir Adam Hay, 14/11/1857.
143 R S Rait, p. 291.
144 *Ibid.* p. 291.
145 R S Rait, pp. 291–2.
146 UB (Glasgow), *Record of Transfers Registered.*
147 UBM *Scroll Book,* 5/1/1846.
148 *Ibid.* 5/5/1847.
149 UBME, 25/5/1847.
150 UBMGB, 19/4/1853.
151 SGC, 1975, p. 467.
152 *Ibid.* p. 468.

Chapter Three *The Union Bank of Scotland at its Zenith 1858–1865*

1 The career etc will be discussed in Chapter 5.5.
2 UB *Annual Report,* 9/5/1861. Despite the directors' words, it would be unwise to say that this firm was that of 'Blackie & Son, publishers at Glasgow', whose main bank was the Clydesdale. So far no evidence is available about the business of the Aberdeen firm.
3 UBM, 20/4/1859.
4 *Ibid.* 10/11/1858.
5 *Ibid.* 10/11/1858.
6 UB *Annual Report,* 8/5/1862.
7 *Ibid.* 8/5/1862.
8 *Ibid.* 8/5/1862.
9 UBM, 2/1/1867, 9/1/1867.
10 UB (Glasgow), MSS, n.d.

11 UBME, 9/8/1858. See also 7/2/1859.

12 UB (Edinburgh), MSS, 6/12/1858.

13 UBM, 4/7/1860, 11/7/1860, 25/7/1860.

14 UBME, 13/8/1860.

15 UBM, 9/11/1859 and *passim*.

16 UB (Edinburgh), MSS, 29/10/1857.

17 Select Committee of 1858, reproduced in: Anon, 1858, *Western Bank Failure and the Scottish Banking System*, p. 52.

18 UBM, 21/10/1863.

19 *Ibid.* 30/12/1863.

20 Metropolitan College, n.d., p. 14. See also W Thomson and R W Jones, 1939, p. 400.

21 UBM, 11/1/1865.

22 UB (Glasgow), *Opinion Books*.

23 UBM, 7/10/1863.

24 R H Campbell, 1955(a), p. 221.

25 D S MacMillan, 1967(a), pp. 340–1.

26 R H Patterson, 1868, p. 571.

27 UBME, 22/10/1860, 29/10/1860.

28 UBM, 23/3/1864.

29 UBSB, 2/7/1862.

30 See Chapter 1.2.

31 UBAAB, —/4/1862.

32 UB (Edinburgh), MSS, 20/5/1862, 30/5/1862.

33 C A Malcolm, 1945, p. 107.

34 BS *Minute of the Board of Directors*, 19/7/1864.

35 BS (Edinburgh), MSS, C Gairdner to D Davidson, 20/1/1866.

36 BS (Edinburgh), MSS, 7/3/1866, *See also*, 'Scheme' attached to UBM, 3/1/1866.

37 R Fulford, 1953, pp. 193–6.

38 *See* Chapter 2.2(2).

39 CWM, *working paper*.

40 SGC, 1975, p. 486.

41 UBGC, 21/12/1860.

42 *Ibid. passim.*

43 *Ibid.* 20/9/1861.

44 *Ibid.* 6/11/1863.

45 *Ibid. passim.*

46 S E Thomas, 1934, p. 555.

47 R H Patterson, 1865, p. 82.

48 UB (Glasgow), *General Quarterly Balance Branch Accounts*, 1/4/1865.

49 UB (Edinburgh), MSS, C Gairdner to S Hay, 22/12/1864.

50 *Ibid.* 22/12/1864.

51 UBM, 16/10/1861, 27/11/1861.

52 *Ibid.* 29/1/1862.

53 *Ibid.* 23/7/1862, 6/8/1862, 3/9/1862.

54 *Ibid.* 30/9/1863.

55 *Ibid.* 3/12/1862.

56 *Ibid.* 1/4/1863.

57 *Ibid.* 22/4/1863.

58 *Ibid.* 10/6/1863.

59 *Ibid.* 30/7/1862, 27/8/1862.

60 *Ibid.* 23/7/1862 and *passim*.

61 See Chapters 4.2 and 5.2.
62 UBM, 10/6/1863, 30/9/1863.
63 W Bagehot, 1873, pp. 285–6.
64 P L Cottrell, 1980, p. 205.
65 UB *Annual Report*, 8/5/1862.

Chapter Four   *Years of Difficulty, 1865–1879*

1 R H Patterson, 1868, pp. 224, 228, 232, 689. W T C King, 1936, pp. 242–51. J Clapham, 1944, vol. 2, pp. 260–1. J Giuseppi, 1966, pp. 119–20. R N Forbes, 1966, pp. 175, 179, 181.
2 H Gairdner, n.d.
3 UBM, 17/1/1866. UBAAB, 2/4/1866.
4 UBM, 16/5/1866.
5 SGC, 1975, pp. 470–1.
6 K MacKenzie, 1909, p. 97.
7 H Gairdner, n.d.
8 *Economist*, 19/6/1875.
9 *Ibid*. 7/8/1875.
10 *Ibid*. 24/7/1875, 7/8/1875. *See also* E T Powell, 1915, pp. 429–30. A W Kerr, 1926, p. 249.
11 H Gairdner, n.d. According to Mrs Gairdner, 'Mr Collie had been introduced to him by one of his most trusted directors.' The name of the director is unknown.
12 *Times*, 10/8/1875.
13 UBM, 20/7/1875.
14 *Ibid*. 20/7/1875.
15 H Gairdner, n.d.
16 R E Tyson, 1974, p. 129.
17 *Times*, 10/8/1875.
18 CWM, 1981, p. 121.
19 UBM, 4/3/1868, 21/3/1868 and *passim*. NB merged with Edinburgh & Glasgow in 1865 (T C Barker and C I Savage, 1974, p. 88).
20 UBM, 17/3/1869, 3/11/1869.
21 *Ibid*. 27/3/1878.
22 For the same purpose, the Bank allowed a credit to Tharsis Sulphur & Copper Co (UBM, 13/5/1874).
23 T C Barker and C I Savage, 1974, p. 85.
24 UBM, 17/1/1866 and *passim*.
25 *Ibid*. 6/12/1865 and *passim*.
26 *Ibid*. 13/12/1876.
27 *Ibid*. 4/10/1871. Merchant House of Glasgow, 1866, pp. 546–8.
28 UBM, 2/5/1866.
29 R E Tyson, 1967, p. 395.
30 R Somers, 1873, appendix III.
31 UBM, 8/11/1878.
32 *Ibid*. 23/3/1876, 23/10/1878, 5/2/1879.
33 *Ibid*. 4/9/1878.
34 See Chapter 5.3.
35 UB (Glasgow), *Charles Gairdner's Note Book*, 30/6/1876.
36 *See* Chapter 5.3.

37 UBC.
38 B R Mitchell and P Deane, 1976, p. 455. S Homer, 1963, p. 288.
39 UBM, 21/9/1876.
40 B R Mitchell and P Deane, 1976, p. 457.
41 UBM, 24/1/1877.
42 T Hankey, 1887, pp. 89–90. UBM, 21/12/1870.
43 *Ibid.* 15/9/1876 and *passim*. UBSB, 19/4/1877.
44 M Gaskin, 1960, pp. 446–7. L S M Munro, 1975, pp. 27, 31.
45 UBGC, 28/3/1873.
46 R Somers, 1873, Appendix III.
47 UBM, 31/12/1873.
48 UBHC, —/2/1875.
49 UBC.
50 J M Reid, 1938, p. 164.
51 M Gaskin, 1960, p. 447.
52 *Minute of Meetings of Bank Managers (Scotland)*, 13/4/1874. See also *ibid.* 23/2/1874.
53 A letter from the chairman of the committee of English country banks, in: *Minute of Meetings of Bank Managers (Scotland)*, 13/4/1874.
54 UBGC, 21/8/1874 and *passim*.
55 UBHC, 25/11/1875.
56 *Minute of Meetings of Bank Managers (Scotland)*, 30/4/1875.
57 UB *Annual Reports*. R H I Palgrave, 1903, pp. 118–23. SGC, 1975, p. 423, Tables 15 and 44. CWM, 1981, pp. 143–4.
58 J M Reid, 1938, pp. 168–70. M Gaskin, 1960, pp. 67–8. M Kita, 1976.
59 UBC.
60 UBM, 20/3/1878.
61 UBHC, 28/6/1878.
62 *Ibid.* 9/8/1878.
63 L S Pressnell, 1956, p. 82.
64 UBM, 30/5/1878.
65 UBC.
66 UBM, 25/4/1877.
67 UBMA, 4/1/1878. UBMB, 14/5/1873 and *passim*.
68 *Ibid.* 24/11/1875.
69 UBC, UBME, 9/5/1870 and *passim*.
70 See Chapter 5.5.
71 UBM, 17/8/1868, 29/9/1869, 25/5/1870.
72 UBMB, 28/8/1872 and *passim*.
73 UBM, 23/8/1873, 17/12/1873, 9/12/1874, 30/8/1876, 6/12/1876.
74 See Chapter 4.2.
75 See Chapter 5.4.
76 UBMB, 3/10/1872.
77 *Ibid.* 13/11/1872. See also *ibid.* 10/9/1873.
78 UB (Glasgow), *Record of Salaries*.
79 *Minute of Meetings of Bank Managers (Scotland)*, 7/10/1878. UBHC, 28/12/1878.
80 UBGC, 3/1/1872 and *passim*.
81 UBM, 5/6/1867.
82 *Ibid.* 3/7/1867, 15/12/1869.
83 *Ibid.* 27/3/1872.
84 *Ibid.* 3/6/1874.

85 *Ibid.* 29/4/1874.
86 UBGC, 5/10/1878, 11/10/1878, 27/2/1879.
87 UB *Annual Report,* 9/5/1867.
88 UBSB, 28/11/1876.
89 G M Bell, 1855, pp. 161–2.
90 A W Kerr, 1926, pp. 241–6. SGC, 1975, p. 493.
91 UBGC, 16/1/1871 and *passim.*
92 *Ibid.* 31/1/1872 and *passim.*
93 *Ibid.* 28/10/1870, 3/12/1872, 28/10/1879, 22/9/1871, 3/7/1878.
94 UBM, 8/4/1874. UBGC, 5/5/1876, 6/11/1877.
95 UBM, 25/4/1866.
96 Appendix to UBM, —/5/1861. UBM, 1/5/1867. UBGC, 13/12/1875. UBSB, 14/5/1878.
97 UBGC, 13/12/1875.
98 G Anderson, 1976, p. 24.
99 SGC, 1975, p. 490.
100 UBHC, 13/11/1872.
101 B R Mitchell and P Deane, 1976, p. 343. See also Chapter 2.3.
102 UBMB, 25/6/1873.
103 UBM, 20/6/1866 and *passim.* UBMB, 14/5/1873 and *passim.*
104 *Minute of Meetings of Bank Managers (Scotland),* 1/10/1878. Anon, 1879, *City of Glasgow Bank Publications,* pp. 5–8. R E Tyson, 1974, p. 126. SGC, 1975, pp. 469–71.
105 C A Oakley, 1946, p. 150.
106 UBM, 2/10/1878 and *passim.*
107 UBHC, 3/10/1878.
108 UB *Annual Report,* 23/4/1879.
109 *Minute of Meetings of Bank Managers (Scotland),* 1/10/1878.
110 UBSB, 12/10/1878.
111 UBHC, 28/10/1878.
112 UB *Special Report,* 16/12/1878.
113 UB (Edinburgh), *General Circular,* 31/10/1878.
114 UB *Special Report,* 16/12/1878.
115 UBM, 13/11/1878 and *passim.*
116 *Ibid.* 4/12/1878.
117 See Chapter 2.5.
118 Anon, 1879, *City of Glasgow Bank Publications,* p. 8.
119 See Chapter 5.1.

Chapter Five   *Stagnation, 1874–1885*

1 SGC, 1975, p. 479.
2 UBC.
3 R E Tyson, 1974, p. 137.
4 C Gairdner to H E Crum Ewing, in: UBM, 10/4/1879.
5 *Ibid.* 10/4/1879.
6 *Ibid.* 12/4/1879.
7 *Ibid.* 12/4/1879.
8 See Chapter 5.5.
9 See Chapter 5.3.
10 W F Crick and J E Wadsworth, 1958, foreword by R McKenna.

11 Anon, 1879, *City of Glasgow Bank Publications*, p. 8.

12 *Times*, 24/4/1879.

13 *GH*, 24/4/1879. See also *Daily News*, 24/4/1879, *Pall Mall Gazette*, 26/4/1879, *Statist*, 26/4/1879.

14 *Economist*, 26/4/1879.

15 S E Thomas, 1934, p. 585. Even the Royal Bank of Liverpool could not claim to be the first in adopting the system. Beyond the Irish Sea, the Provincial Bank of Ireland appointed four auditors at its outset in 1823, though it is unknown whether or not they were outsiders (J W Gilbart, 1836, p. 46).

16 *Pall Mall Gazette*, 26/4/1879.

17 *Scotsman*, 24/4/1879.

18 UB (Glasgow) *Auditors' Memorandum*, 25/4/1879.

19 *Ibid.* 25/4/1879.

20 *GH*, 24/4/1879.

21 SGC, 1975, pp. 480–1.

22 CBS, Minute of Board of Directors, 21/7/1881.

23 UBC.

24 A W Kerr, 1926, p. 268.

25 SGC, 1975, Table,45.

26 S Nishimura, 1971.

27 UBM, 19/11/1879, 11/4/1883 and *passim. See also* Chapter 5.3.

28 UBM, 12/12/1883.

29 L S M Munro, 1975, p. 27. *See also* M Gaskin, 1965, p. 183.

30 BS (Edinburgh), *Report by the Committee on Home Affairs of the Glasgow Chamber of Commerce*, 26/12/1882.

31 UBM, 23/1/1881, 13/11/1882, 17/10/1884. UBPL *passim*.

32 UBM, 30/3/1881.

33 *Ibid.* 4/10/1882, 6/12/1882, GL, 20/1/1884, 22/1/1884, 11/2/1884.

34 GL, *passim*.

35 UBPL, —/3/1881.

36 *See* Chapter 4.2.

37 UBM, 30/7/1884.

38 GL, 20/3/1883, 31/5/1884, 3/10/1884.

39 *Ibid.* 12/12/1883.

40 *Ibid.* 25/6/1884, 30/6/1884, 10/8/1884, 3/10/1884. UBM, 5/11/1884.

41 C A Oakley, 1946, pp. 224–5.

42 W C Jack, 1902, pp. 3–4.

43 GL, 6/8/1883, 24/8/1883.

44 UBM, 26/9/1883, 1/10/1883. This subject will be discussed from another point of view in the last section of this chapter.

45 *See* Chapter 2.2.

46 TP, 1/7/1879.

47 *Ibid.* 1/7/1879.

48 A M Robb, 1958, in: J Cunnison and J B Gilfillan, ed., p. 207.

49 UBM, 3/12/1874.

50 A M Robb, 1958, in: J Cunnison and J B Gilfillan, ed., p. 181. P L Robertson, 1974. M S Moss and J R·Hume, 1977, pp. 117–18.

51 *MacKinnon Report*, in: TP, 3/5/1883.

52 *Ibid.* 3/5/1883.

53 A M Robb, 1958, in: J Cunnison and J B Gilfillan, ed., p. 181.

54 P Mathias, 1969, p. 176.

55 TP, 1/8/1882.

56 *Ibid.* 1/8/1882.
57 UBMA, 25/8/1882. This committee which was almost a sleeping one resumed its activity in this period exclusively on the subject of the Thomson affairs.
58 UBM, 30/8/1882.
59 TP, 27/7/1882.
60 UBM, 11/4/1883.
61 *Ibid.* 8/2/1883.
62 UBM, 8/2/1883.
63 *Ibid.* 14/2/1883.
64 C G D Tennant, 1979, p. 23.
65 UBM, 8/2/1883.
66 *Ibid.* 13/2/1883.
67 *The Bailie,* 2/3/1881.
68 GL, 17/3/1883.
69 *Ibid.* 17/3/1883, 1/5/1883, 3/5/1883, 28/5/1883.
70 *MacKinnon Report,* in: TP, 3/5/1883.
71 *Ibid.* 3/5/1883.
72 UBMA, 14/11/1884.
73 GL, 26/7/1883.
74 *Ibid.* 11/1/1884.
75 *Ibid.* 17/8/1884.
76 UBMA, 17/12/1884.
77 *Ibid.* 17/12/1884.
78 GL, 20/4/1885, 23/4/1885.
79 Anon, 1886, *One Hundred Glasgow Men,* pp. 321–2.
80 GL, 25/3/1884.
81 *Ibid.* 3/4/1884.
82 *Ibid.* 5/4/1884. See also *ibid.* 7/4/1884.
83 See Table 47.
84 GL, 8/4/1884.
85 *Ibid.* 9/4/1884.
86 W F Spalding, 1924, p. 108.
87 GL, 19/4/1884.
88 *See* Chapter 5.1.
89 GL, 25/4/1884.
90 *Ibid.* 16/1/1885.
91 UBM, 25/2/1880.
92 *Ibid.* 25/2/1880, 1/12/1880, 15/2/1882, 17/3/1882.
93 UBM, 21/9/1881, 8/2/1882, UB *List of Branches 1885.*
94 UB *List of Branches 1858–85.*
95 SGC, 1975, Table 44.
96 *See* Chapter 3.2.
97 GL, 12/4/1883.
98 S E Thomas, 1934, p. 299.
99 UBM, 12/10/1881.
100 *Ibid.* 26/7/1882.
101 *Ibid.* 25/8/1880. GL, 30/7/1884.
102 UBM, 27/10/1880 and *passim.*
103 The Union Bank faced difficulties in the Baring Crisis of 1890. (R S Rait, 1930, pp. 324–6).
104 UBM, 28/1/1880.

105 UBSB, 27/4/1883. UBGC, 2/8/1883.

106 UBSB, 27/11/1884.

107 *Ibid.* 17/5/1881. UBGC, 17/5/1881.

108 *Ibid.* 19/10/1882.

109 See Table 41.

110 GL, 8/10/1884 and *passim.*

111 UBSB, 27/4/1883.

112 *See* Chapter 4.3.

113 UB (Edinburgh), *Staff and Salary Records.* See also Table 64.

114 B R Mitchell and P Deane, 1976, p. 344.

115 W J Reader, 1966, p. 202.

116 SGC, 1975, p. 489.

117 *See* Chapter 4.3.

118 UB (Glasgow), MSS.

119 J M Reid, 1938, p. 288. SGC, 1975, p. 543.

120 BS (Edinburgh), MSS, C Gairdner to J A Wenley, 11/1/1883.

121 *The Bailie,* 12/2/1879. Glasgow Stock Exchange Association, 1898, pp. 29, 57. GH, 20/2/1899. Anon, 1904, *Charter, Bye-Laws, Rules and Regulations of the Institute of Accountants and Actuaries in Glasgow,* p. 5. W H Bailey, 1947, p. 24. C G D Tennant, 1979, p. 19.

122 *GH,* 20/2/1899.

123 R Somers, 1873, pp. 135, 146.

124 UB, *List of Shareholders 1858.*

125 *See* Chapter 3.1.

126 UB (Edinburgh), MSS, J A Anderson to A Butter, 2/6/1862.

127 *GH,* 20/2/1899.

128 J W Gilbart, 1849, p. 195.

129 Anon, 1884, *The Adam Smith Club,* pp. 3–4. The author might be Gairdner himself.

130 *Ibid.* pp. 5–6. J A Campbell was the brother of Henry Campbell-Bannerman, the first Prime Minister from Glasgow (see J A Spender, 1923, vol. I, pp. 3, 9, 30).

131 Anon, 1884, *The Adam Smith Club,* p. 8.

132 *Ibid.* p. 21.

133 GL, *passim.* J A Spender, 1923, p. 20. C G D Tennant, 1979, pp. 32–3.

134 Anon, n.d., *Sketch of Life of Charles Gairdner,* p. 437.

135 *See* bibliography.

136 C Gairdner, 1872, p. 12.

137 *Ibid.* p. 36.

138 F W Fetter, 1865, p. 189.

139 *See* Chapter 5.1.

140 M Gaskin, 1955, pp. 17–18. P L Cottrell, 1980, p. 195.

141 *GH,* 27/4/1889.

142 GL, 1/1/1885.

143 *Ibid.* 2/1/1885.

144 UB *Annual Report,* 22/4/1885.

145 GL, −/3/1885.

146 D MacLeod, n.d., p. 80.

147 *See* Chapter 5.3.

148 GL, 6/8/1883.

149 *Ibid.* 24/8/1883.

150 *Ibid.* n.d.

151 *Ibid.* 13/5/1884.

152 *Ibid.* 16/5/1884.
153 *Ibid.* 19/5/1884.
154 *Ibid.* 21/5/1884.
155 *Ibid.* 24/5/1884.
156 UBM, 28/5/1884.
157 *Ibid.* 25/6/1884. GL, 24/7/1884.
158 *Ibid.* A Crum to C Gairdner, 26/4/1883, F Pitman to C Gairdner, 26/4/1883.
159 S E Thomas, 1934, p. 249.
160 GL, 14/5/1884.
161 SGC, 1975, Table 47.
162 G G C Kennedy, 1955, p. 21.
163 A Slaven, 1975, Chapter 7.

Conclusion

1 C P Kindleberger, 1974, p. 1.
2 *Ibid.* p. 16.
3 SGC, 1975, p. 484.
4 *Ibid.* p. 715.

Postscript

1 SGC, 1975, xxiii.
2 See transcript forms of the minute books of the boards of directors of the Scottish banks held in the University of Glasgow Archives.
3 UBM, 26/10/1899.
4 *Ibid.* 1/3/1899, 16/3/1899, 14/3/1901, 17/3/1910, 26/10/1911, 4/12/1912, 7/8/1914.
5 *Ibid.* 4/12/1912.
6 *Ibid.* 3/11/1888. See also *Ibid.* 23/3/1889, 27/3/1889, 14/5/1890.
7 *Ibid.* 27/5/1908, 26/8/1908.
8 *Ibid.* 25/3/1900, 20/5/1908.
9 *Ibid.* 20/11/1918.
10 S Pollard, 1969, pp. 67–9.
11 UBM, 15/1/1890.
12 Giuseppi, 1966, p. 127.
13 UBM, 26/11/1890.
14 *Ibid.* 31/1/1917.
15 *Ibid.* 23/10/1918.
16 *Ibid.* 16/4/1919.
17 *Economist,* 19 July 1919.
18 UBM, 16/4/1919.
19 *Economist,* 17 December 1938. Sayers, 1976, p. 270.
20 UBM, 27/4/1887.
21 More accurately speaking, the Union Bank had another general manager. In the wake of the death of J A Morrison in 1954, the board of directors of the Union Bank appointed William Watson, treasurer of the Bank of Scotland and one of the ordinary directors of the Union Bank, to be general manager. In making this appointment, of course, 'the Board kept in mind that complete fusion of the two Banks was clearly in view' (UB *Annual Report,* 1954), as will be discussed later.

22 Rait, 1930, p. 329.
23 SGC, 1975, p. 512.
24 Rait, 1930, pp. 349–50. SGC, 1975, p. 571.
25 *Ibid.* p. 572.
26 Lenman, 1977, p. 211. SGC, 1976.
27 *Ibid.* pp. 642–4.
28 *Ibid.* p. 641.
29 Committee on the Working of the Monetary System, 1960, *Minute of Evidence,* Q. 4817.
30 Gaskin, 1965, p. 173.
31 Committee, 1960, Q.4819.
32 Gaskin, 1965, p. 159.
33 *Economist,* 23 August 1952.
34 SGC, 1975, p. 643.

Appendices

Appendix A

Balance Sheet, 12 May 1831

Liabilities

Stock	£281,962
Deposit accounts	174,280
Interest receipts	53,305
Bills lodged for collection	2,680
Notes issued	178,000
Greenock agency	44,588
Unpaid accounts	114
Contingent account for loss by protested bills	1,344
Adjusting account	3,751
Profit and loss account	8,780
	£748,804

Assets

Credit accounts	£27,348
Investments in the government funds	22,280
Purchases of the Company's stock	6,014
Property in Greenock belonging to the Bank	60
Bills discounted	364,317
Bills of exchange	54,308
Bills received from agencies for collection	22,142
Bills protested	3,153
Edinburgh agency	125,340
John Marshall	3,144
Manchester & Liverpool District Bank	1,015
Jones Loyd & Company	37,797
Bank of Ireland	654
Country agents accounts	13,134
Bank furniture	463
Agency furniture	436
Stamps	709
Bank note paper	3,991
Provincial Bank of Ireland	924
Balance of cash in safe	61,575
	£748,804

Source: UBM, 12/5/1831

Appendix B

Balance Sheet, 13 May 1858

Liabilities

Capital paid up	£1,000,000
Rest, or undivided profit	200,000
Deposits/including balances at credit of banking correspondents/and notes in circulation	7,529,326
Appropriation of the year's profits as stated in the report	98,224
	£8,827,550

Assets

Bills of exchange, local and country bills	£3,277,997
Cash credits	3,858,501
Bank offices at Glasgow, Edinburgh and Branches	142,818
Consols and other government stocks and railway debentures	982,548
Gold and silver coin, and cash balance at call in hands of London bankers	565,686
	£8,827,550

Source: UB *Annual Report,* 13/5/1858

Appendix C

Balance Sheet, 11 May 1865

Liabilities

Current accounts, deposit accounts, balances due to banking correspondents &c	£7,771,887
Acceptances by London agents and marginal credits	231,023
Note circulation	579,299
Capital paid up	1,000,000
Rest, or surplus profit	109,368
Profit and loss account	143,028
	£9,834,605

Assets

Bills of exchange, local and country bills, cash credits and other advances on securities	£7,507,748
Bank offices at Glasgow, Edinburgh and branches	172,482
Consols and government securities	1,041,024
Other securities and investments	270,625
Gold and silver coin, and notes of other banks, cash balances in hands of London and country bankers	842,726
	£9,834,605

Source: UB *Annual Report,* 11/5/1865

Appendix D

Balance Sheets, 1866–85 (Millions of Pounds)

Liabilities

	Deposits	Notes	Other Public Liabilities	Capital	Reserve	Total Liabilities
1866	8.30	0.68	0.34	1.00	0.30	10.63
1867	8.46	0.74	0.15	1.00	0.37	10.73
1868	8.10	0.73	0.25	1.00	0.39	10.47
1869	8.52	0.81	0.38	1.00	0.41	11.12
1870	8.20	0.62	0.25	1.00	0.43	10.50
1871	8.04	0.69	0.18	1.00	0.44	10.36
1872	8.72	0.88	0.33	1.00	0.46	11.39
1873	9.58	0.95	0.45	1.00	0.54	12.51
1874	9.54	0.89	0.28	1.00	0.55	12.26
1875	9.69	0.78	0.35	1.00	0.55	12.36
1876	9.64	0.75	0.43	1.00	0.56	12.38
1877	9.67	0.84	0.39	1.00	0.45	12.35
1878	8.96	0.79	0.40	1.00	0.47	11.62
1879	8.57	0.76	0.23	1.00	0.47	11.03
1880	9.59	0.77	0.29	1.00	0.47	12.12
1881	10.15	0.72	0.22	1.00	0.48	12.57
1882	10.68	0.74	0.33	1.00	0.49	13.25
1883	10.94	0.83	0.17	1.00	0.51	13.45
1884	10.77	0.80	0.22	1.00	0.53	13.32
1885	10.76	0.78	0.15	1.00	0.52	13.21

Source: SGC and A B MacDonald, 1973

Assets

	Advances	Investments	Liquid Assets	Property	Profit Before Tax	Dividend	Retained Profits	Total Assets
1866	8.16	0.99	1.31	0.16	0.132	0.090	0.041	10.63
1867	8.10	1.07	1.39	0.16	0.160	0.100	0.059	10.73
1868	7.65	1.16	1.50	0.16	0.125	0.103	0.022	10.47
1869	8.18	1.22	1.56	0.16	0.132	0.112	0.019	11.12
1870	7.77	1.14	1.44	0.16	0.138	0.122	0.016	10.50
1871	7.33	1.28	1.60	0.15	0.135	0.123	0.012	10.36
1872	8.20	1.36	1.67	0.16	0.142	0.132	0.010	11.39
1873	9.03	1.50	1.83	0.15	0.162	0.152	0.010	12.51
1874	9.03	1.39	1.68	0.16	0.164	0.151	0.013	12.26
1875	8.64	1.62	1.94	0.15	0.162	0.151	0.011	12.36

1876	9.06	1.45	1.71	0.16	0.158	0.132	0.026	12.38
1877	8.13	1.87	2.18	0.17	0.147	0.132	0.015	12.35
1878	8.14	1.53	1.77	0.18	0.149	0.133	0.016	11.62
1879	7.56	1.45	1.66	0.36	0.134	0.122	0.011	11.03
1880	7.38	2.05	2.32	0.37	0.131	0.123	0.008	12.12
1881	7.52	2.21	2.47	0.38	0.136	0.122	0.013	12.57
1882	7.67	2.47	2.73	0.38	0.140	0.123	0.016	13.25
1883	7.96	2.44	2.67	0.37	0.151	0.122	0.028	13.45
1884	7.95	2.40	2.60	0.37	0.144	0.123	0.020	13.32
1885	7.62	2.52	2.70	0.37	0.125	0.124	0.001	13.21

Appendix E

Balance Sheets, 1886–1952 (Millions of Pounds)

Liabilities

	Deposits	Notes	Other Public Liabilities	Capital	Reserve	Total Liabilities
1886	9.94	0.77	0.12	1.0	0.53	12.36
1887	9.90	0.71	0.14	1.0	0.53	12.28
1888	10.28	0.78	0.20	1.0	0.53	12.79
1889	10.60	0.80	0.15	1.0	0.55	13.11
1890	11.08	0.86	0.25	1.0	0.57	13.77
1891	11.24	0.82	0.11	1.0	0.59	13.76
1892	11.07	0.82	0.07	1.0	0.60	13.56
1893	10.96	0.83	0.11	1.0	0.62	13.53
1894	10.73	0.89	0.19	1.0	0.64	13.45
1895	11.26	0.91	0.16	1.0	0.64	13.98
1896	11.44	0.95	0.17	1.0	0.67	14.23
1897	11.30	0.96	0.20	1.0	0.71	14.17
1898	11.24	0.95	0.22	1.0	0.74	14.15
1899	12.24	1.02	0.28	1.0	0.78	15.32
1900	12.72	1.06	0.22	1.0	0.81	15.82
1901	13.25	1.04	0.19	1.0	0.86	16.34
1902	13.24	1.03	0.21	1.0	0.90	16.39
1903	13.61	1.01	0.10	1.0	0.95	16.67
1904	12.70	0.96	0.14	1.0	0.94	15.74
1905	12.53	0.92	0.06	1.0	0.99	15.50
1906	12.74	0.98	0.15	1.0	1.04	15.91
1907	13.26	0.96	0.12	1.0	1.05	16.40
1908	12.98	0.91	0.16	1.0	1.10	16.15
1909	12.48	0.88	0.27	1.0	1.16	15.78
1910	12.83	0.87	0.35	1.0	1.17	16.22
1911	12.59	0.88	0.20	1.0	1.18	15.85
1912	14.57	0.91	0.39	1.0	1.19	18.07
1913	15.41	0.93	0.97	1.0	1.18	19.50
1914	16.46	0.94	1.03	1.0	1.22	20.65
1915	17.75	1.22	0.50	1.0	1.06	21.53
1916	16.7	1.6	0.9	1.0	1.1	21.3
1917	17.2	1.9	1.2	1.0	1.0	22.3
1918	23.6	2.5	0.5	1.0	1.1	28.8
1919	26.3	3.0	1.1	1.0	1.2	32.6
1920	32.5	3.5	1.3	1.0	1.2	39.5
1921	32.7	3.4	0.6	1.0	1.2	38.9
1922	35.2	2.8	0.4	1.0	1.3	40.8
1923	31.7	2.7	0.6	1.0	1.5	37.5
1924	29.3	2.5	0.7	1.0	1.6	35.1
1925	27.7	2.6	0.6	1.0	1.6	33.5
1926	27.1	2.6	0.8	1.0	1.6	33.2

1927	25.6	2.5	0.7	1.0	1.7	31.5
1928	25.9	2.6	0.7	1.0	1.7	31.9
1929	27.3	2.5	1.2	1.0	1.8	33.8
1930	28.3	2.4	1.1	1.0	1.9	34.7
1931	29.1	2.4	0.7	1.2	2.2	35.6
1932	28.3	2.3	0.5	1.2	2.1	34.5
1933	28.5	2.3	0.5	1.2	2.2	34.7
1934	28.6	2.4	0.4	1.2	2.2	34.7
1935	29.9	2.5	0.4	1.2	2.2	36.2
1936	32.0	2.5	1.9	1.2	2.2	39.8
1937	32.8	2.6	1.6	1.2	2.2	40.4
1938	33.4	2.7	1.0	1.2	2.2	40.5
1939	33.2	2.6	1.1	1.2	2.2	40.4
1940	36.0	2.9	1.0	1.2	2.2	43.3
1941	36.6	3.2	1.2	1.2	2.2	44.4
1942	41.0	4.2	3.0	1.2	2.3	51.7
1943	46.6	5.5	1.3	1.2	2.3	57.0
1944	51.6	6.1	2.5	1.2	2.4	63.8
1945	54.7	6.0	1.4	1.2	2.5	65.7
1946	58.8	5.7	1.2	1.2	2.5	69.4
1947	66.5	6.7	1.7	1.2	2.6	78.6
1948	69.3	6.5	2.1	1.2	2.6	81.6
1949	69.7	6.9	2.1	1.2	2.5	82.4
1950	70.4	7.2	2.9	1.2	2.5	84.2
1951	77.9	7.7	4.7	1.2	2.5	94.0
1952	71.1	7.7	5.0	1.2	2.5	87.5

Assets

	Advances	Invest- ments	Liquid Assets	Property	Profit Before Tax	Dividend	Retained Profits	Total Assets
1886	7.34	2.25	2.39	0.37	0.136	0.124	0.011	12.36
1887	7.42	2.19	2.30	0.36	0.133	0.124	0.009	12.28
1888	7.07	2.63	2.73	0.36	0.139	0.113	0.026	12.79
1889	7.27	2.70	2.78	0.36	0.141	0.113	0.027	13.11
1890	6.52	3.42	3.47	0.35	0.139	0.113	0.026	13.77
1891	6.33	4.17	2.89	0.36	0.135	0.113	0.022	13.76
1892	6.17	4.29	2.74	0.36	0.135	0.113	0.021	13.56
1893	5.98	4.29	2.89	0.36	0.135	0.113	0.021	13.53
1894	6.25	4.07	2.77	0.37	0.139	0.113	0.025	13.45
1895	6.31	3.80	3.51	0.36	0.120	0.103	0.016	13.98
1896	6.84	3.21	3.83	0.36	0.142	0.103	0.038	14.23
1897	7.16	2.65	4.02	0.35	0.150	0.114	0.035	14.17
1898	7.14	2.74	3.93	0.34	0.152	0.114	0.037	14.15
1899	7.96	2.55	4.47	0.33	0.161	0.124	0.035	15.32
1900	8.07	2.67	4.74	0.33	0.167	0.126	0.039	15.82
1901	8.46	2.95	4.61	0.33	0.177	0.126	0.048	16.34
1902	8.42	3.00	4.64	0.32	0.183	0.138	0.042	16.39

1903	8.79	2.88	4.68	0.32	0.191	0.138	0.051	16.67
1904	7.88	2.66	4.89	0.31	0.188	0.136	0.049	15.74
1905	7.79	2.91	4.48	0.32	0.191	0.137	0.051	15.50
1906	7.80	2.93	4.86	0.32	0.196	0.137	0.056	15.91
1907	8.57	2.91	4.60	0.31	0.193	0.137	0.053	16.40
1908	8.24	3.17	4.42	0.31	0.196	0.137	0.056	16.15
1909	7.39	3.58	4.38	0.42	0.212	0.137	0.070	15.78
1910	7.82	3.40	4.59	0.42	0.218	0.148	0.065	16.22
1911	8.11	3.23	4.06	0.44	0.213	0.148	0.061	15.85
1912	9.51	3.07	5.05	0.44	0.217	0.150	0.063	18.07
1913	9.95	3.11	5.99	0.45	0.221	0.150	0.067	19.50
1914	11.34	3.62	5.24	0.45	0.215	0.150	0.060	20.65
1915	10.13	4.95	6.00	0.45	0.239	0.150	0.076	21.53
1916	8.0	7.3	5.5	0.5	0.257	0.150	0.080	21.3
1917	10.6	6.6	4.7	0.4	0.283	0.150	0.100	22.3
1918	15.2	6.7	6.4	0.5	0.234	0.150	0.129	28.8
1919	16.9	7.9	7.2	0.6	0.241	0.150	0.134	32.6
1920	20.4	9.9	8.6	0.5	0.376	0.160	0.151	39.5
1921	21.6	9.3	7.5	0.5	0.377	0.160	0.152	38.9
1922	15.4	16.9	8.0	0.5	0.354	0.170	0.138	40.8
1923	9.9	19.8	7.2	0.5	0.368	0.180	0.146	37.5
1924	11.8	15.4	7.4	0.5	0.371	0.180	0.148	35.1
1925	12.4	14.0	6.6	0.5	0.368	0.180	0.150	33.5
1926	12.5	13.8	6.3	0.5	0.350	0.180	0.136	33.2
1927	13.3	12.1	5.5	0.6	0.311	0.180	0.138	31.5
1928	15.0	10.2	6.1	0.6	0.368	0.180	0.150	31.9
1929	17.4	9.2	6.6	0.6	0.375	0.180	0.156	33.8
1930	17.3	10.8	6.0	0.5	0.385	0.180	0.159	34.7
1931	14.9	13.6	6.6	0.5	0.301	0.216	0.139	35.6
1932	13.7	13.2	7.2	0.5	0.368	0.216	0.114	34.5
1933	10.2	17.4	6.6	0.5	0.355	0.216	0.104	34.7
1934	10.3	17.3	6.6	0.5	0.339	0.216	0.095	34.7
1935	9.9	18.9	7.0	0.5	0.341	0.216	0.097	36.2
1936	11.6	20.1	7.6	0.4	0.348	0.216	0.101	39.8
1937	12.3	21.0	6.7	0.4	0.352	0.216	0.102	40.4
1938	12.7	19.6	7.8	0.4	0.350	0.216	0.097	40.5
1939	12.4	20.0	7.5	0.4	0.361	0.216	0.094	40.4
1940	12.4	21.5	9.1	0.4	0.367	0.216	0.087	43.3
1941	11.2	23.2	9.6	0.4	0.380	0.216	0.082	44.4
1942	14.4	27.2	9.7	0.4	0.392	0.216	0.088	51.7
1943	10.9	32.5	13.2	0.4	0.396	0.216	0.090	57.0
1944	11.2	37.5	14.7	0.4	0.410	0.216	0.097	63.8
1945	10.6	40.7	14.0	0.4	0.432	0.216	0.108	65.7
1946	9.8	43.0	16.2	0.4	0.427	0.216	0.116	69.4
1947	13.0	48.0	17.2	0.4	0.609	0.216	0.123	78.6
1948	16.1	47.3	17.8	0.4	0.604	0.216	0.121	81.6
1949	16.8	46.3	18.8	0.5	0.611	0.216	0.124	82.4
1950	22.1	41.8	19.7	0.5	0.642	0.216	0.127	84.2
1951	25.6	43.4	24.5	0.5	0.779	0.216	0.132	94.0
1952	32.8	33.6	20.5	0.6	0.562	0.216	0.125	87.5

Bibliography

A note on archive materials at the Bank of Scotland

The National Register of Archives (Scotland), a branch of the Scottish Record Office, has compiled the consolidated lists of archive materials including those of the banks. The collection of primary materials at the Bank of Scotland is under,

> No. 945 The Bank of Scotland (includes the British Linen Bank, the Caledonian Bank, the Central Bank of Scotland, the Union Bank of Scotland and the banks merged with the Union Bank).

Section 1
Manuscripts   1.1 The Union Bank of Scotland; Manuscripts held in the Bank of Scotland Glasgow Chief Office
                       1.2 The Union Bank of Scotland; Manuscripts held in the Bank of Scotland Edinburgh Head Office
                       2   The Bank of Scotland; Manuscripts held in the Bank of Scotland Edinburgh Head Office
                       3.1 Manuscripts held in the University of Glasgow Archives
                       3.2 Transcript forms of manuscripts held in the University of Glasgow Archives

Section 2
Periodicals

Section 3
Parliamentary Papers

Section 4
Books, Pamphlets, Articles and Unpublished Writings

Section 1

Manuscripts

1.1 *The Union Bank of Scotland; Manuscripts held in the Bank of Scotland Glasgow Chief Office*

Directors' Minute Books, Glasgow Committee,	1830–85[1]
Directors' Minute Books, General Board,	1843–53
Directors' Minute Books, Glasgow A Committee,	1872–85
Directors' Minute Books, Glasgow B Committee,	1872–85
Directors' Minute Books, Scroll Books,	1837–47
Annual Reports with Balance Sheets,	1831–85
Contract of Co-partnership with Amendments,	1830
Lists of Shareholders with Lists of Branches,	1858, 1885
Abstract Annual Balances,	1860–65
Abstract Profit and Loss Account; Edinburgh,	
London and Branches,	1863–85
Abstract Quarterly Balances,	1838–64
Accountant's Minute Book,	1879–85
Bills discounted,	1831–35
Calculations of Interest,	1855–85
Claim Books,	1847–85
Deposit Money, Interest on Loans and	
Profit and Loss,	1884–85
Envelope containing Details of Salaries,	1884–85
Gairdner's Incoming Letters,	1883–85[2]
Gairdner's Note Book,	*c.*1862–85[2]
General Circulars	1870–85
General Ledgers	1843, 1879–84
General Quarterly Balances; Branches,	1862–65
Glasgow & Ship Bank, Directors' Minute Book,	1836, 1842–43
Head Office Circulars,	1860–79
Journal of Investments,	1879–85
Ledgers of Protested Bills,	1861–85
Memoranda of External Auditors,	1879
MSS Salary Records,	mainly 1860s–1880s
Newspaper Cutting Books,	1875–83
Opinion Books,	1864–85
Perth Bank, Directors' Minute Book,	1852–72[3]
Printed Half Yearly Statements Pursuant to	
the Companies Acts,	1882–85
Printed Interest Tables with MSS Additions,	1836–85
Printed Rates of Discount and Interest,	1854–77
Private Journals,	1830–85
Private Ledgers,	1830–85
Profit and Loss Account,	1865–85

[1] Type-transcript form held in GUA.
[2] Xerox copy held in GUA.
[3] From 1857, Minute Book of the Perth Local Committee.

Protested Bills,	1847–69
Record of Transfers of Stock registered,	1850–85
Secretary's Private Letter Books,	1852–62, 1876–85

1.2   *The Union Bank of Scotland; Manuscripts held in the Bank of Scotland Edinburgh Head Office*

Directors' Minute Books, Edinburgh Committee,	1843–85
Edinburgh Local Committee's Minute Books,	1830–38
Document Books, Memoranda, Notes and Instructions,	1839–85
Documents on 1857 Crisis,	1857
Letter Books,	1853–54
Letters from Coutts on 1857 Crisis,	1857
Letters from Glasgow Head Office,	1849–68
Memoranda on Inspections,	1847–69
Private Letter Books,	1838–69
Profit and Loss Account Ledgers,	1854–61, 1871–73
Staff and Salary Records,	1830–40, 1860–85

2   *The Bank of Scotland; Manuscripts held in the Bank of Scotland Edinburgh Head Office*

Alexander Blair's Confidential Letters,	mainly 1850s
Documents on 1857 Crisis,	1857–58
Documents on Joint London Office,	1866, mainly 1870s
Documents on Scottish Banks in England,	mainly 1870s
Glasgow Chamber of Commerce, Excerpts of Minute Book,	1882, 1884
Meetings of Bank Managers, Excerpts of Minute Book,	1882, 1884
Secretary's Letters,	1857–58
Treasurer's Letters,	1850–79
Western Bank Negotiations,	1857

3.1   *Manuscripts held in the University of Glasgow Archives*

| Gairdner's MSS Papers and Pamphlets, | mainly 1860s–1880s |
| J & G Thomson's MSS Papers, | mainly 1870s–1880s |

3.2   *Transcript Forms of Manuscripts held in the University of Glasgow Archives*

Bank of Scotland, Director's Minute Book	
British Linen Co, Director's Minute Book	
Clydesdale Bank, Director's Minute Book	
Commercial Bank of Scotland, Director's Minute Book	
National Bank of Scotland, Director's Minute Book	
Royal Bank of Scotland, Director's Minute Book	
Union Bank of Scotland, Director's Minute Book	
Meeting of Bank Managers, Director's Minute Book	1872–85

Gairdner's Incoming Letters,   1883–85
Gairdner's Note Book,   c.1862–85
(Transcript forms of the Minute Books of the Banks and Meetings of Bank Managers
have been prepared by Mrs E O A Checkland).

Section 2

Periodicals

Bailie
Blackwood's Edinburgh Magazine
Economist
Edinburgh Almanac
Glasgow Herald
Glasgow University Calendar
Post Office Glasgow Directory
Scotsman
Scottish Bankers Magazine
Times

Section 3

Parliamentary Papers

Select Committee on Banks of Issue,   1841, (366, 410) V
Select Committee on Bank Acts,   1857–58, (381) V
Select Committee on Banks of Issue,   1875, (351) IX

Section 4

Books, Pamphlets, Articles and Unpublished Writings

Acres, W M	1931	*The Bank of England from within.*	London
Alison, A	1883	*Some Account of My Life and Writings.*	Edinburgh
Alison, R	1892	*Anecdotage of Glasgow.*	Glasgow & London
Allan, F H	1931	The Union Bank of Scotland.	*SBM*
Anderson, G	1976	*Victorian Clerks.*	Manchester
Anderson, J L	1910	*The Story of the Commercial Bank of Scotland Limited.*	Edinburgh
Anon (A Scotch Banker)	1841	*Practical Remarks on Currency and Banking.*	Glasgow, Edinburgh & London

	1842	*Mercantile Embarrassments and the Present State of the Banking System.*	Edinburgh
	1858	*The Western Bank Failure and the Scottish Banking System.*	Glasgow
	1863	*The Maze of Banking.*	Edinburgh & Glasgow
	1864	The Economy of Capital.	*BEM*
	1864	The City of Gold.	*BEM*
	1879	*City of Glasgow Bank Publications.*	Edinburgh & London
	1883	*Lord Provosts of Glasgow.*	Glasgow
	1884	*The Adam Smith Club.*	n.p.
	1886	*One Hundred Glasgow Men.*	Glasgow
	1891	*Glasgow and Its Environs.*	London
	1896	*Old Glasgow.*	Glasgow
	1904	*Charter of Incorporation, Bye-Laws, Rules and Regulations of the Institute of Accountants and Actuaries in Glasgow.*	Glasgow
	1910	*Brief Historical Sketch of the Union Bank of Scotland Limited.*	Glasgow
	1910	Robert Blyth.	*SBM*
	1912	Arthur C D Gairdner.	*SBM*
	1930	A Notable Centenary: The Union Bank of Scotland Ltd.	*SBM*
	1935	*The Gas Supply of Glasgow.*	Glasgow
	1942	*Our Bank: The Story of the Commercial Bank of Scotland Ltd.*	Edinburgh
	1957	The Nineteenth-Century Banker's Clerk.	*TBR*
	1960	The Glasgow Financial Scene: Early 19th Century.	*TBR*
	n.d.	*Sketch of the Life of Charles Gairdner.*	n.p.
Ashton, T S	1953	The Bills of Exchange and Private Bankers in Lancashire.	in Ashton & Sayers, eds
Ashton, T S & Sayers, R S, eds.	1953	*Papers in English Monetary History.*	Oxford
Bagehot, W	1873	*Lombard Street.*	London
Bailey, J D	1959–60	Australian Borrowing in Scotland in the Nineteenth Century.	*EcHR*
	1966	*A Hundred Years of Pastoral Banking.*	Oxford
Bailey, W H	1947	*A Chronicle of the Family of Gairdner of Ayrshire, Edinburgh and Glasgow.*	n.p.
Barclay, H	1873	*Memoir of Mr George Baillie.*	Glasgow
Barker, T C & Savage, C I	1974	*An Economic History of Transport in Britain.*	London
Barrow, G L	1975	*The Emergence of the Irish Banking System.*	Dublin
Bell, G M	1855	*The Philosophy of Joint-Stock Banking.*	London
Blackie, A A C	1959	*Blackie & Son.*	London
Boase, C W	1867	*A Century of Banking in Dundee.*	Edinburgh

Bolitho, H & Peel, D	1967	*The Drummonds of Charing Cross.*	London
Bowman, W D	1937	*The Story of the Bank of England.*	London
Brown, J	1848	*Observations on Mr Kinnear's 'History of the Rise of Exchange Companies in Scotland'.*	Glasgow
Brown, P L, ed.	1941	*Clyde Company Papers.*	Oxford
Buchanan, J (Glasguensis)	1884	*Banking in Glasgow during the Olden Time.*	Glasgow
Burke, B	1900	*A Genealogical and Heraldic History of the Landed Gentry of Great Britain.*	London
Byres, T J	1967	Entrepreneurship in the Scottish Heavy Industries.	in Payne, ed.
Cairncross, A K	1954	*The Scottish Economy.*	Cambridge
Cameron, R, ed.	1967	*Banking in the Early Stages of Industrialization.*	London
	1972	*Banking and Economic Development*	London
Campbell, R H	1955	Edinburgh Banks and the Western Bank of Scotland.	*SJPE*
	1955(a)	Developments of the Scottish Pig Iron Trade.	*JEH*
	1965	*Scotland since 1707.*	Oxford
	1967	The Law and the Joint Stock Company in Scotland.	in Payne, ed.
	1980	*The Rise and Fall of Scottish Industry.*	Edinburgh
Campbell, R H & Dow, J B A	1968	*Source Book of Scottish Economic and Social History.*	Oxford
Cargill, A, ed.	1910	*The Centenary of Savings Banks.*	Edinburgh
Carter, E F	1959	*An Historical Geography of the Railways of the British Isles.*	London
Chandler, G	1964	*Four Centuries of Banking.*	London
Checkland, E O A	1980	*Philanthropy in Victorian Scotland.*	Edinburgh
Checkland, S G	1964	*The Rise of Industrial Society in England.*	London
	1967	*The Mines of Tharsis.*	London
	1968	Banking History and Economic Development.	*SJPE*
	1975	*Scottish Banking.*	Glasgow
	1976	*The Upas Tree.*	Glasgow
Checkland, S G & MacDonald, A B	1973	Scottish Banking Data	unpublished
Church, R A	1975	*The Great Victorian Boom.*	London
Clapham, J	1944	*The Bank of England.*	London
Clydesdale Bank	1838	*Contract of Co-partnery.*	Glasgow
Coleridge, E H	1920	*The Life of Thomas Coutts.*	London
Collins, M & Hudson, P	1979	Provincial Bank Lending.	*Bulletin of Economic Research*
Conolly, M F	1869	*Fifiana.*	Glasgow
Corti, C	1928	*The Rise of the House of Rothschild.*	London
	1928	*The Reign of the House of Rothschild.*	London
Cottrell, P L	1975	*British Overseas Investments in the Nineteenth Century.*	London

	1980	*Industrial Finance.*	London
Cottrell, P L	1974	*Money and Banking in England.*	London
& Anderson, B L			
Crathorne, N	1973	*Tennant's Stalk.*	London
Crick, W F &	1958	*A Hundred Years of Joint Stock*	London
Wadsworth, J E		*Banking.*	
Cunnison, J &	1958	*Glasgow.*	Glasgow
Gilfillan, J B S, ed.			
Daiches, D	1977	*Glasgow.*	London
Deane, P &	1969	*British Economic Growth.*	Cambridge
Cole, W A			
Dennistoun, J W	1906	*Some Account of the Family of*	Glasgow
		Dennistoun and Colgrain.	
Devine, T M	1975	*The Tobacco Lords.*	Edinburgh
Dickson, T, ed.	1980	*Scottish Capitalism.*	London
Dilke, M S &	1959	*The County of Dunbarton.*	Glasgow
Templeton, A A, eds.			
Donald, T F	1924	*The Western Club.*	Glasgow
Downie, R	1915	Financial Crises and the	*SBM*
		Lesson they teach.	
Dun, J	1876	On the Analysis of Joint Stock	*JSS*
		Banking in the United Kingdom.	
Ellinger, B	1940	*The City.*	London
Farrow, T	1911	*Banks and People.*	London
Feavearyear, A	1963	*The Pound Sterling.*	Oxford
Fetter, F W	1960	The Economic Articles in	*SJPE*
		Blackwood's Edinburgh Magazine	
		and Their Authors.	
	1965	*Development of British Monetary*	Cambridge
		Orthodoxy.	(Mass)
Fleming, J S	1877	*Scottish Banking.*	Edinburgh &
			London
Fletcher, G A	1976	*The Discount Houses in London.*	London
Forbes, R N	1966	Overend, Gurney & Co.	*SBM*
Forbes, W	1860	*Memoirs of a Banking House.*	Edinburgh
			& London
Francis, J	1849	*Chronicles and Characters of*	London
		the Stock Exchange.	
Freebairn, C F	1924	An Old Banking Institution;	*SBM*
		the Paisley Union Bank.	
	1924(a)	Virginia Street and its	*SBM*
		Environs; A Glasgow Banking	
		Centre of the Past.	
Fulford, R.	1953	*Glyn's*	London
Gairdner, C	1866	*Paper Money.*	n.p.
	1872	*The Rate of Discount and the*	Glasgow
		Bank Acts.	
	1877	*Fluctuations in Trade.*	Glasgow
	1886	*Economy in the Use of Gold as*	Glasgow
		practised in Scotland.	
	1888	*Constitution and Course of the*	Glasgow
		Money Market.	
	1889	*The Royal Commission on Gold*	Glasgow
		and Silver.	
	1890	*National Gold Reserves.*	Glasgow
	1891	*The Making of Gold Reserves.*	Glasgow

	1892	*Mr. Goschen's Scheme for Reform of the Bank Acts.*	Glasgow
Gairdner, C D	1857	*Letter to the Right Honourable the Earl of Eglinton.*	Ayr
	1902	*Autobiography.*	Kilmarnock
Gairdner, H	n.d.	*Stories and Conversations From Real Life &c.*	unpublished
Gaskin, M	1955	*Note Issue in Scottish Banking.*	MA thesis Liverpool
	1960	Anglo–Scottish Banking Conflicts.	*EcHR*
	1965	*The Scottish Banks.*	London
Gilbart, J W	1836	*The History of Banking in Ireland.*	London
	1849	*A Practical Treatise on Banking.*	London
	1907	*The History, Principles and Practice of Banking* (E Sykes, ed.).	London
Gillet Bros Discount Co	1952	*The Bill on London.*	London
Giuseppi, J	1966	*The Bank of England.*	London
Glasgow Stock Exchange Association	1927	*Records of the Glasgow Stock Exchange Association.*	Glasgow
Gourvish, T R	1969	The Bank of Scotland.	*SJPE*
	1980	*Railways and the British Economy.*	London
Gourvish, T R & Reed, M C	1971	Financing of Scottish Railways before 1860.	*SJPE*
Graham, W	1911	*The One Pound Note in the History of Banking in Great Britain.*	Edinburgh & London
Gregory, T E	1929	*Select Statues, Documents and Reports relating to British Banking.*	Oxford
Hall, F G	1949	*The Bank of Ireland.*	Dublin
Hamilton, H	1932	*The Industrial Revolution in Scotland.*	Oxford
Hankey, T	1887	*The Principles of Banking.*	London
Harley, J A	1957	James Lumsden.	*SBM*
Henderson, T	1936	*The Savings Bank of Glasgow.*	Glasgow
Hidy, R W	1949	*The House of Baring in American Trade and Finance.*	Cambridge (Mass)
Hogg, J	n.d.	*Fortunes Made in Business.*	London
Holgate, H C F	1948	*English Bank Accounting.*	London
Homer, S	1963	*A History of Interest Rates.*	New Jersey
Horne, H O	1947	*A History of Savings Banks.*	Oxford
Horsefield, J K	1953	The Origins of the Bank Charter Act.	in Ashton & Sayers, eds
Hughes, J	1906	*Liverpool Banks and Bankers.*	Liverpool & London
Hume, J R	1976	*Industrial Archaeology of Scotland.*	London
Hume, J R & Moss, M S	1975	*Clyde Shipbuilding.*	London
Irving, J	1881	*The Book of Eminent Scotsmen.*	Paisley
Jack, W C	1902	*Correspondence &c respecting Sir Donald Currie and his Management.*	n.p.
Jeans, J S	1872	*Western Worthies.*	Glasgow
Jenks, L H	1963	*The Migration of British Capital to 1875.*	London
Johnston, T	1929	*A History of the Working Classes in Scotland.*	Glasgow

Joplin, T	1827	*An Essay on the General Principles and Present Practice of Banking in England and Scotland.*	London
Keir, D, ed.	1966	*The City of Edinburgh.*	Glasgow
Keith, A	1936	*The North of Scotland Bank.*	Aberdeen
Kellas, J G	1980	*Modern Scotland.*	London
Kellett, J R	1968	*Glasgow.*	London
	1979	*Railways and Victorian Cities.*	London
Kennedy, G G C	1955	The Union Bank of Scotland Ltd.	*SBM*
Kennedy, I M	1956	Charles William Boase.	*SBM*
Kerr, A W	1898	*Scottish Banking during the Period of Published Accounts.*	London
	1926	*History of Banking in Scotland.*	London
Kindleberger, C P	1974	*The Formation of Financial Centers.*	Princeton
King, W T C	1936	*History of the London Discount Market.*	London
Kinnear, G	1847	*Banks and Exchange Companies.*	Glasgow
	1848	*A History of the Rise of Exchange Companies in Scotland.*	Glasgow
Kinnear, J G	1847	*The Crisis and the Currency.*	London
Kita, M	1977	The Scottish Banking Invasion of England.	*Soka Economic Studies Quarterly,* Tokyo
Knowles, L C A	1930	*The Industrial and Commercial Revolutions in Great Britain during the Nineteenth Century.*	London
Knox, J	1927	*The Triumph of Thrift.*	Airdrie
Lawson, W J	1855	*A History of Banking.*	London
Leighton-Boyce, J A S L	1958	*Smiths the Bankers.*	London
Lenman, B	1977	*An Economic History of Modern Scotland.*	London
Leslie, J O	1955	Alexander Blair.	*SBM*
Liquidator of Western Bank	1872	*Debate in Causa.*	Glasgow
Livingstone, P K	1955	*A History of Kirkcaldy.*	Kirkcaldy
Logan, W H	1844	*The Scottish Banker.*	Edinburgh
Malcolm, C A	1945	*The Bank of Scotland.*	Edinburgh
	1950	*The History of the British Linen Bank.*	Edinburgh
Malloch, D M	1912	*The Book of Glasgow Anecdote.*	Edinburgh & London
Marriner, S, ed.	1978	*Business and Businessmen.*	Liverpool
Marwick, W H	1936	*Economic Developments in Victorian Scotland.*	London
Mathew, E	1958	James Dennistoun of Golfhill.	*SBM*
Mathias, P	1969	*The First Industrial Nation.*	London
Marchant House of Glasgow	1866	*View of the Merchant House of Glasgow.*	Glasgow
Metropolitan College	n.d.	*The Banking Students' Note Book.*	St Albans
Miller, R & Tivy, J, eds	1958	*The Glasgow Region.*	Glasgow
Mitchell, B R & Deane, P	1976	*Abstract of British Historical Statistics.*	Cambridge
Mitchell, J O	1905	*Old Glasgow Essays.*	Glasgow

Mitchell, W	1878	*Our Scotch Banks.*	Edinburgh
Mitchison, R	1962	*Agricultural Sir John.*	London
Michie, R C	1979	*The Scottish Stock Exchanges in the 19th Century.*	PhD thesis, Aberdeen
Morgan, E V & Thomas, W A	1962	*The Stock Exchange.*	London
Morris, J A	1940	*A Romance of Industrial Engineering.*	Kilmarnock
Moss, M S & Hume, J R	1977	*Workshop of the British Empire.*	London & Edinburgh
Munn, C W	1975	The Origin of the Scottish Note Exchange.	*TBR*
	1976	*The Scottish Provincial Banking Companies.*	PhD thesis, Glasgow
	1981	*The Scottish Provincial Banking Companies.*	Edinburgh
	1981(a)	Scottish Provincial Banking Companies; An Assessment.	*BH*
	1981(b)	Scotland: The Coming of Joint Stock Banking.	Monetary History Group Conference
Munro, A	1960	*Book-Keeping and Accountancy.*	London
Munro, L S M	1975	The Scotch Banks in London (The first prize-given essay of the Institute of Bankers in 1878).	*SBM*
Munro, N	1928	*The History of the Royal Bank of Scotland.*	Edinburgh
Murray, N	1978	*The Scottish Hand Loom Weavers.*	Edinburgh
M'Dowall, J K	1899	*The People's History of Glasgow.*	Glasgow
MacFarlan, J F	1866	*Our Monetary Affairs.*	Edinburgh
M'Kechnie, S M	1951	Ayrshire Banking Companies and their Successors.	*SBM*
MacKenzie, H	1953	*The City of Aberdeen.*	Edinburgh
MacKenzie, K	1909	Scottish Bank Crises.	*SBM*
MacKenzie, P	1866	*Reminiscences of Glasgow.*	Glasgow
MacKinnon, J	1921	*The Social and Industrial History of Scotland.*	London
MacLeod, D	n.d.	*Historic Families, Notable People and Memorabilia of Leven, Loch Lomond and Cardross.*	Dumbarton
MacLeod, H D	1889	*The Theory of Credit.*	London
MacMillan, D S	1967	*Scotland and Australia.*	Oxford
	1967(a)	Scottish Enterprise in Australia.	in Payne, ed.
	1970	The Transfer of Company Control from Scotland to London in the Nineteenth Century.	*BH*
Nevin, E & Davis, E W	1970	*The London Clearing Banks.*	London
Nishimura, S	1971	*The Decline of Inland Bills of Exchange in the London Money Market.*	Cambridge
Oakley, C A	1946	*The Second City.*	London & Glasgow
Palgrave, R H I	1903	*Bank Rate and the Money Market.*	London
Patterson, R H	1865	*The Economy of Capital.*	Edinburgh & London

	1868	*The Science of Finance.*	Edinburgh & London
	1882	*The New Golden Age.*	Edinburgh & London
Payne, P L, ed.	1967	*Studies in Scottish Business History.*	London
	1974	*British Entrepreneurship in the Nineteenth Century.*	London
	1979	*Colvilles and the Scottish Steel Industry.*	Oxford
	1980	*The Early Scottish Limited Companies.*	Edinburgh
Pennycook, P W	1910	Early Banking in Glasgow.	*SBM*
Pollard, S	1969	*The Development of the British Economy.*	London
Powell, E T	1966	*The Evolution of the Money Market.*	London
Pressnell, L S	1956	*Country Banking in the Industrial Revolution.*	Oxford
Rae, G	1885	*Country Banker.*	London
Rait, R S	1930	*The History of the Union Bank of Scotland.*	Glasgow
Ramsay, A A W	1928	*Sir Robert Peel.*	London
Reader, W J	1966	*Professional Men.*	London
Reed, M C, ed.	1969	*Railways in the Victorian Economy.*	Devon
	1975	*Investment in Railways in Britain.*	Oxford
Reid, J M	1938	*The History of the Clydesdale Bank.*	Glasgow
	n.d.	*A History of the Merchants House of Glasgow.*	Glasgow
Renwick, R	1908	*Glasgow Memorials.*	Glasgow
	1916	*Extracts from the Records of the Burgh of Glasgow,* vol. XI.	Glasgow
Richardson, R	1900	*Coutts and Co.*	London
Robertson, P L	1974	Shipping and Shipbuilding.	*BH*
Saul, S B	1978	*The Myth of the Great Depression.*	London
Sayers, R S	1957	*Lloyds Bank in the History of English Banking.*	Oxford
	1976	*The Bank of England.*	Cambridge
Scammell, W M	1968	*The London Discount Market.*	London
Sellar, E M	1907	*Recollections and Impressions.*	Edinburgh
Senex,	1856	*Glasgow Past and Present.*	Glasgow
Simpson, N	1975	*The Belfast Bank.*	Belfast
Slaven, A	1975	*The Development of the West of Scotland.*	London
Smellie, T	1931	The First Banks and Bankers of Kilmarnock.	*The Kilmarnock Standard*
Smith, A	1776	*The Wealth of Nations* (ed. A Skinner 1974).	Harmondsworth
Smout, T C,	1972	*A History of the Scottish People.*	Glasgow
ed.	1979	*The Search for Wealth and Stability.*	London
Somers, R	1873	*The Scotch Banks and System of Issue.*	Edinburgh
Somerville, T	1891	*George Square.*	Glasgow

Spalding, W F	1924	*The London Money Market.*	London
Spender, J A	1923	*The Life of the Right Hon. Sir Henry Campbell-Bannerman.*	London
Stewart, G	1881	*Curiosities of Glasgow Citizenship.*	Glasgow
	1883	*Progress of Glasgow.*	Glasgow
Stirling, J	1865	*Practical Considerations on Banks and Bank Management.*	Glasgow
Sykes, J	1926	*The Amalgamation Movement in English Banking.*	London
Tamaki, N	1981	*The Union Bank of Scotland.*	MLitt thesis, Glasgow
Tennant, C G D	1979	The Gairdner Correspondence.	*SIH*
	1980	The Gairdner Letters.	*SBM*
Thomas, J	1971	*Scotland: The Lowlands and the Borders (A Regional History of the Railways of Great Britain, VI).*	Devon
Thomas, S E	1934	*The Rise and Growth of Joint Stock Banking.*	London
Thomson, W & Jones, R W	1939	*Dictionary of Banking.*	London
Tyson, R E	1967	Scottish Investment in American Railways.	in Payne, ed.
	1971–72	The Failure of the City of Glasgow Bank.	*Newsletter, Business Archives Council of Scotland*
	1974	The Failure of the City of Glasgow Bank and the Rise of Independent Auditing.	*Accountants' Magazine*
Union Bank of Scotland	1947	*The Arms Granted to the Union Bank of Scotland, Limited.*	Glasgow
Vamplew, W	1970	Sources of Scottish Railway Share Capital before 1860.	*SJPE*
	1971	Financing of Scottish Railways before 1860: a reply.	*SJPE*
Viner, J	1937	*Studies in the Theory of International Trade.*	London
Wallace, A	1889	*Popular Traditions of Glasgow.*	Glasgow & London
Wallace, W, ed.	1905	*Trial of the City of Glasgow Bank Directors.*	Glasgow
Whale, P B	1953	A Retrospective View of the Bank Charter Act, 1844.	in Ashton & Sayers, eds
Ward, J T	1968	Charles W. Boase.	*Dundee Abertay Historical Society*
Whitehead, M A	1978	*The Western Bank and the Crisis of 1857.*	MLitt thesis, Strathclyde

Index

Figures in bold type indicate whole chapters or sections.
Alphabetical order: word-by-word, to first comma or colon.
Collected entries: BANKS, RAILWAYS, STATUTES.
'*bis*' means twice; '*p*' means *passim*; '*n*' means note.

Salmon, Backhouse, R, Leeds, 137
Scott, G J, 190 *bis*
Scott, James, 80
Scott Moncrieff, Robert, 4 *& n.*
Scottish Amicable Life Assurance
 Society, 190 *& n.*
Scottish Banking—A History, 1975,
 (Professor S G Checkland), xvii
Scottish Banks, 1800 and 1829, (Table
 1), 1
Scottish Banks, Number of Branches
 Ranking in 1848, 1856 and 1857,
 (Table 60), 162
Scottish Total: Growth Rates,
 Advances, Investments and Profits,
 1866–79, (Diagram 3), 97
Sectoral Preference, 1866–79, (Table
 35), 101
Select Committee on Banks of Issue:
 1841, 34 *& n.*, 40 *& n.*, 53, 62; 1875,
 109 *bis & n.*
Servia, SS, 142 *& n.*
Sewers, Commissioners of, City of
 London, 138 *& n.*
Shand, A B, 156 *bis & n.*
Shareholders, 1830: Occupation
 Distribution, (Table 5), 11; Regional
 Distribution, (Table 4), 11
Sharp, J D, 116
Sharpe, John, 12 *& n.*
Sheffield, Brown & Co, 188
Sherman, Duncan, & Co, 47
shipbuilding, 64 *& n.*, **141–7** *p. & nn*
Sinclair, Sir John, 4 *& n.*
Smith, Adam, 80, 168
Smith, Fleming & Co, 97 *& n.*, 119 *& n.*
Somerwell, G, 71 *bis & n.*
Special Advances, 1879–85, (Table 54),
 138
STATUTES: Joint Stock Bank Act, 1826,
 2; Bank Act, 1708, 7 *& n.*; Peel's
 Charter Act, 1844, 40, *quoted* 41 *p. &
 n.*, 42, 69 *& n.*, 167; Bank Act, 1845,
 56, 165; Companies Act, 1880, 129 *bis
 & n.*
Stewart, Robert, wine and spirit
 merchant, 8 *& n.*, 10–11 *p. & nn.*,
 quoted 19 *& n.*, 37, 181
Stirling, P., 149–50
Stock Exchange, London, 94, 105
stock, Government, 57 *& n.*
stock, offers of Union Bank, 1878–79,
 (Table 45), 122

stock, railway company, 46–7, 50 *& n.*
Structure of the Union Bank, 1885,
 (Diagram 11), 163
Syme, James, 79, 115 *& n.*

Tennant, Sir Charles, *quoted* 146 *bis &
 n.*, 149, 172
Tennant, John, chemical industrialist,
 56
Thames, SS, 143 *& n.*
Thomson, J & G, shipbuilders; 49 *& n.*,
 103 *bis*, (Table 36) *& nn.*, 124, 139;
 financing, 141–7, (Table 57), *& nn.*,
 179–80, 188 *p. & n.*
Thomson, Seton, *quoted* 140 *& n.*,
 quoted 148 *& n.*, 149, 169 *bis & n.*
Thomsons', Estimated Profits, (Table
 57), 146
Times, The, 70, *quoted* 127 *& n.*
tobacco trade, 2, 4
Tooke, Thomas, 40, 41
Total Liabilities, Growth Rates of:
 Union Bank and Scottish Total,
 1866–79, (Diagram 1), 96; Proportion
 of, Edinburgh, North and Glasgow
 Based Banks, 1866–85, (Diagram 5),
 122
trade, foreign, 47 *& n.*, 48, 54

Union Bank, History of, 1830–1930 (R T
 Rait), 6
US Investments in the mid 1870s, (Table
 38), 106

Veitch, Professor John, 166 *& n.*
Virginia Street, Glasgow, 32 *& n.*, 37

Walrond, Theodore, iron merchant, 24
 & n., 48 *& n.*, 56
Watson & Smith, 137
Wauchope, D B, (Table 42), 112, (Table
 68), 168, 169 *bis & nn.*
Wenley, J A, *quoted* 164 *& n.*
West of Scotland Malleable Iron Co, 48
 & n.
White, Peter, stockbroker and
 accountant, 165
Wilkie, David, WS, 10
Wright, J Innes, & Co, 119 *& n.*
Wyllie, David, 76 *& n.*, 87 *& n.*, 115

Young, Professor John, 56, 166